Parents, Schools,
and the Law

David Schimmel
Louis Fischer

Published by

The National Committee for Citizens in Education

Published by

The National Committee for Citizens in Education

10840 Little Patuxent Parkway, Suite 301

Columbia, MD 21044

Cover Design by Bette Lucey

Copyright 1987 by David Schimmel and Louis Fischer
ISBN 0-934460-29-9
ISBN 9-934460-31-0 Pbk
Library of Congress Catalog Number 87-61370

Manufactured and printed in the United States of America.

For our children

Josie, Jonathan, and Suzanne;

Judy, Cathy and Valerie.

And all other children–

the ultimate beneficiaries

of parents' rights.

About the Authors: David Schimmel (J.D.,Yale University) and Louis Fischer (L.B.,Ph.D., Stanford University) are both lawyers and Professors of Education at the University of Massachusetts, Amherst. They are coauthors of several books on school law, the most recent of which is *Teachers and the Law*, Longman (1987).

Special Dedication

The staff of the National Committee for Citizens in Education would like to dedicate this book to the memory of César Ramirez, our good friend and translator of several of our publications into Spanish. César was a tireless worker for the rights of parents and children. We will not forget his service, nor his friendship.

ACKNOWLEDGMENTS

This book could not have been produced without the help of many people:

William H. Cosby, Jr., whose concern for children and their parents is demonstrated almost daily in his fine work in the entertainment and education fields, who took time from his busy schedule to write a "Foreword" for us;

Our manuscript readers, those parents, advocates, and members of the NCCE Governing Board who spent untold hours in critical review of each question and answer: Gloria Allen, Dale Berlin, Carol Furman, Anne Carlson Hallett, Paul Weckstein, and Ruth Zweifler;

Members of the NCCE staff and their consultants: Vicki Agee, Chrissie Bamber, Nancy Berla, Diane Coyte, Pat Fort, Bette Lucey, Bill Rioux, Al Staats, and Cathy Wolkow.

And our colleagues and family members: Barbara Fischer, Barbara Morgan, Rick Morrill, and Joanna Schimmel. Our thanks to one and all.

We also wish to acknowledge that some of the material in this book is drawn from our earlier writing, especially *Teachers and the Law*, Fischer, Schimmel and Kelly (©1987 Longman, Inc.), and *School Law for Counselors, Psychologists, and Social Workers*, Fischer and Sorenson (©1985 Longman, Inc.).

CONTENTS

FOREWORD

David Schimmel and Louis Fischer, the authors of this comprehensive work, *Parents, Schools, and the Law*, have provided an important and much-needed service to our educational system and the children it serves. Parents, teachers, and students will benefit by consulting this volume as a reliable source of information. Indeed, I believe that it will become a definitive handbook for parents on the subject of education and the law. Every school and community library should have a copy on hand as a reference for professional educators and the public.

To the authors' credit, they have addressed complex legal issues and presented them with clear language and a simple format. The book is remarkably free of jargon, and the presentation (unlike many legal texts) is non-intimidating and understandable by even the legally unsophisticated readers.

A thoughtful, introductory overview of the chapters is provided by the authors. Each chapter begins with a series of pertinent questions about the rights or restrictions surrounding a particular legal issue. These are questions we have all wondered about, or heard or read about in the media. For example, a key question in Chapter 2 is, "Must 'due process' be used before a child is suspended from school?" There are thirty related questions covered in this chapter on "Discipline and Due Process" and the text answers them in order, succinctly but thoroughly. This question-and-answer format is used throughout the book, making it quite easy for the reader to look up a particular issue. Along the way, we are told about laws relating to education and the legal rights of parents and children.

It is important to note that legal issues have played an increasingly critical role in our public educational system during the past several decades. During my own years in public school, the only legality people seemed aware of was universal compulsory education; school boards and parents were expected to abide by that fundamental requirement. Since the 1950s, however, many statutes have been enacted or redefined by the courts and by federal, state and local legislative bodies.

Perhaps the most sweeping and critical decisions came in 1954 when the United States Supreme Court declared "separate but equal" education to be unconstitutional and thereby gave the green light to the desegregation of all public schools in the country. That decision brought about new opportunities for black Americans but the continued *de facto* segregation in many cities and towns reminds us that laws themselves can take us only so far. Social structures and attitudes must also change if the spirit of the law is to be carried out.

Similarly, the spirit of the law must capture the minds of our citizens if recent legislation is to become fully effective. Laws such as the Family Educational Rights and Privacy Act of 1974 and the Education of All Handicapped Children Act of 1975 are examples of statutes that require the cooperation of educators, parents, and community agencies to fulfill their good intentions. Students and parents have acquired many new rights; but their effective implementation will depend on careful negotiation with authorities, rather than an approach that is antagonistic and confrontational.

One strong message of this book is that basic legal literacy on the part of both parents and educators can lead to the negotiated settlements of conflicts, eliminating expensive and time-consuming court procedures. In fact, it has become imperative that parents become more knowledgeable about, and involved in, their children's education. It is clear that with new rights go new responsibilities, demanding our personal commitment and energy.

This book will enable those who are responsible for the education of our children to carry out their charge with greater enthusiasm and effectiveness; this can only serve to improve the American educational system. Our nation's strength ultimately depends upon a strong bond among students, parents, and educators. Politicians and other officials can help, in their direction of social policies, to reinforce those bonds. But better comprehension of the issues at stake is critical to the process. With this work, David Schimmel and Louis Fischer are filling a critical gap in public understanding of education and the law.

William H. Cosby, Jr., EdD

January 1987

CHAPTER 1

Overview

T his book is about the legal rights that parents have in the education of their children from kindergarten through high school. These rights are of two kinds, both equally important: the rights that parents have on their own, as parents, and the rights they have as guardians of their children, who also have legal rights as students. The first kind was established by the Supreme Court in 1924 when it ruled that parents have the right to direct the education of their children,*[1] and was reaffirmed in 1972.[2] The second was established in 1969 when the Court held that students do not shed their rights "to freedom of speech or expression at the schoolhouse gate"[3] and was expanded in 1975 to include due process rights when a student faces suspension or expulsion from school.[4]

In addition to these constitutional protections, parents and students have been granted a wide range of rights under state and federal statutes.

What are these rights? In brief, they include:

The right to a free education, the right to be protected against harm, the right to inspect student records, the right to special education for students with special needs, the right to due process of law, the right to equal educational opportunity, the right to freedom from unreasonable search and seizure, the right to freedom of expression, and the right to freedom of religion and conscience.

All these rights have now been established by law. But none

---

* Numbered footnotes refer to publications and to court cases. These have been grouped at the back of each chapter.

of them will have any practical significance unless parents know
about them and are willing to do what is necessary to see that
they are protected.

But it is not the purpose of this book to encourage parents to
go to court. On the contrary, its goal is to help resolve educational conflicts without going to lawyers or resorting to the
courts. How? By helping parents to become legally literate—
by informing you about your rights, about the way the legal
system works, and about the way it can work for you in the
public schools. With this kind of information, parents will be
able to practice "preventive law." This does not mean you will
be able to be your own lawyer, but that you will know when
the rights of your children are violated and how to protect your
children within the educational system, or when to seek the
help of experts.

Why will parents succeed without going to court? Because
although some administrators may deliberately break the law,
most unlawful school practices are the result of legal ignorance
or misunderstanding, and because most administrators are
anxious to avoid lawsuits—especially those they would probably lose. Where parents are able to show that school policies
are unlawful, administrators would rather change them voluntarily than as a result of a court order.

Why are many educators poorly informed about the rights of
parents and students? Because most of these rights did not exist
when the educators were students and because they learned
almost nothing about this subject during their educations. As
a result, they have had little training in applying these rights
in their schools, and little has been written that could assist
them. It is our hope that this volume will help fill the gap—for
educators, as well as for parents.

In addition, our book will try to demystify the law for
parents—to break through the barrier of professional jargon and
legalese that lawyers use among themselves by translating that
legalese into English.

In short, the purpose of this book is to enable you as a parent
of public school students to constructively take the law into your
own hands—to provide you with the knowledge necessary to
assert your rights and to bring violations to the attention of
teachers, administrators, and other parents so that you can help
your children receive the kind of education to which they are

legally entitled.

The rights that parents have spring from three main sources: (1) the federal and state constitutions and bills of rights (e.g., freedom of speech and due process of law); (2) statutes of the federal and state governments (e.g., the Family Educational Rights and Privacy Act giving parents access to their children's school records); (3) the legal tradition called the common law, as it is reflected in the written decisions of our state and federal courts (e.g., the *Brown* decision prohibiting segregated schools), regulations of departments of education, and local school board policies.

The United States Constitution is the basic law of the land, and when it is interpreted by the Supreme Court, the interpretation is binding on all state and federal courts. Moreover, since 1975, when the Supreme Court ruled that school officials could be held personally liable for damages if they violated a student's clearly established constitutional rights[5], teachers and administrators have become more responsive to legitimate complaints that are based on these rights. Chapters 2 through 6 and Chapter 12 of this book focus on rights that derive from the U.S. Constitution, as established by the Supreme Court and other federal courts.

Chapter 2 is about a student's right to be treated fairly by a school disciplinary system. It covers the procedural protections required by the Constitution before a public school can suspend or expel a student or search his locker and discusses the question of whether corporal punishment violates a student's constitutional rights.

Chapter 3 deals with the First Amendment protections of freedom of speech and press. It considers the extent and limits of a student's right to say and print whatever she* wishes—in the classroom and on the campus, in underground papers and in school publications.

Chapter 4 deals with freedom of religion and the separation of church and state as it affects the public schools, examining such issues as prayer in the classroom, state aid to parochial

---

* Although it is customary to use the pronoun "he" to refer to the third person singular, we prefer to alternate "she" and "he" throughout the book, except where individuals are specifically identified.

schools, and whether parents may disregard compulsory attendance laws for religious reasons.

Chapters 5 and 6 focus on the constitutional right of equal
educational opportunity and the violation of this right because
of racial or sexual discrimination. They examine such controversial issues as busing to achieve desegregation and whether all
school athletic teams should be open equally to boys and girls.

Chapters 7 to 9 focus on the common law and state control
of education. The common law, with its origin in English law
that predates the Constitution, is the oldest source of parental
rights. These chapters deal with state laws, regulation and court
decisions concerning student injuries and the balance between
parental and state control over education. The laws and regulations in this area vary considerably from state to state.

Chapter 7 deals with the rights of parents to recover compensation when their children are injured and indicates what
parents have to prove to hold schools liable for negligence.

Chapter 8 considers whether parents can collect damages
from schools for poor teaching and discusses minimum competency exams for students and teachers. It also examines the
extent to which concerned parents can influence the school curriculum in such areas as sex education, religious values, and the
use of vulgar language.

Chapter 9 deals with conflicts between individual parents
who wish to control the schooling of their own children and the
responsibility of the state to educate all children. It considers
such issues as the right of parents to educate their children
at home or to withdraw them from objectionable classes or
dangerous schools.

Federal statutory rights are the subject of chapters 10 and 11.
Education has traditionally been a state function, and hundreds
of statutes in different states provide parents with specific rights
in the education of their children. Since these provisions are so
diverse, we focus on parental rights that are based on powerful federal statutes enacted by Congress during recent years.
Although federal legislation in education is not comprehensive,
many of its provisions are far reaching and may be a model for
parental involvement in the education of their children. The law
concerning handicapped children, for example, gives parents
the right to be involved in the development of individualized
educational plans for their handicapped youngsters; it also

guarantees their right to object to a plan they believe is unsatis-factory and to seek one they think meets their child's special needs. Many parents believe these rights would be useful in the education of every child.

Chapter 10 is about the rights of parents in connection with their children's school records. It outlines the major provisions of the Family Educational Rights and Privacy Act of 1974, which limits access to student records by outsiders, guarantees access to parents, and provides procedures for parents to challenge and correct false or misleading information contained in the records.

Chapter 11 discusses the federal law mentioned above, which covers the rights of parents of children with special educa-tional needs. It focuses on the Education for All Handicapped Children's Act of 1975 and explains its broad provisions, which spell out the rights of parents and students for whom special individualized education is now mandated.

Chapter 12 is about personal appearance. It considers whether students have a constitutional right to wear the hairstyle and clothing of their choice and when schools have the right to restrict dress and grooming.

Chapter 13 confronts several other topics related to parents' rights. It considers two federal statutes which provide special rights to poor parents and their children and to parents and children who do not speak English. It also considers such issues as the meaning of a "free" public education; the financing of public schools; the openness of school board meetings; the use of school facilities by parents' groups; and tracking and testing.

Our final chapter is about legal literacy for parents: it dis-cusses ways parents can learn more about the law and ways that legal literacy can be improved throughout the country.

Each chapter begins with a listing of the major questions to be examined. Most chapters then present a few important judi-cial decisions that outline the major legal principles involved, describing the court's reasoning in reaching its decision. This is usually followed by a series of questions and answers about issues of interest to parents. Each chapter ends by summarizing the law on the subject.

While the chapters are designed to be read in sequence, we have tried to write each one so that it can be understood if read alone. The choice is yours—whether to read the book straight through or to skip among the chapters that interest you. Although most constitutional rights and educational laws are mainly applicable to public schools, we hope the book will also be useful to parents of private school students who want to encourage these schools to shape their policies according to constitutional standards. (Contract law and some due process principles apply to private schools, but generally the Bill of Rights prohibits only *Public* officials from interfering with individual freedom.)

The Appendix includes the constitutional amendments most relevant to the rights of parents and their children. It also includes excerpts from landmark Supreme Court cases. In addition, it explains how you can look up the full text of the cases cited in the book. Although we do not always agree with the decisions we discuss, we try to present an objective picture of what the law is rather than our personal views of what it ought to be.

This short volume cannot address all major conflicts involving parents and education. It does not, for example, explore the difficulties that arise when parents and children disagree about student rights, responsibilities, and educational goals. Nor does it examine ways to resolve disagreements among competing groups of parents who hold reasonable, sincere and strong, opposing views.

Furthermore, there are some important rights that parents have as citizens that are not discussed here. These include the right to meet and organize as parents, generally the right to elect school board members, and the right to talk with teachers and school administrators. These rights have been discussed more fully in other NCCE publications such as *Parents Organizing to Improve Schools* (1985) and *How to Run a School Board Campaign and Win* (1982).

The law examined in this book is neither simple nor unchanging. Many of the cases are as difficult to resolve for lawyers and judges as they are for parents and educators. This is because they do not involve simple conflicts of right against wrong, but complex issues of rights in conflict. And when the constitutional rights of parents and educators collide, the job of the courts is not to choose one over the other but to try to balance and protect both. Moreover, education law is constantly changing. New legislation is passed, regulations are changed, school boards revise their policies, and the Supreme Court may reverse the decision of a lower court.

Because of the diversity and change, our discussion of the cases and laws in each chapter is intended to be illustrative, not exhaustive. We have chosen to highlight major cases and legislation of general interest to parents rather than to focus on legal details.

To summarize, this book is an introduction to legal literacy for parents. It examines a wide range of constitutional, statutory, and common law rights that you as a parent can assert on behalf of your child. Since no two cases are exactly alike, and since the law is constantly changing, the book cannot be a substitute for legal advice.

Any parent who contemplates legal action should first consult a knowledgeable lawyer or a legal services office. But since the judicial resolution of an educational dispute is often an unhappy, expensive, difficult, and time-consuming process, bringing suit should be a last resort. Parents and educators usually share many goals. If this book does its job properly, it should help resolve disputes through mutual education, discussion, and negotiation.

Notes for Chapter 1

1. *Pierce v. Society of Sisters*, 268 U.S. 510 (1925).

2. *Wisconsin v. Yoder*, 406 U.S. 205 (1972).

3. *Tinker v. Des Moines*, 393 U.S. 503 (1969).

4. *Goss v. Lopez*, 419 U.S. 565 (1975).

5. *Wood v. Strickland*, 420 U.S. 308 (1975).

CHAPTER 2

Discipline
and Due Process

Do children have a right to attend school?

Must due process be used before a child is suspended from school?

Does the length of the suspension make a difference?

What does due process require before long suspension or expulsion?

Can a student be suspended until her parents come to school for a meeting?

Is it legal to suspend a student for an undetermined length of time for reasons other than a meeting with parents?

Must students be given a "Miranda Warning" before they are questioned by school officials?

Should the hearing be held before suspension begins?

May the student remain in school during the appeal process?

May schools put students into "double jeopardy"?

Do students have a right to education while suspended?

May work missed during suspension be made up?

Do parents have the right to use lawyers in school disciplinary procedures?

May schools use corporal punishment?

May parents request that their children not be spanked?

May corporal punishment be used for very minor infractions?

Is excessive punishment unconstitutional?

Do child abuse laws apply to physical punishment inflicted by school personnel?

May students and their lockers be searched?

May lockers be searched at any time?

May schools conduct body searches or strip searches?

May trained dogs be used in school searches?

May contraband found in school searches be used by the police?

May police conduct searches in school?

May administrators or the police interrogate students?

May schools punish students for behavior away from school?

May a student be disciplined for breaking rules he or she didn't know about?

May grades be lowered for improper conduct?

May participation in graduation ceremonies be denied as a means of discipline?

May grades be lowered or course credit denied because of absences from school?

What about excessive absences due to illness or injury?

May grades be reduced when a student is truant or suspended?

May participation in extracurricular activities be denied because of low grades?

May students and their parents challenge the grades given by a teacher?

Due process simply means fair procedure. It is now the law that schools should use fair procedures with students and their parents in all serious disciplinary matters. If your child is threatened with suspension for disturbing classes by handing out supposedly obscene newspapers, for starting fights in the cafeteria, or for any other reason, fair procedures (due process) must be used to determine his innocence or guilt. Thus, due process applies to all the issues discussed in this book. In this chapter, however, we focus specifically on the relationship between due process and discipline.

Do children have a right to attend school?

Yes, they do. Since the national Constitution is silent about education, schooling falls under the powers reserved to the states. Pursuant to such reserved powers, every state provides schooling, at public expense, to children between the ages specified by state law. Where such schooling is provided by state law, children have a right to attend school and to be fairly treated there.

Schools should use fair procedures with students and their parents in all matters, and they must use them in disciplinary procedures. In this chapter we focus on the relationship between fair procedures (due process) and discipline. In brief, fairness requires that students and their parents be notified of an alleged offense and the possible punishment for the behavior. Students should also have the opportunity to present their side of the story, and they and their parents, in serious cases, should be informed of their right to appeal if they consider the punishment unfair or unjustified.

Much of the discussion in this chapter focuses on suspension since that penalty, and the more severe penalty of expulsion, are serious in that they deprive students of an education. While many educators consider suspension as a penalty to be used only for serious offenses, some use it for trivial offenses as well. Parents may wish to question the fairness and wisdom of suspension or expulsion policies and practices, but they should also be informed about the due process requirements which must be followed by the school in order to comply with the law.

Suspension and Expulsion

Must due process be used before a child is suspended from school?

Nine high school students were suspended without a hearing for up to 10 days each by the Columbus, Ohio, Board of Education in 1971. Some were suspended for disruptive or disobedient conduct, some "for demonstrating in the school auditorium while a class was being conducted there," others for physically attacking police officers who were in the school to help control demonstrations, and still others for "disturbance in the lunchroom which involved some physical damage to school property."

An Ohio law gave the officials the right to suspend students without a hearing for up to 10 days provided that parents were notified of the suspension within 24 hours and given the reasons for it. The students and their parents claimed the law was unconstitutional. In the *Goss v. Lopez*[1] case, the Supreme Court agreed with them.

In a 5-to-4 decision, the Court held that once a state provides public schools for its children, the students have a "property right" in attending them. (In legal terms, a property right is a benefit or something of value to which a person is entitled). A property right may not be taken away without at least some minimal fair procedures. Furthermore, held the Court, suspension or expulsion damages a student's reputation. And since "the Due Process Clause also forbids arbitrary deprivation of liberty 'Where a person's good name, reputation, honor, or integrity is at stake because of what the government is doing to him,' the minimal requirements of the clause must be satisfied." Thus the Court found that the students' liberty as well as their property rights were violated by the denial of fair procedures.

School officials argued that a short-term suspension is a trivial matter that does not merit constitutional protection. But the Court disagreed. Asserting that "education is perhaps the most important function of state and local governments," the Court ruled that although some suspensions might be trivial, the power to suspend for up to 10 days is certainly important to the student and cannot be exercised arbitrarily.

Does the length of the suspension make a difference?

Yes, it does. While both short (one to ten days) and long (more than ten days) suspensions must be preceded by some kind of hearing, the type of hearing required by the courts differs according to the length of the suspension. In the *Goss* case, the justices were well aware of the complexities of our schools and of the need for order and discipline. They recognized that school officials need the power of suspension, but they saw no reason such power could not be exercised fairly.

As a minimum, they ruled, fairness would require an informal notice and a hearing. This means that the student should be told of the charges against him, orally or in writing, and if he denies them, must be given "an explanation of the evidence the authorities have and an opportunity to present his side of the story." This procedure can be carried out quite informally; as the Court pointed out, good teachers and administrators have followed such fair procedures for a long time in their efforts to reach fair resolutions of disputes in school, without being forced by law.

What if parents consider the informal hearing to have been unfair, or the student did not tell her side of the story? Can parents request a full hearing if they are dissatisfied? Such requests can always be made, and some administrators will reexamine the issues involved. Courts, however, have not required such reexamination in minor disciplinary matters as long as school officials provided at least some minimal due process prior to the short suspension.

Some emergencies can occur at school in which prior notice and hearing are not necessary—when, for example, danger to persons or property requires a delay in the hearing. In such cases the Court requires only that fair procedures be followed as soon as practicable after the danger has been removed. Otherwise, an informal notice and hearing should be provided before any suspension, and the longer the probable suspension the more careful the procedures should be.

What does due process require before long suspension or expulsion?

The courts have established no strict formula or procedure for all serious disciplinary matters. They generally hold, however, a notice must be given and a hearing held prior to long-term suspension (more than 10 days) or expulsion; the accused student must be given the right to counsel, to present evidence on his behalf, and to cross-examine witnesses; and must also be given a statement of the findings, conclusion and recommendation, as well as the right to appeal.

The following is a model that has been suggested before severe penalities are imposed:

1. Notice of hearing, including
   a. the time and place
   b. a statement of the alleged infraction(s)
   c. a declaration of the student's right to legal counsel
   d. a description of the procedures to be followed in the hearing
   e. adequate time to prepare
   f. notice of and access to the evidence against the student
2. Conduct a hearing, including
   a. advisement of student's right to remain silent
   b. the presentation of evidence and witnesses against the student
   c. right to confront and cross-examine the witnesses
   d. the presentation of witnesses on behalf of the student
   e. the recording (either by tape or in writing) of the proceedings
3. Finding(s) of hearing, including
   a. recommendation(s) for disciplinary action, if any
   b. report of findings to appropriate school authorities (e.g., the board of education) and to the student
4. Prompt application of disciplinary measure(s), if any, including the right to appeal.[2]

Can a student be suspended until her parents come to school for a meeting?

Yes, but not indefinitely. School officials often attach this condition to a student's return to school following a suspension, and most courts consider it a reasonable requirement when used by school officials to plan with parents ways to overcome the student's difficulties with schooling. But if the parents are unable or unwilling to come to the school within the term of the suspension (say three days), the student cannot be punished for the parents' inaction. Suspensions which are lengthened because of parents' failure to become involved discriminate against children of low-income and working parents who may not be able to quickly arrange for a school visit, and may punish a student excessively for a stated offense. Furthermore, since due process must precede the suspension, except for emergencies, hearings or other elements of due process may not be used to prolong the student's suspension from school.

Is it legal to suspend a student for an undetermined length of time for reasons other than a meeting with parents?

Courts have not looked favorably upon this practice, especially when suspensions have run longer than ten days. Students have successfully challenged open-ended suspensions for illegal use of alcohol at school[3], as well as those tying their return to class to the payment of repairs for damage to school property[4], or the resolution of pending juvenile court action.[5] Indefinite exclusion from school for these reasons was seen as being too harsh for the students' misdeeds. In these cases, the courts ruled that the interests of students to receive an education outweighed the need of the school to discipline. School systems which fail to develop and publish the time limits for suspension in line with state guidelines risk charges that they have overstepped their authority and failed to treat all students equally. What is more, when conditions required of a returning student turn a short-term suspension into a long-term suspension (more than ten days), the extension must be preceded by more due process procedures, including a formal hearing. (For special considerations related to the length of suspension for handicapped students, see Chapter 11.)

Must students be given a "Miranda Warning" before they are questioned by school officials?

No. The so-called "Miranda rights" apply to those under questioning while in police custody related to criminal investigations.[6] This means that when police take people into custody, they must inform them of their right to remain silent, that anything they say may be used against them, and that they have a right to the assistance of a lawyer.

Since school disciplinary proceedings are not criminal proceedings, Miranda does not apply to them.[7] In fact, in ordinary school disciplinary procedures, students don't even have the right to have their parents present. This, of course, changes in serious situations, that might result in long-term suspension or expulsion.

Independently of any "Miranda warning," students have the right to remain silent when charged with infraction of the school rules. The First Amendment guarantees not only freedom of expression, but also its corollary, the right not to speak. However, if a student remains silent when given a fair opportunity to respond to charges against him, the administrator may consider this behavior as corroborating evidence in the total assessment of the situation.

Should the hearing be held before suspension begins?

Yes. Guilt or innocence is determined during or after the hearing, where the student has an opportunity to explain his side of the controversy. If the suspension begins before the hearing, he is pre-judged and determined guilty without due process. The student may continue his schooling until after the hearing. The only exception to this is when there are grounds to conclude that there is danger to persons or property if the student is not immediately removed from the school. In such a case, immediate suspension is proper, but it should be followed by due process hearings as soon as practicable.

May the student remain in school during the appeal process?

Yes, she may, unless her presence constitutes a danger to others or to property. Guilt or innocence is not determined until all appeals are exhausted; therefore, a student has a right to attend school until appeals are completed.

May schools put students into "double jeopardy"?

"Double jeopardy" is a technical legal concept used in criminal law when one is brought to trial twice for the same offense. Since schools do not conduct criminal proceedings, the concept of double jeopardy does not apply to them. Questions still arise when a student has received punishment such as detention for some unacceptable behavior, and the same offense is taken into account in a subsequent disciplinary situation. Is that double punishment, and is it legal?

Breaking a rule repeatedly is often considered more serious than breaking it only once. That is true in and out of school. Punishment for the first offense is supposed to prevent its repetition. Thus, when later offenses occur, it is reasonable to consider the entire history of the particular student's behavior. If one important purpose of school punishment is to help students change their behavior, then it makes sense to consider their pattern of behavior over time before deciding on an appropriate punishment for a particular infraction of rules. Courts respect the decisions of school administrators in these matters as long as they follow the basics of due process.

School officials also have broad discretion in the use of short-term suspension, which might be anywhere from one to ten days, depending on state law or local policy. Most schools do not use suspension for trivial infractions and tend to use other forms of punishment, such as detention, extra homework, denial of privileges, or notices to parents for minor misbehavior like tardiness, interrupting class, or not handing in homework assignments. Courts are very reluctant to intrude into the ordinary daily life of schools and do not want school activities to become overly legalistic.

Some schools also use a disciplinary technique known as "in-school suspension," whereby students are removed from regular classes and placed temporarily in a study hall under supervision of a teacher. Whether this is considered a punishment or a way of teaching students to be disciplined, courts have not interfered with the reasonable use of such in-school suspension.

Do students have a right to education while suspended?

As a general rule, they do not. This may not apply to handicapped students covered by special laws which we discuss later in Chapter 11. The power and threat of suspension would be somewhat diminished if schools were obligated to continue educating students who were under suspension. There are good reasons to argue that when a student, within the compulsory age of schooling, is suspended from attendance for any length of time, the school should provide some alternative education for him during the period of suspension. While the law in general does not require this, some states, such as New York, require by state law that the board of education provide such alternative instruction.[8] Courts in the District of Columbia and in New York have so ruled, and even in the absence of a specific statute, a strong argument to the same effect can be made in states whose constitutions indicate that education is a "fundamental state interest" or constitutional right.[9]

Similar arguments can be raised regarding expulsions where, in general, courts have so far not required the out-of-school education of expelled students. Expulsions generally last until the end of the semester during which the serious infraction occurred. If an expulsion goes beyond that, a good case could be made that such expulsion violates the state constitution. In such situations, the specific state statutes related to compulsory attendance as well as expulsion would have to be examined.

A parent whose child is expelled from school for serious misbehavior might also investigate whether or not that child would qualify under Public Law 94-142 or its state counterpart as a child with some special need. Handicapped students may not be expelled without an alternative educational placement, as we explain in Chapter 11.

May work missed during suspension be made up?

That depends on the nature of the offense that brought on the suspension and the stated policies of the school. Denying an opportunity to make up work missed on top of the suspension seems like double punishment. The wisdom of such policy is an educational and not a legal matter. Therefore, courts usually will not disturb such school policies and practices,[10] and it is more advisable for parents to try to influence such policies through their own advisory boards, PTAs, or other forms of local political action.

Do parents have the right to use lawyers in school disciplinary procedures?

That depends on the situation. As a general rule, in minor disciplinary matters, where the punishment is likely to be suspension for a short period of time, there is no right to be represented by a lawyer. On the other hand, if the likely punishment is long-term suspension or even expulsion, students and parents can insist on representation by counsel. As in almost every other conflict, courts attempt to balance the competing interests of the schools against those of the parents and students. Because elaborate legal procedures for minor violations would be expensive, time consuming, and cumbersome, relatively simple procedures are acceptable. On the other hand, when a severe punishment might befall a student, the balance tilts the other way, and fairness requires more careful, meticulous procedures.

Corporal Punishment

May schools use corporal punishment?

Many parents are adamant that schools must never spank their children, while others subscribe to the time honored maxim, "spare the rod and spoil the child." Depending on where you live, the law may allow or forbid school officials to use corporal punishment.

The basic legal principle, established in common law and still with us today, is that a teacher or administrator may use such force as a reasonable educator would believe to be necessary for the proper control, training, or education of the child. If the force is excessive or unreasonable, the educator in almost all states is subject to a civil suit for damages as well as possible criminal liability. In order to determine whether a punishment is reasonable, all the circumstances of the case must be considered. The important factors are: the seriousness of the offense; the student's attitude, past behavior, age and strength; the nature and severity of the punishment; and the availability of alternative, less severe means of punishment.

Not all states have legislation on the subject, but of those that do, most allow the use of moderate corporal punishment in public schools. Some require that the parents be notified, some require an adult witness, and some permit only the school principal or vice principal to administer the punishment. As of this writing, nine states prohibit all corporal punishment in public schools. They are: California, Hawaii, Maine, Massachusetts, New Hampshire, New Jersey, New York, Rhode Island, and Vermont. Some of these states prohibit corporal punishment by legislation, others through statewide policy of a school board. The New York State Board of Regents, for example, created a policy banning such punishment as of September 1, 1985, defining corporal punishment as "any act of physical force upon a pupil for the purpose of punishing that pupil." The policy excludes from the definition of corporal punishment the use of reasonable force for self-defense, in the defense of other persons or property, or to restrain or remove a disorderly student who refuses to comply with a request to stop disorderly conduct.

In states that have no laws prohibiting corporal punishment, local boards of education have the power to ban corporal punishment in their schools, and many have done so. Therefore, it is important for parents to express their convictions through local organizations and thus help influence local school policy.

Where state laws or local rules do not prohibit it, courts have uniformly preserved the common law rule that permits the reasonable use of force to discipline children in schools.

May parents request that their children not be spanked?

Such requests can be made, but schools are not necessarily bound by them, and they do not have to get approval from parents. This was affirmed by the Supreme Court in 1975, in the case *Baker v. Owens.*[11]

Mrs. Virginia Baker of North Carolina had requested that her son's teachers or principal not use corporal punishment, because she opposed it in principle. Nevertheless, after her sixth-grader, Russel Carl, violated an announced school rule against throwing kickballs during certain times, he "received two licks in the presence of a second teacher and in view of other students."

Although the law of North Carolina allows the use of reasonable force "to restrain or correct pupils and to maintain order," Mrs. Baker claimed the law was unconstitutional since it allows such punishment over parental objections. The district court ruled against her, and when she appealed, the Supreme Court affirmed this ruling. While recognizing the basic rights of parents to supervise the upbringing of their children, the court also recognized "the state's legitimate and substantial interest in maintaining order and discipline in the public schools." Since both popular and professional opinion are divided on the question of corporal punishment, the court refused to allow "the wishes of a parent to restrict school officials' discretion in deciding the methods to be used in...maintaining discipline."

May corporal punishment be used for very minor infractions?

Psychologists generally agree that corporal punishment should not be used in schools, and certainly psychologists and educators agree that corporal punishment should not be used for trivial breaking of rules or for such minor matters as forgetting to bring pencils or notebooks to class or for innocently giving wrong answers on a test. Educationally it is unjustifiable to beat children for such behavior. However, the wisdom of an educational practice is not a legal matter, and courts will not usurp the authority or power of educators in such situations. If a teacher uses reasonable corporal punishment for trivial infractions or academic errors in school districts that still allow such punishment, courts will not interfere. It is up to educators and parents to examine such practices and to create policies that eliminate their use.

Is excessive punishment unconstitutional?

It is illegal but not unconstitutional, ruled the Supreme Court in 1977.[12] In a Dade County, Florida, case, two junior high school boys were paddled until one of them "suffered a hematoma requiring medical attention and keeping him out of school for 11 days"; the other lost the use of his arm for a week. The parents of both boys claimed that this was cruel and unusual punishment and a violation of due process, since the boys had been given no prior notice and hearing.

By a 5-to-4 vote, the Court ruled that the Eighth Amendment prohibition against cruel and unusual punishment does not apply to students, even when school punishment is excessive. After examining the history of cruel and unusual punishment, the Court explained that it was meant to apply only to criminal matters. Although the Court deplored excessive use of force in the schools, it concluded that adequate remedies are available against educators who use it, since they can be sued for money damages and even prosecuted in criminal action.

The Court further held that situations calling for corporal punishment do not require prior notice and hearing, pointing out that the traditional common law remedy of suit for money damages is fully adequate against those who abuse their discretion as educators.

Parents who are dissatisfied with this ruling can reduce its effect on their children by working for state legislation or local board rules that will control educators in disciplining students. Parents who support the position of the Court, of course, have the same opportunities to influence state law and board rules.

At least one federal circuit court ruled, however, that brutal and excessive corporal punishment violates substantive due
process*, guaranteed by the Fourteenth Amendment. Since this
issue was not raised in the Supreme Court case discussed
above, at this time we do not know whether the Court would
take the same position. The 4th Circuit Court relied on cases
that held that individuals have a right to be "free of state in-
trusions into realms of personal privacy and bodily security
through means so brutal, demeaning, and harmful as literally
to shock the conscience." This ruling came in a case where the
parents claimed that their grade school student was so badly
beaten by the teacher that the severe injuries suffered required
ten days of hospitalization and may have caused permanent
injuries to her lower back and spine.[13]
To summarize, whether corporal punishment is allowed is
first a question of state law. If your state allows it, as most
states do, check whether your school follows the requirements
for witnessing or notice to parents or other conditions specified
by the state statute. Futhermore, even if a state allows such
punishment, a local school board policy may either limit or
prohibit its use. If neither state law nor district policy controls corporal punishment, the law allows its reasonable use
in schools. Excessive use can lead to a civil suit for damages
and even a criminal charge of battery. Brutal, malicious corporal
punishment may well be a violation of due process that could be
grounds for legal action as a constitutional "tort"** (see Chapter
8).

**Do child abuse laws apply to physical punishment inflicted
by school personnel?**

The answer to date is no. Definitions of child abuse vary from

---

*Courts speak of *procedural* due process and *substantive* due process.
The former has to do with fairness in procedures used while the latter requires that official action not be arbitrary, capricious, unfair, or
excessively severe when less severe alternatives are available.

**A "tort" is a wrong committed against an individual for which a suit
for money damages can be filed.

state to state*, but they generally apply to acts of parents or other persons responsible for the welfare of the child. While it is clearly arguable that teachers and administrators are responsible for the welfare of children and that they stand in *loco parentis* (in the place of parents) while children are in school, no parent has successfully prosecuted an educator under child abuse statutes for administering corporal punishment. There have been cases, however, where teachers have been arrested on charges of sexual molestation and pornography.**

Search and Seizure

May students and their lockers be searched?

As a byproduct of recent widespread drug use and violence in the schools, the practice of searching students' lockers and even their persons has become highly visible. Police usually need a court order or a person's consent to search his house, person, or car. Are school officials similarly bound in conducting searches in school?

In general, the answer is no. Courts have given educators broader leeway than police when it comes to searching school lockers and even the students themselves. This is because of the special nature of a school environment. In a New York case, for example, a judge said: "Not only have the school authorities the right to inspect *but this right becomes a duty when suspicion arises* that something of an illegal nature may be secreted there."[14] Courts in other states have come to similar conclusions.

But school officials do not have blanket power to search students at any time and for any reason. Such power would be

---

*Although state laws vary, they all use two or more of the following elements in defining child abuse and neglect: (1) physical injury, (2) mental or emotional injury, (3) sexual molestation or exploitation. See Frazier, *A Glance at the Past, a Gaze at the Present, a Glimpse of the Future: A Critical Analysis of the Development of Child Abuse Reporting Status*, 54 Chi. Kent L. Rev. 641, 643 (1978)

**See, for example, a news item in *The New York Times*, March 25, 1986, p. A20.

too broad and arbitrary. The Supreme Court so ruled in 1985 in the well-publicized case of *New Jersey v. T.L.O.*[15] In that case a teacher, upon entering the girls' bathroom, found T.L.O. and a friend holding lighted cigarettes. The girls were taken to the assistant vice principal's office, since school rules forbade smoking in bathrooms. When T.L.O. denied smoking, she was asked to open her purse. There, along with cigarettes, were found drug paraphernalia and evidence that she had sold drugs. After examining the purse, the administrator summoned T.L.O.'s mother and the police.

The case ultimately reached the U.S. Supreme Court, whose majority said that school searches are justified "when there are reasonable grounds for suspecting that the search will turn up evidence that the student has violated either the law or the rules of the school." Thus, the "probable cause" requirement that is applied before the police may search your car or your home is not applicable to school officials' search of student lockers or purses. If the administrators have reasonable grounds to suspect a violation of the law or of school rules, they may search, but their search itself must be reasonable in scope. While the Supreme Court has not yet ruled on some other aspects of searching students, lower federal courts, including some appeals courts, provide us with some guidance.

Following *T.L.O.*, courts often ask two questions in search and seizure cases: first, was the initial search based on reasonable suspicion, and second, was the scope of the search appropriate, under the circumstances? In a California case illustrating this two-step approach, a student without a pass to be out of the classroom behaved suspiciously when questioned by the boys' dean in the restroom. He was directed to empty his pockets, which turned out to contain cigarettes and cocaine. These materials and the student were turned over to the police. Was the search legal?

The court first held that it was proper for the boys' dean to be in the restroom and to quiz the student who lacked a proper pass and behaved suspiciously. Thus, the initial questioning was reasonable. Second, the court found the boy's illicit conduct justifiably led to the more thorough search. The scope of the search was not too intrusive nor excessive.[16]

May lockers be searched at any time?

There is no uniform law on this question. The Supreme Court has never ruled on the search of a school locker, and lower courts are divided on the issue. Since school lockers are school property, and the administration usually has keys or combinations to all locks, some courts hold that students have no expectation of privacy for their lockers.

Other courts disagree and hold that lockers may be examined only if there are reasonable grounds to suspect contraband in specific students' lockers. They may also be searched for library books or other school materials if advance notice is given for the upcoming search.

Parents may well wish to find out the policies of their school district, as well as how courts in their jurisdiction have ruled on locker searches.

May schools conduct body searches or strip searches?

Our Constitution, as interpreted by the courts, provides more protection as a search becomes more personal and invasive of one's privacy. Thus, a body search that includes the search of a student's clothing is more invasive than a locker search, and a strip search is more invasive than either of the foregoing. A higher degree of reliable evidence must exist before courts will allow such searches; in fact, for a strip search the "probable cause" standard is used by the courts. This is the same standard as the courts apply to requests for search warrants by the police.

Thus, a court found that educators violated students' constitutional rights when they conducted a strip search of an entire fifth grade class over a missing $3.[17] Moreover, a court awarded $7,500 in damages to a student in connection with a strip search a federal court found to be illegal.[18] Similarly, a school policy requiring that all students submit to urine samples for drug testing was held to be unconstitutional as violative of due process, right of privacy, as well as the prohibition against unreasonable search and seizure.[19]

May trained dogs be used in school searches?

The law is not completely clear on this issue since federal circuit courts are somewhat divided in their answers, and the

Supreme Court has not yet ruled on a case involving search dogs in schools.

A case that arose in Indiana held that the use of sniffing dogs is not a search, even though school personnel, the police, and trained dog-handlers spent two-and-a-half to three hours in a room-by-room inspection of the students. The dogs sniffed almost 3,000 students, alerting 50 times. Eleven students were strip searched, including a 13-year-old girl who had been playing with her dog before school. The Seventh Circuit Court ruled that only the body searches were unreasonable, and that the general use of sniffing dogs is not a search.[20] If the use of sniffing dogs does not constitute a "search," the constitutional prohibition against unreasonable or warrantless searches does not apply.

A similar issue arose more recently in the Goosecreek School District in Texas, where trained Doberman pinschers and German shepherds were used to sniff students, lockers, and cars in a search for drugs. The Fifth Circuit Court rejected the reasoning of the previously discussed Indiana case. It held that there is a difference between the use of dogs to sniff objects and persons.

Legal doctrine provides that no search warrant is needed when something is in "plain view." The courts reasoned that odors are similar to seeing something in "plain view." Therefore, merely sniffing cars or lockers does not constitute a search. Moreover, when dogs alert school officials to lockers or cars, they have reasonable grounds to check them for contraband. Persons, however, receive greater protection than objects. Therefore, the court held that the use of dogs to sniff students is a search, and a general sniffing of all students is objectionable. Before a body search could be conducted, educators must have probable cause to believe that a particular student possessed drugs or other illegal substances.

Because of the prevalence of problems related to illegal materials in school lockers, purses, pockets, and cars, an increasing number of schools have established written policies on school searches. Parents can request copies of these policies.

May contraband found in school searches be used by the police?

That depends on how the contraband was obtained. The so-called "exclusionary rule" holds that illegally obtained evidence may not be used in court. However, if school administrators in a proper search find drugs or other contraband and turn them over to the police, they may be used in court. In fact, in most places the school officials are obligated to turn such materials over to the police.

May police conduct searches in school?

Yes, they may, if they have a proper search warrant. There is no uniform law when police conduct a search without a warrant, but with permission from the school adminstration. In such situations, courts disagree, some accepting the evidence on the theory that schools own the lockers and may give permission for the police search, while others reject the evidence unless school administrators had reasonable grounds to suspect specific students' lockers.

May administrators or the police interrogate students?

Yes, they may, in the proper performance of their duties. However, the student does not have to answer the police if he or she doesn't want to. Similarly, when questioned by the administrator, the student may remain silent. Our First Amendment right to freedom of expression also protects our right not to speak. Students should not be punished for such refusal to respond, but the school official may enter an accurate description of the event in the student's record, and consider the student's refusal to respond along with other evidence in reaching a conclusion.

May schools punish students for behavior away from school?

As a general rule they may not. Exceptions include school-sponsored field trips and athletic activities. Furthermore, if there is a close connection between schooling and the particular away-from-school misbehavior—as, for example, when a group of students attacked a girl on her way home, one block away from school—courts have upheld the rights of schools to administer reasonable discipline.

May a student be disciplined for breaking rules he or she didn't know about?

That depends. If the rules were generally known or if they were posted or available in student handbooks, a student can be held responsible for knowing them. The rules should be clear and understandable to ordinary students; rules that are too vague or overly broad will not hold up either in practice or in court, since students can't tell what is expected of them. For example, a rule calling on students "to behave and be good citizens" is so vague as to be useless and unenforceable.

May grades be lowered for improper conduct?

Increasingly, the courts are separating conduct from academic achievement. Since schools have procedures for dealing with improper conduct, grades, which are supposed to reflect school achievement, should not be altered by good or bad behavior. Many schools assign separate grades for conduct and for scholastic achievement.

This is especially the case when the alleged misconduct occurs away from school. A Pennsylvania court so ruled in a case involving Deborah Katzman, an 11th-grade honors student with an excellent school record. While on a field trip to New York City sponsored by her humanities class, Deborah and her four classmates each had a glass of wine, in violation of school policy. When she admitted her guilt, Deborah was suspended from school for five days, expelled from the cheerleading squad, expelled from the National Honor Society, and her grades in each of her classes were reduced by ten percent (two percentage points for each day of suspension). When Deborah and her parents went to court to challenge her grade reduction, the court ruled in their favor. According to the court, the school cannot base the student's grade on behavior not related to academic performance. The reduction of her grades, according to the court, could misrepresent her academic achievement, and such misrepresentation would be both improper and illegal.[21]

In one case, a school attempted to withhold a student's diploma for alleged misbehavior. The court denied the school this right, pointing out that since the diploma is earned through academic achievement, poor behavior cannot be used to deny it. Separate disciplinary procedures are legitimate to address the

question of misbehavior, but the diploma cannot be denied.[22]
The same logic would hold for lesser school penalties such as
the withholding of credit for improper conduct or the retention
of a student. Course credits reflect academic achievement, and
increasingly the courts differentiate such achievements from
questions of misbehavior. Of course, schools still have the
authority to specify reasonable rules of conduct for students
and create appropriate mechanisms for their enforcement.

**May participation in graduation ceremonies be denied as a
means of discipline?**

That depends on the reasons for the denial. If, for example,
the student refuses to wear the specified academic dress but
insists on wearing an Indian headdress or football helmet instead, he or she can be excluded.[23] But school officials may
not exclude a student for past misconduct where there is not
clear evidence that such misconduct will recur to disrupt the
ceremonies.[24]

Courts consider graduation to be a significant experience for
students who earned it through years of schooling. One who
has fulfilled all requirements should not be excluded from it for
past misbehavior.

**May grades be lowered or course credit denied because of
absences from school?**

Schools usually specify the types of absences that are excused
and those that are not. School handbooks or other policy statements also inform students and parents of the consequences of
unexcused absences. At times, parents disagree with the school
policies and approve school absences for their children which
are not acceptable by the school. For example, parents in a small
New England town took their children to a special exhibit at
the Museum of Fine Arts in Boston on a school day, after the
school denied permission for such a trip. Parents may not override school policy in such matters, and if the school has a stated
policy that informs students and parents that grades or course
credit will be affected by unexcused absences, even if the absence is approved by parents, generally the school may enforce
such policy.

These questions have arisen over brief absences and lengthy
ones, for example, when parents took their children on a three-

week trip to Mexico or Europe during the school term. In most situations, informal agreements are reached with teachers that make it possible for the students to keep abreast of the work or to make up what they missed. These arrangements, however, are at the discretion of the school officials, and there is no law that requires them to make such accommodations. In these situations, it's best not to resort to legal technicalities, but to proceed through friendly negotiations with school personnel.

Unexcused absences may be used to lower students' grades if such a school policy is clearly stated and announced in advance. Behavior, including regular school attendance, may be considered by schools in calculating grades and credit, if clear notice of such policy has been announced to the school community.

What about excessive absences due to illness or injury?

When students miss too many school days due to chronic illness, hospitalization or other medical reasons, they may lose school credit, may have to repeat a course, or even an entire grade in school. Such unfortunate circumstances may be no one's fault, just a reality of life. Schools may assess the progress of such students and give them credit for the coursework missed if the student can demonstrate knowledge of the materials. On the other hand, the schools may require a repetition of the grade or the course. Either alternative would be considered reasonable in the eyes of the law, and local school policy will control the situation.

May grades be reduced when a student is truant or suspended?

Some courts have upheld grade reduction penalties for truancy, holding that grading can be used to reflect both academic achievement and behavior.[25] Some other courts, however, held that grade reduction because of truancy is not legitimate because it exceeds the rule-making authority of the school board.[26] (It is an *ultra vires* act.) How the courts rule will be influenced by relevant state statutes, if any exist, as well as the existence of school board policies controlling such matters.

May participation in extracurricular activities be denied because of low grades?

As a general rule, yes. Participation in extracurricular activities, school dances, and athletic events is generally not considered to be an essential part of compulsory schooling. If educators create reasonable conditions for participating in them, courts are likely to uphold such conditions. The rationale behind this is that students should use their time and energies on their studies first. Extracurricular activities should be a second priority. Some educators claim that such a precondition will motivate some students to pay more attention to their studies.

The state of Texas, for example, has created the so-called "no pass, no play" rule which was held to be constitutional by the Texas Supreme Court. The rule required that students, except the mentally retarded, must receive grades of at least 70% or "C" or above in order to participate in extracurricular activities, including athletics. The rule was attacked as a violation of the Equal Protection and Due Process Clauses of the Texas Constitution. The court held that there were good reasons for the rule and that it did not discriminate against any protected class of students; therefore, the court held the rule did not violate the state constitution.[27]

May students and their parents challenge the grades given by a teacher?

In general, legal challenges to grades assigned for academic work will not succeed. Courts are most reluctant to substitute their judgment for that of teachers, for they feel incompetent to judge the quality of such work and to assign grades to it. It has been a time-honored practice for educators to make the final decisions about the quality of academic work. Exceptions to this general rule may arise where parents and students can show racial, ethnic, or gender prejudice on the part of the teacher, or discrimination based on religion or other protected constitutional rights. The burden of proving such discrimination would be on the parents, a very difficult burden to satisfy.

Some schools provide machinery for an internal review of alleged grade discrimination or unfair evaluation of student work. Such review is usually conducted by a department head or appropriate administrator. If schools have such review mechanisms, students and parents have a right to request them,

but courts will only see to it that the school procedures were
followed. Judges will not examine the substantive merits of
such disagreements and will not overrule the judgments of
educators. If a school has no process to address such disagreements, parents and administrators can work together to
create one.

Summary

During recent years, due process has become one of the most
important constitutional rights of parents and students. In this
chapter we focused on those aspects of due process that relate
to disciplinary matters in schools.

As exclusion from schools, whether by suspension, expulsion
or some other action, became a widely used form of discipline,
parents and students challenged some school procedures, lead-
ing to a ruling by the United States Supreme Court that a minimum of due process is required—even in cases involving short-
term suspensions. This, the Court said, is not an unreasonable
burden for schools, since only such rudimentary elements of
fairness as informal notice and hearing are required, and this
requirement is met if the student is told orally or in writing what
his alleged wrongdoing was and what the evidence is against
him, and if he is given a chance to tell his side of the story.
In emergency situations, where there is danger to persons or
property, the hearing will not be insisted upon until after the
removal of the danger.

If a long-term suspension is the punishment, the courts require more complete procedures. In such situations, parents
may insist on a notice and a hearing, and the right to be represented by a lawyer, to cross-examine witnesses and to be given
a record of the proceedings. Parents and students also have the
right to appeal—usually to higher school authorities and to the
school board. (A guidance conference is not a disciplinary action, nor is an ordinary transfer of a student from one class to
another. But if a transfer is for purposes of punishment, due
process should be followed.)

Constitutional attacks on corporal punishment have had
limited success. The Supreme Court ruled that even excessive
use of force in school does not violate the Eighth Amendment's
prohibition against cruel and unusual punishment, because that

amendment was never intended to apply to schools. However, at least one circuit court ruled that some punishment may be so excessive and brutal as to violate the Fourteenth Amendment's Due Process Clause. There are nine states that forbid any use of corporal punishment, and even in states that allow it, many communities prohibit its use by local policy. Furthermore, no court protects unreasonable or excessive use of force. Educators who use excessive force can be sued for money damages and can be subject to criminal liability. The Supreme Court has ruled that procedural due process is not required prior to corporal punishment. Parents should get to know the laws of their state and the local rules regulating corporal punishment, since they are usually more specific and helpful than court rulings based on the Constitution.

School officials may search student lockers or even the students themselves if they have a reasonable suspicion that illegal or dangerous drugs, weapons or other material is hidden there. They may cooperate with law enforcement officials, but must have a factual basis for their suspicions before they may proceed. The use of trained dogs to search students' lockers, cars, and students themselves for drugs has led to several court cases. No uniform law exists on this issue, but the trend of opinion is to allow the use of trained dogs to smell objects, such as lockers and cars. If drugs emit a "public smell" detected by dogs, the lockers and cars may be searched by school officials. Dogs may be used to smell students only if there are reasonable grounds to suspect individuals possess contraband. Body searches or strip searches may not be conducted on the basis of a dog's alert, and school officials must have "probable cause" to conduct such a search, which is the same standard as judges apply to policemen who seek a search warrant.

In general, your children cannot be punished by the schools for behavior away from school unless a clear and close connection can be shown to school activities. Students are held responsible for rules they should have known, even if they do not know them. And schools ought not lower grades or withhold diplomas for reasons of poor behavior.

History shows that parents and students have made significant gains in recent years in the recognition of their rights to due process. Many educators recognized these rights in the past, and today the courts, state laws and local policies are making them increasingly a part of the daily life of the schools. (Race discrimination in suspension practices by schools is discussed in Chapter 5.)

Notes for Chapter 2

1. *Goss v. Lopez*, 419 U.S. 565 (1975).

2. Robert L. Ackerly, *The Reasonable Exercise of Authority*, Washington, D.C.: National Association of Secondary School Principals, 1969, pp. 14-16.

3. *Cook v. Edwards*, 341 F. Supp. 307 (D.N.H. 1972).

4. *Perkins v. Independent School District*, 56 Iowa 476, 9.N.W. 356, 357 (1880).

5. *Brown v. Bd. of Ed. of Tipton Co.*, C.A. No. 79-2234-M (W.D. Tenn, 5/3/79)

6. *Miranda v. Arizona*, 384 U.S. 436 (1966).

7. *Pollnow v. Glennon*, 594 F. Supp. 220 (S.D.N.Y. 1984), aff. 757 F.2d 496 (2d cir. 1985).

8. Education Law, Section 3214, Subsection 3(e).

9. *Pacyna v. Board of Education*, 204 N.W. 2d 671 (Wisc. 1973).

10. *New Braunfels Independent School District v.Armke*, 658 S.W.2d 330 (Tex. App. 1983).

11. *Baker v. Owens*, 423 U.S. 907 (1975).

12. *Ingraham v. Wright*, 97 S. Ct. 1401 (1977).

13. *Hall v. Tawney*, 621 F.2d 607 (4th Cir. 1980).

14. *People v. Overton, 249 N.E.2d 366 (N.Y. 1969).*

15. *New Jersey v. T.L.O.*, 105 S.Ct. 733 (1985).

16. In re Bobby B., 218 Cal. Rptr. 253 (Cal. Ct. App. 1985).

17. *Bellnier v. Lund*, 438 F.Supp. 47 (N.D.N.Y. 1977).

18. *M.M. v. Anker*, 607 F.2d 588 (2nd Cir. 1979).

19. *Odenheim v. Carlstadt-East Rutherford Regional School Dist.*, 510A.2d 709 (NJ Super. Ct. App. Div. 1985).

20. *Doe v. Renfrow*, 631 F.2d 91 (7th Cir. 1980), *cert. denied* 451 U.S. 1022 (1981).

21. *Katzman v. Cumberland Valley School District*, 479 A.2d 671 (Pa. Commw. Ct. 1984).

22. *Matter of Carroll, Decision of Chancellor*, (N.Y., Dec. 6, 1971).

23. *Fowler v. Williamson*, 448 F.Supp. 497 (W.D.N.C. 1978).

24. *Ladson v. Board of Education*, 323 N.Y.S.2d 545 (Sup. Ct. 1971).

25. *Knight v. Board of Education*, 348 N.E.2d 299 (Ill. App. 1976).

26. See, for example, *Blackman v. Brown*, 419 N.Y.S.2d 796 (1978); *Katzman v. Cumberland Valley School District*, 479 A.2d 671 (Pa. Cmwlth. 1984).

27. *Spring Branch Independent School District v. Stamas*, No. C-4184, slip. op. (Tex. 1985).

CHAPTER 3

Freedom of Expression

Does the *Tinker* decision apply only to the classroom?

Can schools legally limit freedom of expression or symbolic speech?

Must officials wait until a disruption has occurred?

Are "fighting words" protected?

Can school officials prohibit vulgar and indecent speech?

Do students have a right of "curricular choice"?

Can administrators cancel a school play because of its theme?

Can students be prohibited from discussing controversial issues in a student newspaper?

May school personnel restrict the distribution of student newspapers?

Can students be required to submit publications to school officials for review prior to distribution?

Is the distribution of obscene or libelous materials protected by the Constitution?

Can student newspapers be prohibited from criticizing school policies or administrators?

Can schools restrict newspaper activities that could cause emotional harm?

Can schools ban ads about controversial issues?

Can schools ban newspapers that contain advertisements for drug paraphernalia?

Can schools regulate newspapers published by the journalism class?

Can school officials control the content of publications if they pay the costs?

Does the First Amendment apply to a high school yearbook?

Can schools regulate off-campus publications?

Can schools prohibit students from inviting or listening to controversial speakers?

Does the First Amendment protect teachers' communications with parents?

_____

During the first half of this century, the Bill of Rights rarely assisted parents and students who challenged the constitutionality of school rules. Courts generally used the so-called "reasonableness" test to judge school policies. If there was any reasonable relationship between the rule and the goals of the school, the rule would be upheld— even if many parents and educators believed it was unwise or unnecessary. Judges felt that school boards should have wide discretion and that courts should not substitute their judgment for that of school officials, who were presumed to be experts in educational matters.

In 1969, the U.S. Supreme Court handed down a historic decision that challenged the reasonableness test. In *Tinker v. Des Moines*, a suit initiated by a few concerned parents, the Court ruled that students do not shed their constitutional right to freedom of expression "at the schoolhouse gate." This chapter begins with a description of that important case, which changed the direction of education law in America. It then considers the extent and limits of a student's freedom of expression—in the classroom and on the playground, in school newspapers and in underground publications.

The Tinker Case[1]

In 1965, when there was heated disagreement about American involvement in the Vietnam War, a group of students in Des Moines, Iowa, decided to wear black armbands to publicize their anti-war views. Upon learning of the plan, the Des Moines principals established a policy prohibiting the armbands in order to prevent any possible disturbance.

Although they knew about the policy, several students nevertheless wore the armbands to school and refused to remove them. They were then suspended. The parents of these students argued that the school policy was unconstitutional and took their case to court. The trial judge ruled that the anti-armband policy was reasonable, but the parents did not give up. They pursued the case to the Supreme Court, presenting it with a conflict between the rights of students and the rules of the school. While the Court recognized that school officials must have authority to control student conduct, it held that neither students nor teachers "shed their constitutional rights to freedom of speech or expression at the schoolhouse gate." The First Amendment protects symbolic as well as pure speech,* the Court said, and the wearing of an armband to express certain views is the type of symbolic act protected by that amendment.

Moreover, after reviewing the facts of the case, the Court found that there was "no evidence whatsoever" that wearing armbands interfered "with the school's work or with the rights of other students to be secure or to be left alone." School officials might have honestly feared that the armbands would lead to a disturbance, but the Court said that this fear was not sufficient to violate student rights. "In our system," wrote the Court, "undifferentiated fear or apprehension of disturbance is not enough to overcome the right to freedom of expression."

While the Court recognized that free speech in the schools may cause problems, it noted:

> Any word spoken in class, in the lunchroom, or on the campus that deviates from the views of another person may start an argument or cause a disturbance. But our Constitution says we must take this risk; and our history says that it is this sort of hazardous freedom—this kind of openness—that is the basis of our national strength and of the independence and vigor of Americans who grow up and live in this relatively permissive, often disputatious society.

In a provocative comment about education and freedom, the Court wrote:

---

*See Appendix A for the wording of the First Amendment and other constitutional amendments most relevant to parents and students.

In our system, state operated schools may not be enclaves of totalitarianism. . . .Students in schools as well as out of school are possessed of fundamental rights which the State must respect, just as they themselves must respect their obligations to the State. In our system, students may not be regarded as closed-circuit recipients of only that which the State chooses to communicate.

In sum, the *Tinker* case held that school officials cannot prohibit a particular opinion merely "to avoid the discomfort and unpleasantness that always accompany an unpopular viewpoint." On the contrary, unless there is evidence that the forbidden expression would "materially and substantially" interfere with the work of the school, such a prohibition is unconstitutional.* Thus the willingness of a few Iowa parents to assert the rights of their children led to a Supreme Court decision which expanded the rights of all students in the United States.

Does the *Tinker* decision apply only to the classroom?

No. The Court ruled that the principles of this case are not confined to the curriculum or to classroom hours. On the contrary, a student's right to freedom of expression applies equally "in the cafeteria, or on the playing field" and in all other school activities.

Can schools legally limit freedom of expression or symbolic speech?

Yes. There are limits to all constitutional rights. In *Tinker*, the Court stated that any student conduct which "materially disrupts classwork or involves substantial disorder or invasion of the rights of others is, of course, not immunized by the constitutional guarantee of freedom of speech."

On the other hand, symbolic speech cannot be prohibited simply because of threatened disruption. For example, if some students threaten to attack protesters who peacefully wear controversial symbols, it is the responsibility of school officials to discipline those who threaten violence, not those exercising their constitutional rights.[2] However, where officials make a

---

* For a more complete report of the *Tinker* decision, see Appendix C.

good faith effort to control disruption and fail, they can then restrict student speech.

Must officials wait until a disruption has occurred?

No. In the case of a student demonstration inside a high school, a federal judge ruled that the First Amendment does not require administrators to wait until actual disruption takes place before they act.[3] The judge explained that schools may restrict student expression when evidence indicates a "reasonable likelihood of substantial disorder." In a related case, students were suspended for distributing leaflets calling for a "School Walkout." A court upheld the disciplinary action saying student expression is not protected where officials can present evidence which reasonably leads them "to forecast substantial disruption" of school activities.[4] However, if the disruption is not caused by the protesters but by others, officials should first try to discipline the disrupters, not those participating in a peaceful protest.

Are "fighting words" protected?

No. In a Pennsylvania case, a high school senior was punished for calling his teacher "a prick" off campus. The court said the student's conduct involved an invasion of the right of the teacher "to be free from being loudly insulted in a public place." The court concluded the "fighting words," expressions which are not intended to communicate ideas but which "by their very utterance inflict injury," are not protected by the constitutional guarantee of free speech.[5] In some situations, these might include racial, religious, or ethnic insults.

On the other hand, all insulting gestures are not "fighting words." Thus in a 1986 Maine case, a federal judge ruled that a student could not be suspended for violating a school rule against "vulgar language directed at a staff member" for "extending the middle finger of one hand" toward a teacher in an off-campus parking lot.[6] According to the court, "giving the finger" to a person who happened to be a teacher in a situation that had nothing to do with school activities did not violate the school rule against discourtesy to teachers. Nor did it constitute "fighting words" that would cause a violent reaction and

strip the gesture of First Amendment protection. The court concluded that freedom of expression "may not be made a casualty
of the effort to force-feed good manners to the ruffians among
us."

Can school officials prohibit vulgar and indecent speech?

Yes. In a 1986 decision, the U.S. Supreme Court ruled that it
was "highly appropriate" for public schools "to prohibit the use
of vulgar and offensive" language.[7] The case arose after Matthew Fraser, a high school senior, was suspended for making a
nominating speech in support of a friend who was running for
vice president of the student body. The speech was filled with
sexual allusions. Chief Justice Burger distinguished the "sexual
content" of Fraser's speech from the "political message" in the
Tinker case. Justice Burger concluded that school officials acted
within their authority in punishing Fraser for his "offensively
lewd and indecent speech."

Do students have a right of "curricular choice"?

No. Although many schools allow students choice in courses,
assignments, and even teachers, this is an educational, not
a constitutional, matter. Thus, a federal appeals court ruled
that students have no constitutional right to challenge a school
board's decision to eliminate a popular course or remove certain
books from the curriculum.[8]

Can administrators cancel a school play because of its theme?

The answer may depend on whether it is an extracurricular
activity or part of the academic program. Thus, a court upheld
the right of a Delaware superintendent to cancel a high school
production of *Pippin* because of "its sexual theme" on the
grounds that the play was "an integral part of the school's
educational program" over which the administration has wide
discretion.[9] On the other hand, a federal court reached a different result in a 1985 Ohio case involving a third grade production of *Sorcerer and Friends*. The board cancelled the play because
it "glorifies cowardice, denigrates patriotism, and disparages
the aged."[10] Since the play was a voluntary extracurricular activity (and not part of the curriculum), the court ruled that the

cancellation (because board members "disagreed with some of the ideas expressed therein") was a violation of the participants' First Amendment rights.

Can students be prohibited from discussing controversial issues in a student newspaper?

No, not just because they're controversial. In a Texas case involving an underground paper which discussed controversial subjects (such as current drug laws and where to get information about birth control, venereal disease, and drug counseling), a federal court ruled that "in a democracy 'controversy' is, as a matter of constitutional law, never sufficient in and of itself to stifle the views of any citizen."[11] Similarly, a federal court ruled that a Virginia principal could not ban an article entitled "Sexually Active Students Fail to Use Contraception."[12] The judge noted that schools could exclude the topic of birth control from its courses but not from the student newspaper which was not part of the curriculum. A school's financial support of the newspaper does not give it total control over its contents.

May school personnel restrict the distribution of student newspapers?

They may, but not in order to suppress the ideas they contain. Schools can establish reasonable rules limiting the "manner, place, or time" that students can distribute publications in school. Such rules should be applied equally and drawn narrowly to prevent disruption. Thus, schools may prohibit distribution in classrooms, during assemblies, or on crowded stairways. But students cannot be punished for writing articles or distributing publications solely because they are considered controversial or because teachers, administrators, or parents disagree with their content. As one federal judge wrote: ". . .the purpose of education is to spread, not to stifle, ideas and views. Ideas must be freed from despotic dispensation by all men, be they robed as academicians, or judges, or citizen members of a school board."[13]

Can students be required to submit publications to school officials for review prior to distribution?

One court has ruled that such requirements are an unconstitutional prior restraint. The court acknowledged that schools can punish students who distribute materials that are libelous, obscene or cause substantial disruption; but it held that administrators cannot require their approval in advance or prevent distribution.[14]

Most courts, however, hold that school rules *can* require prior review of student publications if the rules are clear and provide due process safeguards.[15] Due process usually requires that rules for administrative review of publications before distribution should include: (1) a brief period within which the review should take place so as not to interfere with timely distribution; (2) clearly stated standards, e.g., definitions of obscenity, libel and disruption; (3) a reasonable method for appeal; and (4) the time within which the appeal must be decided.

Is the distribution of obscene or libelous materials protected by the Constitution?

No. But a publication is not obscene merely because it contains blunt, vulgar, or "dirty" words, nor is it libelous merely because it is highly critical. According to current Supreme Court standards, material for students would be obscene only if the work (1) "appeals to the prurient interest" of minors, (2) describes sexual conduct "in a patently offensive way," *and* (3) "lacks serious literary, artistic, political, or scientific value."[16] In applying these tests, the publication must be judged as a whole, rather than by particular passages selected out of context.

A written statement about another person is libelous if it injures the person's reputation, and it is not true. If the injured person is a "public figure," she also must prove that the defamatory statement "was made with knowledge of its falsity or in reckless disregard of whether it was false or true."*[17] A person who is libeled can sue for damages, but truth is generally a defense against such a suit.

In short, student publications can't be banned simply because a school official *thinks* they are libelous or obscene; they can't, for example, be banned merely because they criticize the quality of teaching or use "dirty" words. But material that is,

---

*For libel purposes, a "public figure" is anyone who has assumed a role of special prominence in society, including a community's educational leaders.

in fact, legally obscene or libelous is not protected by the First Amendment.

Can student newspapers be prohibited from criticizing school policies or administrators?

No. In an Illinois case, a student was suspended for writing an editorial in an underground paper that strongly criticized some of the school's procedures and one of the administrators. The judge acknowledged that the editorial reflected a "disrespectful. . .attitude toward authority." However, the court ruled that the critical statements did not justify suspending the student. In fact the judge wrote that "prudent criticism" by high school students may be socially valuable.[18]

In a similar Texas case, officials defended their ban of an unofficial student newspaper because of its "negative attitude" and criticism of the administration. But the court explained that "aversion to criticism" is no justification for restricting student publications and that the First Amendment gives citizens "the right and even the responsibility" of commenting on the officials who regulate them.[19]

Can schools restrict newspaper activities that could cause emotional harm?

Perhaps. In one New York case, administrators prohibited a high school newspaper survey about students' sexual attitudes, knowledge, and experience. Since some evidence indicated that answering the questions could create anxiety among some students, a divided federal appeals court ruled that officials could stop the survey to protect students from peer pressures that might cause emotional harm.[20]

Can schools ban ads about controversial issues?

It depends on the facts of the case. A school newspaper has the right to prohibit all advertisements. But when the newspaper prints an ad about an issue of public controversy, it cannot prohibit ads by groups with opposing views. This principle was illustrated in a California case that arose when the San Diego schools rejected all ads from CARD (The Committee Against Registration and the Draft). School officials claimed that the newspaper was not a public forum and that the ads encouraged illegal failure to register. But a federal appeals court disagreed.[21]

The divided court ruled against the school district for two reasons. First, since the schools allowed ads advocating military service, they created a limited public forum and, therefore, could not prohibit ads sponsored by opponents in this political dispute. Second, the CARD ads informed students of lawful alternatives to the draft and did not advocate illegal activity. Thus the prohibition of the CARD ads violated the organization's First Amendment rights.

Can schools ban newspapers that contain advertisements for drug paraphernalia?

Yes. In a Maryland case, a federal appeals court upheld a principal's seizure of an "underground" publication because it contained an ad for waterpipes used to smoke marijuana and hashish.[22] The court ruled that the free press rights of students "must yield to the superior interest of the school" in prohibiting publications "that encourage actions which endanger the health or safety of students."

Can schools regulate newspapers published by the journalism class?

This issue recently came before the U.S. Supreme Court. It arose when a St. Louis principal ordered two "highly sensitive" stories deleted from a journalism class newspaper.[23] The first article was about pregnant students at the school; the second was about the effects of divorce on some of the students. Since the newspaper was produced as a "laboratory exercise" by the journalism class as part of the school curriculum, a trial court ruled that it could be restricted by school officials if there was a "reasonable basis" for their action. According to the court, the principal met this test by showing that his deletions were based on a "legitimate and reasonable" concern for the "unwarranted invasions of [students'] privacy" and for "the rules of fairness which are standard in the field of journalism."

In 1986, a federal appeals court reversed the trial court's ruling.[24] It held that the school newspaper was not simply an academic project of the journalism class but was a public forum for all students and, therefore, was entitled to First Amendment protection. A majority of the court found that the two controversial articles would not have been substantially disruptive and would not have invaded the rights of the pregnant students. Therefore, the appeals court ruled that the censorship of the newspaper by the principal violated the newspaper staff's freedom of the press. When our book went to press, the Supreme Court was reviewing this St. Louis case, and its decision probably will determine whether First Amendment principles apply to newspapers published by journalism classes.

While officials can regulate the spelling, grammar, and technical quality of a newspaper produced by a journalism class, they probably cannot censor reasonable student criticism or unpopular views. Thus, a federal court ruled that Georgia school officials were not justified in censoring controversial stories in a journalism class paper because of their technical errors. Removing controversial articles because they are not in "proper journalistic form," wrote the court, "too closely resembles censorship of content in the guise of correcting technical defects, a practice which has been disapproved as violative of freedom of expression."[25]

Can school officials control the content of publications if they pay the costs?

It depends on what is meant by "control." As noted above, administrators cannot censor student news and views, but they can decide whether or not to sponsor a student publication and what level of financial support to give it. The limits of administrative control are not precise; but they are not total. Thus one court ruled that students could not be prohibited from placing an advertisement that was critical of U.S. government policy in a school-sponsored newspaper,[26] and another held that a student editor could not be prohibited from publishing responsible criticism about public officials.[27] In sum, school officials have some control over publications they sponsor, but they cannot suppress or censor student views or withdraw support from student newspapers simply because they do not like the views expressed in them.

Does the First Amendment apply to a high school yearbook?

Yes. This was illustrated by a 1984 case involving a Maine

high school that usually allowed each senior to select a short quotation for the yearbook.[28] But when Joellen Stanton selected a "shocking" quotation about capital punishment, ("to provoke" her classmates to think more deeply about the subject), school officials rejected her choice as "not appropriate" and "in poor taste." However, a federal court ruled that it was unconstitutional to restrict Stanton's freedom of expression on the basis of "vague" and "completely subjective" standards such as "poor taste" and "appropriateness." Although a quotation could be prohibited if it were libelous or obscene, officials could not reject Stanton's choice because it used "graphic language to convey her convictions."

Can schools regulate off-campus publications?

Not according to a federal appeals court decision in a New York case.[29] The controversy concerned students in a small, rural community who produced a satirical publication that was "indecent" but not legally obscene. Although the "objectionable" publication was written, printed, and sold off campus, administrators penalized the student publishers. But the court ruled that the First Amendment "forbids public school administrators and teachers from regulating the material to which a child is exposed after he leaves the school."

Can schools prohibit students from inviting or listening to controversial speakers?

School officials apparently have authority to bar all outside speakers from school. But if they provide a forum for controversial outside speakers, they must allow opposing views to be presented and may not discriminate among proposed speakers or censor their ideas. For example, in a high school where Republican and Democratic candidates were allowed to present their views, it was ruled unconstitutional for the principal to prohibit a Socialist Workers candidate from speaking.[30]

Does the First Amendment protect teachers' communications with parents?

Not necessarily. Teachers may have a right to communicate with parents about broad matters of public concern, but they have no First Amendment right to complain to parents about their own personal concerns. In a Massachusetts case, a teacher wanted to bring to the attention of parents a problem she was having with school officials. Therefore, on Parents' Night, she posted on her classroom bulletin board several letters she had received from school officials together with her own critical comments. As a result she was disciplined for "conduct unbecoming a teacher."[31] She claimed that her conduct should be protected by the First Amendment, but a federal appeals court disagreed. The court ruled that posting the letters was not protected speech since it was about an individual problem and not a matter of public concern.*

Summary

Since the landmark case of *Tinker v. Des Moines*, all courts recognize that the Bill of Rights applies to students in the public schools. Individual rights, however, are not absolute. When a student's rights come in conflict with the rights of other students or with the obligation of the school to keep order, judges weigh these competing interests in light of the circumstances of each case.

In *Tinker*, the Supreme Court held that restricting a student's freedom of expression is unconstitutional unless there is evidence that the forbidden conduct would "materially and substantially interfere" with school activities. Some courts have used the *Tinker* case to restrict symbolic expression where such symbols caused material disruption in the recent past or would probably cause an already tense situation to explode. On the other hand, courts have indicated that an "expectation of disruption" is not enough to justify suspension of a student's rights unless (1) such an expectation is "based on fact, not intuition"; and (2) school officials first make an honest effort to restrain those who might cause the disruption.

Before *Tinker*, administrators generally had "broad discretion" to censor school newspapers and punish students for distributing publications that "damaged school discipline" unless students could show that the school's actions were clearly

---

*For more on teachers' freedom of speech, see *Teachers and the Law*, Fischer, Schimmel, and Kelly. (NY, Longman, Inc. 1987)

unreasonable. This is no longer the law. Today, the First Amendment protects both school-sponsored newspapers and "underground" student publications. This means that students are free to write about controversial topics and to criticize school policies and personnel—especially in unofficial newspapers. Moreover, even if a school finances a student publication, administrators do not have total control over its contents. And if parents question the constitutionality of rules that restrict their child's freedom of expression, it is up to school officials to justify the restriction.

This does not mean that the constitutional rights of students are always the same as those of adults. Because there must be order as well as freedom of expression in the schools, authorities can impose reasonable restraints on the time, place and manner in which student publications are distributed. Nor does the First Amendment protect students who are abusive and seriously disrespectful to school officials, or those who distribute materials that cause disruption, or are legally obscene or libelous. Furthermore, schools have greater control over newspapers published by a journalism class than those published as an extracurricular activity. However, the opinions of students cannot be censored nor can they be punished solely because teachers, administrators, parents, or other students disagree with what they say or because the subject itself is unpopular or controversial.

Notes for Chapter 3

1. *Tinker v. Des Moines Independent School District*, 393 U.S. 503 (1969).

2. *Butts v. Dallas Independent School District*, 436 F. 2d 728 (5th Cir. 1971).

3. *Karp v. Becken*, 477 F.2d 171 (9th Cir. 1973).

4. *Dodd v. Rambis*, 535 F. Supp. 23 (S.D. Ind. 1981).

5. *Fenton v. Stear*, 423 F.Supp. 767 (W.D.Penn. 1976).

6. *Klein v. Smith*, 635 F.Supp. 1440 (D.Me.1986).

7. *Bethel School District 1 v. Fraser*, 54 LW 5054 (1986).

8. *Zykan v. Warsaw Community School Corporation*, 631 F.2d 1300 (7th Cir. 1980).

9. *Seyfried v. Walton*, 668 F.2d 214 (3rd Cir. 1981).

10. *Bowman v. Bethel-Tate Board of Education*, 610 F.Supp. 577 (D.C. Ohio 1985).

11. *Shanley v. Northeast Independent School District*, 462 F.2d 960 (5th Cir. 1972).

12. *Gambino v. Fairfax County School Board*, 564 F.2d 157 (4th Cir. 1977).

13. *Shanley v. Northeast Independent School District*, 462 F.2d 960 (5th Cir. 1972).

14. *Fujishima v. Board of Education*, 460 F.2d 1355 (7th Cir. 1972) *Riseman v. School Committee of Quincy*, 439 F.2d 148 (1st Cir. 1971).

15. *Shanley v. Northeast Independent School District*, op. cit.; *Eisner v. Stamford Board of Education*, 440 F.2d 803 (2nd Cir. 1971).

16. *Miller v. California*, 413 U.S. 15 (1973).

17. *Garrison v. Louisiana*, 379 U. S. 64 (1964).

18. *Scoville v. Board of Education of Joliet Township*, 425 F.2d 10 (7th Cir. 1970).

19. *Shanley v. Northeast Independent School District*, op. cit..

20. *Trachtman v. Anker*, 563 F.2d 512 (2d Cir. 1977).

21. *San Diego Committee v. Governing Board*, 790 F.2d 1471 (9th Cir.1986).

22. *Williams v. Spencer*, 622 F.2d 1200 (4th Cir. 1980).

23. *Kuhlmeier v. Hazelwood School District*, 607 F. Supp. 1450 (D.C. Mo.

1985).

24. *Kuhlmeier v. Hazelwood School District*, 795 F.2d 1368 (8th Cir. 1986).

25. *Reineke v. Cobb County School District*, 484 F.Supp. 1252 (N.D. Ga. 1980).

26. *Zucker v. Panitz*, 299 F.Supp. 102 (S.D. N.Y. 1969).

27. *Dickey v. Alabama State Board of Education*, 273 F.Supp.613 (M.D. Ala. 1967).

28. *Stanton by Stanton v. Brunswick School Department*, 577 F.Supp. 1560 (D.Me. 1984).

29. *Thomas v. Board of Education, Granville Central School District*, 607 F.2d 1043 (2d Cir. 1979).

30. *Vail v. Board of Education of Portsmouth*, 354 F.Supp.592 (D.N.H. 1973).

31. *Alinovi v. Worcester School Committee*, 777 F.2d 776 (1st Cir. 1985).

CHAPTER 4

Freedom of Religion and Conscience

May parents choose to send their children to religious schools?

If a given state requires children to attend school until the age of 16, may parents object to that requirement on religious grounds?

May parents ask to have their children excused from the daily flag salute and Pledge of Allegiance?

May schools conduct daily prayers or read selections from the Bible?

May schools begin the day with a minute of silence?

Is Transcendental Meditation allowed in public schools?

Can schools give students Bibles or other religious materials?

Can schools have Christmas programs, celebrations, and nativity plays?

Do parents have the right to have their children excused from Christmas programs or assemblies?

May there be religious invocations or prayers at graduation ceremonies?

May students stay out of school on religious holidays without penalty?

Can student religious groups meet in school facilities?

Can parents conduct a religious school at home in place of sending their children to public schools?

May children receive religious instruction during school hours?

Can parents who send their children to private parochial school expect the school to receive public funds?

Can states allow income tax credits for private school costs?

Can states regulate private religious schools?

I t is a generally accepted principle in our culture that parents have the right to determine and guide the religious upbringing of their children. This principle was given the force of law in 1925 when the Supreme Court upheld the right of parents to educate their children in parochial rather than public schools. After declaring that the State may not "standardize its children by forcing them to accept instruction from public teachers only,"[1] the Court stated: "The child is not the mere creature of the State" and thus placed in the hands of parents the right and even the obligation to guide the moral, religious and civic upbringing of their children. In this chapter we consider various issues involving religion and the public schools—among them court decisions related to religious objections to school attendance; controversies related to saluting the flag and reciting the Pledge of Allegiance; and others connected with prayers, Bible reading and silent meditation.

The issues in this chapter relate to the First Amendment's provision that "Congress shall make no law respecting an establishment of religion, or prohibiting the free exercise thereof." (Related questions concerning parents who object to textbooks for religious reasons are discussed in Chapter 8.)

May parents choose to send their children to religious schools?

Yes, they may. The U.S. Supreme Court's 1925 decision made it clear that parents could, if they chose, send their children to public or private schools and, if private, to either religious or secular. But the question still remained: just how long must children attend school?

If a given state requires children to attend school until the age of 16, may parents object to that requirement on religious grounds?

This was precisely the question raised by several Amish parents who challenged Wisconsin's compulsory attendance law.[2] Messrs. Yoder, Miller, and Yutzy, devout members of the Amish community in Green County, Wisconsin, decided not to send their 14- and 15-year-old children to school beyond the eighth grade. They believed that their own as well as their children's religious salvation would be jeopardized if the children attended high school and were exposed to a worldly and scientific curriculum that emphasized values quite different from those of the Amish community. On the basis of their 300-year history of close-knit religious and communal life, the Amish believed that after their children mastered basic literacy in the elementary school, their further education should be occupational, and should take place on Amish farms and in Amish shops, under the close supervision of adult members of the community.

The State of Wisconsin, on the other hand, wanted to enforce its compulsory attendance laws, which required that students remain in school until they were sixteen.

The Supreme Court ruled in favor of the Amish parents, basing its reasoning primarily on the protection the First Amendment gives to the free exercise of religion, and citing its earlier decision protecting the right of parents to guide the religious development of their children. But this First Amendment right had to be balanced against the state's interest in having educated citizens. Here the evidence showed that the Amish youngsters had mastered basic school skills as well as other students, had been given excellent vocational training in their own communities, and had an impressive record of general citizenship and self-reliance.

Since freedom of religion is one of the fundamental freedoms the Constitution guarantees, and since the evidence concerning the accomplishments of the Amish was quite favorable, the Court felt that the state's interest should not prevail. But the Court clearly warned that this type of exemption from the requirement of compulsory education would be only rarely granted. "It cannot be over-emphasized that we are not dealing with a way of life and mode of education by a group claiming to have recently discovered some 'progressive' or more enlightened process for rearing children for modern life." The exception granted the Amish was based on a demonstration that their religious beliefs and mode of life were inextricably related, that they had relied on these religious beliefs for three centuries, that they formed a successful and self-sufficient group in American society, and that the enforcement of the state law would threaten their survival.

May parents ask to have their children excused from the daily flag salute and Pledge of Allegiance?

Yes, said the Supreme Court.   In a West Virginia case,[3] Jehovah's Witness parents sued on behalf of their children, objecting to the daily flag salute required by state law. The Court, while recognizing the legitimate interest of the state in developing patriotic citizens and thus building national unity, ruled in favor of religious freedom, which it recognized as fundamental, to be overridden only by a compelling need of the state. In a powerful paragraph, Justice Jackson set forth a guiding principle of our nation:

> If there is any fixed star in our constitutional constellation it is that no official, high or petty, can prescribe what shall be orthodox in politics, nationalism, religion, or other matters of opinion or force citizens to confess by word or act their faith therein. If there are any circumstances which permit an exception, they do not now occur to us.

While the Supreme Court in this case upheld the right to refuse to salute the flag on the grounds of freedom of religion, more recent cases have held that similar protection is extended to someone who objects as a matter of conscience.   In fact, students don't even have to stand while a salute is being conducted.   A controversy arose over this in Coral Gables High School in Florida when a student had a deeply felt objection to saluting the flag and was reluctant to express his respect by standing up.   While the school board policy allowed him not to participate, it did require that nonparticipants stand quietly during the salute. The student claimed that such a requirement violated his right to freedom of expression. The court, while upholding the claim of the student, noted that "standing is an integral portion of the pledge ceremony and is no less a gesture of acceptance and respect than is the salute or the utterance of the words of allegiance."[4]

Similarly, a New York Court held that nonparticipating students have the right to remain in the room and wait quietly for the end of the pledge. They may not be excluded even if others will imitate their behavior.[5] This case noted that the First Amendment protects successful dissent as well as ineffective protest.

May schools conduct daily prayers or read selections from the Bible?

No, they may not. The Supreme Court has ruled that Bible reading and school prayers violate the First Amendment's separation of church and state, and this ruling applies even if the prayers are non-denominational and participation is voluntary.[6] Furthermore, excusing students from participating in these exercises does not cure the constitutional defect because the prayers are still conducted under the auspices of the school, and the school is an agency of the state. This ruling, made in 1963, has been consistently reaffirmed by the Court. While recognizing that the "place of religion in our society is an exalted one," the Court noted that under our Constitution the place for religion is in "the home, the church, and the inviolable citadel of the individual heart and mind," and that the Constitution "has never meant that a majority could use the machinery of the State to practice its beliefs."[7]

Various attempts have been made in Congress to enact constitutional amendments legalizing official prayers in public schools, but none have yet succeeded. In place of such prayers, many states have enacted laws providing for a minute of silence at the beginning of the school day, during which time students may voluntarily engage in prayer or meditation.

May schools begin the day with a minute of silence?

That depends on the purpose of the law or policy that requires such a period of silence. To test the constitutionality of such a law or policy, the courts apply a three-part test: (1) Is the purpose or intent religious or secular? (2) Will the primary effect be to advance religion or be hostile to it? (3) Does it create excessive entanglement between church and state, that is, between religion and the schools?[8]

To be constitutional, the law or policy must not have a religious purpose, should not advance or be hostile to religion, and must not create too much of an administrative entanglement between the school and the religious activity. Thus, courts examine the legislative intent or purpose behind the creation of the minute of silence. In various cases, courts have found that state legislators intended those periods of silence to be used for prayers, and this violates both of the first two tests listed above. Courts have so ruled in Louisiana,[9] Alabama,[10] and in other states. In light of such rulings, Massachusetts changed its law in 1985, a law that used to provide for a period of silence for meditation or prayer, to provide that a ". . .period of silence not to exceed one minute in duration shall be observed for personal thoughts, and during any such period, silence shall be maintained and no activities engaged in."[11]

In sum, schools may provide a brief period of silence at the beginning or during the school day. If courts determine that the intention or purpose of such a period of silence is to encourage prayer, it is likely to be declared unconstitutional. On the other hand, if genuinely secular purposes motivate the provision of silence, it will be upheld.[12] (An authoritative ruling on this issue might be forthcoming soon, since the Supreme Court agreed to review New Jersey's moment of silence law.)

Is Transcendental Meditation allowed in public schools?

No, it is not. Transcendental Meditation (TM) is believed by many parents to be a religion, and it uses many religious symbols. A court so ruled in a New Jersey case after TM was introduced into a school because of its alleged beneficial physical effects. There was conflicting testimony in the case concerning whether or not TM was a religion. When the judge saw that a mantra (a special word) was assigned to each student together with a special textbook at an out-of-school religious ceremony, he ruled that this was a religious use of TM and therefore unconstitutional in the public schools.[13]

Can schools give students Bibles or other religious materials?

As a general rule they cannot, for religious purposes, for such activities violate the Establishment Clause of the First Amendment. Even the posting of the Ten Commandments in public school was struck down by the Supreme Court. The Court declared unconstitutional a Kentucky law requiring the posting of the Commandments, purchased with private contributions, on the classroom walls of public schools. The Court applied the three-part test we mentioned previously and held that the law served a religious purpose and was, therefore, unconstitutional.[14] Parents must be aware that public schools are to be neutral toward religion; they must not advance religion nor be hostile to it.

Most controversies concerning religious celebrations in public schools seem to arise in connection with Christmas assemblies and nativity plays. Many schools, sensitive to these controversies, make special efforts to emphasize educational rather than religious aspects of the in-school experiences and use the occasion to develop intercultural and interreligious understandings. The involvement of a diverse group of parents can be quite helpful in these efforts.

Can schools have Christmas programs, celebrations and nativity plays?

Schools must be sensitive to the distinction between teaching about religion and conducting religious celebrations. Education is incomplete if it does not include the importance of religion in human affairs, in history, literature, art, music, architecture, and perhaps other aspects of life. According to the Supreme Court, schools may, indeed they should, teach about this, but religious ceremonies must not be conducted in schools "under the guise of study." The federal courts so spoke when public school Christmas programs were challenged in Sioux Falls, South Dakota, in 1979. Although the courts upheld the program, they urged schools to be sensitive to the "religious beliefs and disbeliefs of their constituents and should attempt to avoid conflict. . .but they need not sacrifice the quality of the students' education."[15]

Do parents have the right to have their children excused from Christmas programs or assemblies?

Only if they can show a genuine religious objection to their children participating in the program or class. If the activity is a legitimate learning activity and not a religious celebration, schools may require participation. If it is not an educational activity, it has no proper place in school. Yet some programs, even though primarily educational and built around a secular purpose, may have portions that are objectionable to some people's religious views. While we have seen no court cases on this issue, schools generally excuse students from observing or participating in such programs when parents request it.

May there be religious invocations or prayers at graduation ceremonies?

The law is not settled on this issue. During recent years several lawsuits challenged these widespread practices with conflicting results. In the two most recent cases, federal district courts reached opposing conclusions. A court in Iowa found the practice to be unconstitutional since its primary purpose and effect were religious[16], while a district court in Michigan recognized a dual purpose in such practices. It found one such purpose to be secular, namely the provision of a solemn opening and closing for the graduation consistent with a long tradition.[17] The Michigan court relied on an earlier Supreme Court ruling related to a nativity scene where the Court upheld the practice as long as it served a dual purpose, one secular and one religious. The Oregon Court of Appeals declared such a traditional practice unconstitutional since it created the impression that the state sponsored or endorsed religion.[18]

May students stay out of school on religious holidays without penalty?

Yes, they may. This question is often asked by parents whose religious holidays do not coincide with school holidays. Children from Jewish and Seventh-Day Adventist homes, as well as some others, may need to miss school on some religious holidays. These students have a right, under the Free Exercise Clause of the First Amendment, not to attend school on their religious holidays. Schools must not punish them for exercising their constitutional rights. They should not receive unexcused absences and, if tests are given during their absence, they have a right to a fair make-up test within a reasonable time upon their return to school. Any unfair treatment would constitute hostility toward religion.

Can student religious groups meet in school facilities?

There is no clear legal answer to this question right now. During recent years, controversies arose in various communities when student religious groups wanted to meet before or after school, on school premises, to pray or to share religious readings and experiences. School administrators, believing such practices to violate the law, denied these students access to school facilities, whereupon they went to court.

In a college-level case, the Supreme Court held that if a public university made its facilities available to a variety of student groups, it created an open forum which could not be denied to religious groups.[19] This ruling was based on the free speech guarantee of the First Amendment, the Court ruling in effect that free expression cannot be limited by the content of the speech. However, the Court distinguished colleges from lower level educational institutions which do not have open forums available to everyone. Other cases arose, however, in high schools that had rich and varied extracurricular programs. Such schools have what has been called "limited open forums."

May student religious groups meet on school premises where such limited open forums exist? There is no clearly settled law on this issue. Several circuit courts ruled that they may not, distinguishing high schools from colleges. When a federal district court upheld the students' right to conduct religious meetings, the 3rd Circuit Court overruled it, based on the Establishment Clause of the First Amendment, reasoning that high school students are still quite impressionable and many will believe that the school itself is supporting the religious activity creating an appearance of state support for religion. Thus, the state's compelling interest to remain neutral in matters of religion outweighs the students' right to freedom of expression.[20] This case, *Bender v. Williamsport*, was accepted for review by the Supreme Court, and everyone expected the controversy to be settled by an authoritative decision. However, on March 28,

1986, the Court dismissed the case on procedural grounds. In a 5-to-4 decision, the Court ruled that the appeals court erred when it allowed a single member of the Williamsport School Board to appeal the lower court's ruling. Thus, for the time being, students in Williamsport may meet in student-initiated prayer groups during extracurricular periods. Courts in the 2nd, 5th, 10th, and 11th Circuits have forbidden the practice. In areas where no courts have yet ruled on the issue, educators may follow local legal advice which might mean abiding by the Equal Access Act of 1984.

As a result of intensive political interest in the issue of equal access, Congress passed the Equal Access Act in 1984,[21] which makes it possible in secondary schools for student religious, political, or ideological groups to meet in school facilities before or after school hours. The group must be voluntary and student-initiated; schools, school employees, or outsiders may not sponsor or participate in the meetings and school employees may attend only to provide basic supervision. The constitutionality of the Act is yet to be determined. Several cases are currently under litigation which may lead to a clarification of the constitutional principles related to equal access, including the constitutionality of the Equal Access Act of 1984.

Can parents conduct a religious school at home in place of sending their children to public schools?

That depends on the laws of the state they live in and on the kind of home school they propose. In one Florida case the home school was disallowed on the grounds that it was not a school in the generally accepted sense of the word, and the parents involved were not qualified tutors under Florida law.[22] Parents who are interested in creating their own schools should, therefore, check their state laws carefully to be sure that the projects comply with minimal requirements. (For further discussion of this topic, see Chapter 9.)

May children receive religious instruction during school hours?

Yes, they may, but not in the public schools, and not from public school teachers. The Supreme Court has ruled it constitutional for schools to let students leave the campus during the school day for religious instruction as long as no school facilities or personnel are used and as long as all costs are borne by the religious organization.[23] The practice that has developed out of this ruling is known as "released time" religious education. A variation is the so-called "dismissed time" program, where all students are dismissed early on certain days, and those who wish, go to religious education programs.

Can parents who send their children to private parochial schools expect the school to receive public funds?

The answer is yes and no, depending on the nature of the aid sought. In 1947 the Supreme Court upheld a state law by which New Jersey used tax funds to pay the bus fares of all pupils attending school.[24] Similarly, a New York statute was upheld that provided for lending textbooks free of charge to all students, including those at private, parochial schools.[25] Neither of these rulings was unanimous, but both of them still stand.

Many other ways have been attempted to provide government support for the parochial schools—so-called parochiaid— and these efforts have aroused much controversy among parents. Under the efforts to grant parochiaid, state statutes have attempted to pay teachers' salaries, the cost of pupil testing, auxiliary school services, school maintenance and repair, tuition grants, tuition reimbursement, and to give tax credits and to pay other school costs. The Supreme Court has ruled each of these unconstitutional, a violation of the Establishment Clause of the First Amendment.[26]*

On June 24, 1977 the Supreme Court handed down a major decision related to parochiaid. In ruling on a case that originated in Ohio, the Court held that states may finance therapeutic, remedial and guidance counseling for parochial school children provided that such services are rendered at a "neutral" site—that is off the school premises (at converted mobile homes, for example). On the other hand, diagnostic services, such as speech and hearing tests, can be provided in the parochial schools. Furthermore, states may provide parochial

---

*The Establishment Clause prohibits the government from making any law "respecting an establishment of religion."

schools with standardized tests and test-scoring services, if they provide them to public schools. In this same decision, the Court disallowed the financing of field trips for parochial school students as well as the provision of wall charts, slide projectors and other instructional materials.[27]

It is not exactly clear why it is proper to provide texts and transportation for parochial school students but not some other types of parochial schools aid. Earlier decisions had claimed that texts and transportation benefit students, not the religion that supports the school. This so-called child benefit theory turned out to be very controversial, since it is difficult to draw the line between those benefits the students should have and those they should not, and the judges who opposed it argued that it would break down the wall of separation between church and state as it applies to public schools. Today, the question by which the Court guides itself in these cases is whether the proposed arrangement has the "purpose or effect" of helping a religion and/or whether it leads to excessive "entanglement" between government and religion. The application of these tests excluded most parochiaid for elementary and secondary schools, while allowing for the provision of texts, transportation, testing and diagnostic and therapeutic guidance services at "neutral" sites.*

In 1985, the Supreme Court ruled unconstitutional programs in New York and Michigan in which public school teachers were sent into private and parochial schools to teach remedial classes to economically disadvantaged children under a federal Chapter 1 program. In identical close votes in the two cases (5-4), the Court struck down the programs as calling for excessive entanglement between church and state. This is the case because when public school teachers go into religious schools to work, both they and these schools must, in the opinion of the Court, be subjected to "comprehensive discriminating and continuing

---

*This discussion does not apply to college level education. Courts have allowed certain kinds of financial aid to church-related colleges that might not be allowed to elementary and secondary schools. Similarly, clubs sponsored by religious organizations are allowed on public college campuses, but would not be allowed in primary or secondary schools.

surveillance." This cooperation might also create the impression of a "symbolic union of church and state" and would help subsidize the religious function of the church schools by taking over portions of their responsibility to teach secular subjects.[28]

Can states allow income tax credits for private school costs?

Yes they can, depending on the type of credits involved. An important case related to this issue arose in Minnesota and was decided by the Supreme Court in 1983. A Minnesota statute provided that parents may deduct on their state income tax returns actual expenses for tuition, textbooks, and transportation of dependents attending any elementary or secondary schools[29]. The deductions could not exceed $500 for dependents in grades kindergarten through six and $700 for dependents in grades seven through twelve.

To decide the case, the Supreme Court applied its three-part test. First, did the statute have a secular purpose? Clearly yes, said the Court, that purpose being the creation of an educated populace by reducing the cost of education. Was the primary effect religious or secular? Since the statute made deductions available to all parents including those attending public schools, private non-sectarian as well as sectarian schools, it satisfied the Court on the primary effect test. (The Court did not consider significant the fact that the public schools were free and that 96% of private school attendance in the state was at religiously-affiliated institutions.) The "excessive entanglement" test was satisfied since the state was not called upon to exercise significant surveillance and only had to decide which textbooks would qualify for the deduction. Thus, the Court was satisfied that the law would not violate the Establishment Clause. Many commentators consider the Minnesota tax credit case to be one of the most important developments in the area of public aid to private schools, including church-related schools.

Can states regulate private religious schools?

To a limited extent they can. Since the state also has a serious interest in the health and welfare of children, reasonable regulations to protect such interest have been upheld by the courts. In fact, all health and welfare legislation, including laws related to child abuse and neglect, is based on the premise that society has serious interests in its citizens, including children. However, since parents have the basic right and responsibility in the rearing, care, and education of their children, state regulations must be justified, clear, and not overly broad.

Few controversies arise when health and safety regulations are applied to religious schools. Controversy flares when states attempt to regulate the curriculum, teacher qualifications, and some employment practices considered discriminatory by state agencies.

A case arose in Maine, for example, where state laws and regulations required that students may be excused from attending public schools only if they received ". . .equivalent instruction in private school. . .if the equivalent instruction is approved by the commissioner." Members of fundamentalist Christian churches in Maine challenged the law and claimed that it violated their right to free exercise of religion. A federal district court ruled that the state regulations did not interfere with the free exercise of religion in any substantial manner. The state has a compelling interest in the education of all children and as long as its regulations are reasonable, clear, and do not substantially restrict constitutionally-protected conduct, they will be upheld by the courts.[30]

An interesting case arose in Ohio, when charges of sexual discrimination were brought against a religious school pursuant to a state statute that forbids discrimination in employment based on sex. When the church school objected to a state agency investigating them, the trial court held that the state had a right to investigate charges of discrimination. A federal appeals court, however, held otherwise on the grounds that the controls exercised by the state civil rights commission would place a heavy burden on the church school's exercise of freedom of religion and would require the kind of continuous supervision that would lead to excessive entanglement between church and state.[31] This case was accepted for review by the Supreme Court which ruled in 1986 that the state agency may examine the claims of sex discrimination and that the religious group may raise its constitutional objections during this process. Ultimately, the courts will have to decide on the merits of such objections. Thus, the Supreme Court sent the case back to the administrative agency for further proceedings.

Perhaps the most complex of these cases arose in Nebraska

where controversy focused on the applications of state licens-
ing and teacher certification requirements to a fundamentalist
school operated by Faith Baptist Church, of Louisville, Nebraska. During the long process attempting to resolve this conflict,
various strategies were used by Christian educators to change
requirements imposed by the state of Nebraska. During the
protracted conflict, ministers went to jail, lawsuits were filed,
negotiations conducted and new legislation enacted. This case
study is an excellent example of the complexity of the church-
state-education issue in America as well as an illustration of the
use of courts, legislation, and political processes in the resolution of complex social problems.[32]

Summary

From the earliest days of the Republic, disagreements have
abounded concerning the proper relationship between religion
and public institutions. Some parents have attempted to use
public schools and public funds to further religion, while others
have sought to keep the schools neutral and separate from
religious influences. These conflicting efforts have inevitably
ended up in the courts, and the U.S. Supreme Court has ruled
on many aspects of the controversy. The Court has ruled that
although a state may require children to attend school, parents
may satisfy this requirement by sending their children to private
or public schools and, if private, either to religious or secular
ones. Further, in the case of the Amish, the Court permitted
parents to withdraw their children from schools after the eighth
grade, since the facts showed that the Amish religion would
be significantly threatened by "worldly" high-school education.
But this decision is not likely to apply to other groups. In the
case of that sect, the Court was very impressed by its self-
sufficiency and by the close relationship that has existed for
more than 300 years between the Amish religion and the Amish
way of life. Recently formed religious groups are not likely to
succeed in their attempts to be exempt from schooling.

Students need not salute the flag or recite the Pledge of Allegiance if their objections are based on religion or conscience.
But such students should not interfere with others' rights to
participate in these exercises.

Courses on religion are perfectly legal, but prayers or Bible reading in schools have been declared violations of the First Amendment. Legislation providing a minute for silent prayer is also unconstitutional, but a brief period of silence for a secular purpose may not be objectionable. Voluntary, student-initiated prayer or religious groups may use school facilities at the college level if the college has an open forum policy. There are conflicts concerning whether high schools with a limited open forum may make school facilities available to student religious groups. The Supreme Court has not ruled on this question, and the Equal Access Act of 1984 allows such use of school facilities.

Public funds for elementary and secondary parochial schools have, with some exceptions, been declared violations of the First Amendment. The exceptions make it legal for states to provide bus transportation for parochial school students, to lend them books, and to provide diagnostic services, standardized tests, and scoring services. The state may pay for therapeutic, remedial, and guidance counseling services, provided they are rendered away from the parochial school at some neutral site. Other efforts to secure parochiaid have been declared unconstitutional. Nevertheless, these efforts continue, particularly in state legislatures.

Parents have a constitutional right to send their children to church schools. Such schools may be subject to reasonable regulation by the state as long as the regulations are clear, not too broad or vague, and do not intrude in any substantial way into the religious beliefs of the group sponsoring the school. It is safe to predict that controversy over the application of those sections of the First Amendment that relate to religion will be with us for many more years, for it is difficult to determine what constitutes an "excessive entanglement" that would threaten the wall of separation between Church and State.

Notes for Chapter 4

1. *Pierce v. Society of Sisters*, 268 U.S. 510 (1925).

2. *Wisconsin v. Yoder*, 406 U.S. 205 (1972).

3. *West Virginia v. Barnette*, 319 U.S. 624 (1943).

4. *Banks v. Board of Public Instruction of Dade County*, 314 F.Supp. 285

(S.D. Fla. 1970).

5. *Frain v. Barron*, 307 F.Supp. 27 (E.D. N.Y. 1969).

6. *Abington School District v. Schempp*, 374 U.S. 203 (1963) and *Engel v. Vitale*, 370 U.S. 421 (1962).

7. Ibid. 226.

8. *Lemon v. Kurtzman*, 403 U.S. 602 (1971).

9. *Karen B. v. Treen*, 653 F.2d 897 (5th Cir. 1981); affirmed on appeal, 455 U.S. 913 (1982).

10. *Jaffree et al. v. Board of School Commissioners of Mobile County*, 459 U.S. 1314 (1983).

11. Chapter 690, General Laws of Massachusetts, 1985.

12. Justices Powell and O'Connor so noted, dissenting in *Jaffree v. Wallace*, 1059 Ct 2479 (1985).

13. *Malnak v. Yogi*, 440 F.Supp. 1284 (D.N.J. 1977); affirmed 592 F.2d 197 (3rd Cir. 1979).

14. *Stone v. Graham*, 449 U.S. 39 (1981).

15. *Florey v. Sioux Falls School District*, 49-5, 619 F.2d 1311 (1980); *cert.* denied, 449 U.S. 897 (1980).

16. *Graham v. Central Community School District*, 608 F.Supp. 531 (S.D.Iowa 1985).

17. *Stein v. Plainwell Community Schools*, 610 F.Supp. 43 (W.D. Mich. 1985).

18. *Kay v. David Douglas School Dist. No. 40*, 719P.2d875 (Or Ct App 1986)

19. *Widmar v. Vincent*, 454 U.S. 263 (1981).

20. *Bender v. Williamsport Area School District*, 741 F.2d 538 (3rd Cir. 1984); *cert.* granted 105 S. Ct. 1167 (Feb. 19, 1985).

21. 20 U.S.C.A. 4071 (1985).

22. *F. and F. v. Duval County*, 273 So. 2d 15 (Fla 1973).

23. *Zorach v. Clausen*, 343 U.S. 306 (1952).

24. *Everson v. Board of Education*, 330 U.S. 1 (1947).

25. *Board of Education v. Allen*, 392 U.S. 236 (1968).

26. See for example *Meek v. Pittinger*, 421 U.S. 349 (1975).

27. *Wolman v. Walter*, 433 U.S. 229 (1977).

28. *Aguilar v. Felton*, 105 S. Ct. 3232 (1985); *Grand Rapids v. Ball*, 534 U.S.L.W. 3430 (1985).

29. *Mueller v. Allen*, 463 U.S. 388 (1983).

30. *Bangor Baptist Church v. State of Maine*, Department of Educational & Cultural Services, 549 F.Supp. 1208 (D. Maine 1982).

31. *Dayton Christian Schools v. Ohio Civil Rights Commission*, No. 84-3124 Slip.Op. (6th Cir. 1985), 54 U.S.L.W. 2034 (7-16-85).

32. For analysis of this controversy see Binder, Timothy J. *"Douglas v. Faith Baptist Church"* Under Constitutional Scrutiny. 61 Nebraska Law Review 74 (Spring 1982); Carper, James C., and Devins, Neal E., "The State and the Church School," "Religion and the State: Essays in Honor of Leo Pffefer", James E. Wood, Ed., Waco: Baylor University Press, 1985.

CHAPTER 5

Racial Discrimination and Education

What does desegregation require?

Must each school be racially balanced?

Must one-race schools be eliminated?

Is busing necessary for desegregation?

Can courts order busing across district lines?

Can parents choose the schools their children will attend?

Have the courts gone too far in controlling the schools?

Must schools continually redraw attendance lines?

May a state repeal its desegregation laws?

May private schools exclude black students?

Must schools desegregate faculties as well as students?

Can parents challenge discriminatory disciplinary practices?

Can parents challenge discriminatory testing and placement of students?

Are grouping or tracking practices unconstitutional?

What can parents do if they believe that local school policies discriminate against blacks, Hispanics, or other minorities?

What will the Office of Personnel Management do after receiving a complaint?

Over thirty years have passed since the Supreme Court of the United States declared that racial discrimination in the public schools is unconstitutional, and that racial segregation of students is unacceptable. In the well known *Brown*[1] case, Chief Justice Warren announced the principle that has since become a nationwide standard:

> In the field of public education the doctrine of 'separate but equal' has no place. Separate educational facilities are inherently unequal.[2]

While this general principle has become the accepted rule of law, disagreements over ways to carry it out have already spawned thousands of lawsuits and promise to continue to be controversial in the future. In this chapter, we consider several important issues related to this aspect of schooling.

In the *Brown* case of 1954, the Court recognized that our national history of racial discrimination and segregation, together with wide variations in local conditions, would make any single remedy unworkable. Therefore, it called for arguments on the question of proper relief: the kind of order to issue to help schools overcome widespread, massive racial segregation.

The case known as *Brown II*[3] provides the general principles by which this question has been answered. Recognizing the diversity of local conditions, the Supreme Court assigned primary responsibility for desegregation to local school authorities, supervised by local courts, to ensure "good faith implementation of governing constitutional principles." Schools were to proceed reasonably and in good faith toward "compliance at the earliest practicable date" and to make progress, according to the now famous phrase, "with all deliberate speed." Since the speed in many communities matched that of a snail, lawsuits multiplied to enforce speedier compliance.

During the years since the *Brown* decision, parents have raised various questions concerning desegregation. This chapter addresses those questions.

What does desegregation require?

Swann v. Charlotte-Mecklenberg Board of Education[4]: In 1965, the

Charlotte-Mecklenberg school system of North Carolina placed a desegregation plan in effect. Under this plan, 84,000 students were enrolled in 107 schools during the 1968-69 school year. Of these, about 24,000 were black and of these black students 14,000 attended 21 schools that were at least 99% black. One of the black students, James Swann, with the support of his parents and others, requested the local school board to plan a more effective desegregation, since both he and his parents believed that many black students were not getting an equal educational opportunity in their racially imbalanced schools.

A new plan proposed by a court-appointed expert included controversial recommendations concerning grouping of schools and busing for racial balance, and went beyond the rezoning suggested by the school board:

> . . .and desegregates all the rest of the elementary schools by the techniques of grouping two or three outlying schools with one black inner city school; by transporting black students from grades one through four to the outlying white schools; and by transporting white students from the fifth and sixth grades from the outlying white schools to the inner city black school.
>
> Under the. . .plan, nine inner city Negro schools were grouped in this manner with 24 suburban white schools.[5]

The dispute over this plan was appealed to the U.S. Supreme Court.

Must each school be racially balanced?

No, said Justice Burger, who wrote the opinion in the *Swann* case. "The constitutional command to desegregate schools does not mean that every school in every community must always reflect the racial composition of the school system as a whole." The Constitution does not require particular ratios or degrees of racial mixing. However, in school systems with a proven history of discrimination, it is proper for the courts to make use of mathematical ratios as starting points in proposing remedies, though not as fixed requirements.

Must one-race schools be eliminated?

Not necessarily. Large cities tend to contain racial or ethnic neighborhoods in which one-race schools are often found,
and the mere existence of these schools does not automatically constitute illegal segregation. But they should be carefully examined, Justice Burger urged, to determine whether
they are the results of deliberate school assignments that create
segregation.

Courts presume that one-race schools are the result of discrimination and school officials, therefore, have the burden
of proving that students' assignments to such schools were
genuinely nondiscriminatory. This is particularly the case in
communities which in the past had dual school systems, one
black and one white. As they change to unitary systems, they
must satisfy the courts that their racial composition is not the
consequence of past or present discrimination.

Is busing necessary for desegregation?

The big yellow school buses have in recent years become
the controversial symbols of parental disagreements about
desegregation. Although they are successfully used in many
communities, they have been used and abused, burned and
destroyed in Massachusetts and Michigan, Colorado, North
Carolina, California, and a score of other states.

Courts have applied the same general principles to the question of busing as they have to other aspects of desegregation.
Since conditions in different localities vary widely, no rigid rules
can be laid down to govern all situations. The courts closest to
the situation are, therefore, in the best position to consider such
factors as local highways, traffic patterns, travel time, the ages
of the children involved, health hazards, and costs to the school
district. Any busing plan should be tailored to the particular
needs of the situation.

Justice Burger noted that busing has played a significant role
in the history of American education. In *Swann*, he wrote:

Bus transportation has been an integral part of the public
education for years, and was perhaps the single most important factor in the transition from the one-room schoolhouse to the consolidated school. Eighteen million of the

Nation's public school children, approximately 39%, were transported to their schools by bus in 1969-1970 in all parts of the country.[6]

Where should the line be drawn on busing to achieve desegregation? The Supreme Court indicated that objections are valid when "the time or distance of travel is so great as to either risk the health of the children or significantly impinge on the educational process. It hardly needs stating that the limits on time of travel will vary with many factors, but probably with none more than the age of the students."[7]

Can courts order busing across district lines?

In a suit brought by Detroit parents, the district court found a history of unconstitutional racial segregation and sought acceptable remedies. In 1973, student enrollment in the Detroit school district was 69.8% black and 30.2% white. It was, therefore, impossible to achieve substantial racial desegregation within the city limits.   On the other hand, since the 1970 census showed a metropolitan area racial composition of 81% white and 19% black, it was possible to draw up a desegregation plan which covered both Detroit and its suburbs by sending some suburban children to city schools and some city children to schools in the suburbs. The district court accepted such a plan, and the appeals court upheld its ruling. The Supreme Court, however, disagreed in a 5-to-4 decision.[8]

Since the unconstitutional practices occurred in the city of Detroit, the majority of the court held that the remedy must be confined to the city limits.   The dissenting four justices saw the situation differently. Since education is a function of the state government in Michigan, they wrote, the state had the primary responsibility to correct violations of the Constitution in schooling. Furthermore, since a proper remedy could not be achieved within the city limits of Detroit, they did not see sufficient reasons to respect municipal boundaries if this frustrated efforts to achieve school desegregation. But the majority prevailed and metropolitan area cross-district busing was struck down.

Under certain circumstances, however, such cross-district busing is necessary and legally acceptable. This would be the case where district lines were purposely created to avoid racially mixed schools or where new districts were created to avoid court-ordered desegregation.

As Justice Burger said in the Detroit case:

> Before the boundaries of separate and autonomous school districts may be set aside by consolidating the separate units for remedial purposes or by imposing a cross-district remedy, it must first be shown that there has been a constitutional violation within one district that produces a significant segregative effect in another district.

> Thus an inter-district remedy might be in order where the racially discriminatory acts of one or more school district lines have been deliberately drawn on the basis of race. In such circumstances, an inter-district remedy would be appropriate to eliminate the inter-district segregation directly caused by the consitutional violation. Conversely, without an inter-district violation and inter-district effect, there is no constitutional wrong calling for an inter-district remedy.[9]

Little Rock, Arkansas, and Benton Harbor, Michigan, are two examples. In the Little Rock case in 1984, the U.S. District Court was presented evidence that proved that three school districts engaged in racially discriminatory acts resulting in inter-district segregation. Since these violations of the law could be cured only by an inter-district plan that included court-supervised busing and magnet schools, the court ordered such a consolidated plan that covered all three districts.[10]

It should be of particular interest to parents that the court also ordered the schools to hold no less than three public meetings within their districts to explain the consolidation plan to their patrons and to allow constructive criticism.

Similarly, in Benton Harbor, Michigan, the court ordered a consolidated desegregation plan for four school districts, because evidence showed that they all collaborated in unconstitutional acts that led to segregation. Moreover, the court even held the state of Michigan responsible for violating both the U.S. and Michigan constitutions and ordered the state to pay a substantial cost of the transportation necessary to carry out the inter-district desegregation plan.[11]

Thus, remedies in desegregation cases consider the history of the community and its racial and ethnic composition, the intentions and motives behind the actions related to schools, as well as such factors as local geography, traffic patterns, highways, costs, special health hazards, and certainly the age of the children.*

Can parents choose the schools their children will attend?

To some extent. As explained in Chapter 1, parents have the right to choose whether their children attend private or public schools, secular or religious ones. Furthermore, within the public school system, school boards and school officials may provide parents with a wide range of choices. This is not a legal matter, but an administrative-educational policy to be determined in each community. But public schools are state agencies; board members, administrators, and teachers are public officials; and the policies they establish must be consistent with constitutional principles.

Parental freedom, for example, cannot be used to re-segregate the schools. Such arrangements were struck down repeatedly when the so-called "freedom-of-choice" plans were used as a subterfuge to continue segregated schooling. As the Supreme Court said in the *Green* case:

Freedom-of-choice is not a sacred talisman: it is only a means to a constitutionally required end—the abolition of the system of segregation and its effects. If the means prove effective, it is acceptable, but if it fails to undo segregation, other means must be used to achieve this end. The school officials have the continuing duty to take whatever action may be necessary to create a "unitary, non-racial system."[12]

Nor may parental freedom be used to keep an ethnic group segregated in the public schools even if the parents want to

---

*Title VI of the 1964 Civil Rights Act empowers the Attorney General to file suit on behalf of parents if they are denied equal protection for reasons of race, religion, sex, or national origin.

do so to maintain their own ethnic identity, language, and culture. The courts so ruled in a case that arose in San Francisco, where Chinese parents sued to exclude their children from a citywide desegregation plan. The parents wanted their children to continue attending neighborhood schools that enrolled mostly Chinese-American students. They feared that if the students were dispersed by busing through a citywide desegregation plan that would make it more difficult to teach their children the Chinese language, and eventually their culture would be destroyed.

When evidence showed that school officials drew attendance lines in a way that would maintain and even heighten racial imbalance, the Court ruled these actions unconstitutional. The Court held that Chinese students, along with others, must participate in the overall desegregation plan. However, the Court also recommended bilingual classes for Chinese-speaking students, as well as courses that would help all students understand the culture and heritage of various ethnic and racial groups.[13]

Have the courts gone too far in controlling the schools?

Some parents, as well as educators, lawyers and judges have raised this question in recent years, during which judges have exercised supervision over such details of schooling as pupil and teacher placement, teacher and administrator selection, curriculum content, building maintenance, grading practices, and disciplinary procedures. In some instances receiverships have been created with court-appointed "experts" in charge of schools and special "Masters" advising the judges.[14] The recent history of the Boston schools exemplifies some of these arrangements.

These extreme measures are exceptional and are imposed on the schools only in highly unusual circumstances. Although the federal courts have wide-ranging powers, as a general principle they wish to avoid entanglement in educational policy and administrative activities. They are willing to examine these activities to see that they comply with the Constitution, but they readily admit their lack of competence in educational matters, and they have no interest in becoming substitute school boards. Nevertheless, if a community has a history of racial discrimination and if it exhibits a continuing resistance to desegregation, judges have wide discretion in the means and methods at their disposal to enforce the law. It is never a happy solution when courts exercise substantial supervision over the details of schooling, but it may be legally necessary. Such situations are always highly controversial, with parents on each side of the controversy.

Must schools continually redraw attendance lines?

If, after a community desegregates its schools, population changes again create racial imbalance, must the school board redraw attendance lines to compensate for such imbalance? In a Pasadena case, the Supreme Court said no.[15] Justice Rehnquist, who wrote the decision, relied on the *Swann* case (see page 72) and stated that the duty to rearrange attendance zones exists only as long as there is a constitutional violation. Once the duty to desegregate has been satisfied, there is no further constitutional requirement to make year-by-year adjustments.

May a state repeal its desegregation laws?

Yes, but it must continue to satisfy the requirements of the federal law. Questions about states repealing their own laws arose in California and Washington.

The California Supreme Court held that the state constitution forbade all segregation whether *de facto* or *de jure**. Thereafter, in 1979, the people of California ratified Proposition I, an amendment to their constitution that repealed state antidiscrimination laws. When the constitutionality of Proposition I was challenged, the U.S. Supreme Court held that the people of a state may add and repeal laws as they experiment with ways of solving their problems. However, they may not alter the requirements of the Fourteenth Amendment of the U.S. Constitution. The net result of the repeal of the California laws related to desegregation was that in California, as elsewhere, it

---

De facto segregation means that segregation resulted from voluntary actions of individuals in the absence of laws or any type of official, government action. *De jure* segregation means that segregation resulted from law, official policy or regulations, or some action by government or school officials.

is necessary to prove intentional segregation to establish a claim of unconstitutional action.[16]

By contrast, the people of the state of Washington passed a statewide initiative that allowed pupils to be assigned beyond their neighborhood for various purposes, but not for achieving racial integration. They could be bused for special education, to avoid overcrowding, to benefit from special programs, but not for racial balance. The U.S. Supreme Court held this initiative to be unconstitutional, and it is obviously different from the simple repeal involved in the California case previously discussed.[17]

May private schools exclude black students?

As a general rule they may not. This is the law because a federal statute protects the equal right to enter into contracts.[18]

When parents want to enter into an agreement with a private school for the education of their children, they are forming a contract with the school. The U.S. Supreme Court ruled that private non-sectarian schools may not deny admission to black or other minority children simply on the basis of race or ethnicity.[19] If a private religious school wants to exclude minority race students based on genuine religious principles, it can do so, but its tax-exempt status may be denied by the Internal Revenue Service.[20]

This is so, ruled the Court, because tax exemption applies only to "charitable" institutions consistent with the public interest. Since racial discrimination is against public policy, institutions that practice it are not "charitable" within the meaning of our Internal Revenue code, as intended by Congress.[21]

Must schools desegregate faculties as well as students?

Yes. The law requires that all aspects of the school environment be seriously considered in any plan to desegregate. This requirement certainly includes the faculty, administration, and support staff. Courts have so ruled in the North and South, in the East and the West. Such desegregation cases arose in Alabama[22] and Michigan,[23] Massachusetts,[24] and California,[25] and the courts have consistently held that faculties, administration and staff must also be desegregated consistent with the principles announced in the original *Brown* case. Segregation in public schooling must be eliminated "root and branch."

Can parents challenge discriminatory disciplinary practices?

Yes, they can. The best known case that found illegal racial discrimination in school disciplinary practices arose in Dallas, Texas.[26] In the *Hawkins* case, the school officials claimed that what appeared to be a larger number of suspensions, expulsions, and other disciplinary actions against black students simply reflected greater misbehavior on their part rather than discrimination. The federal district court, however, found that the disparity in discipline was caused at least in part by (1) selective reactions on the part of the school staff whereby black students were punished more severely and more frequently for the same behavior than white students, (2) punishment for cultural differences such as wearing hats or different styles of verbal and physical interactions, none of which were really disruptive, and (3) provocation of black students by insensitivity and lack of access to school decision-making. The court ordered the schools to create a plan to eliminate racial disparities in discipline.

A more comprehensive settlement was reached in Newburgh, New York, in 1980 where a suit challenged the disproportionate suspension of black and Hispanic students.[27] (Various studies have shown the national suspension rate for blacks to be approximately twice the rate for whites.) The settlement was reached the day before the scheduled trial and incorporated into a consent decree.

In the New York case of *Ross v. Saltmarsh*, a comprehensive plan was created that modified the student discipline code in order to reduce suspensions, provided for greater involvement by students, parents and guidance counselors in the discipline process, and made improvements in the school's psychological services, extracurricular activities, and the grouping of students.

The constitutional principle is clear and settled that it is illegal for schools to practice racial or ethnic discrimination in disciplinary procedures. To prove such discrimination is often difficult and so is the creation of new, nondiscriminatory approaches to schooling. (The *Ross* case might be a useful guide to parents. Information about the case is available from the Children's Defense Fund, 1520 New Hampshire Avenue, NW, Washington, DC 20036.)

Can parents challenge discriminatory testing and placement of students?

Yes, they can. Various lawsuits have been filed by parents challenging school testing and placement practices that landed a disproportionate number of minority students in special education classes. Since the passage of the Education of All Handicapped Children Act of 1975 there are legal safeguards against such mistakes in testing and placement. We discuss these in Chapter 2.

Probably the best known case that challenged the use of IQ tests, the results of which were used to place black children into classes for the retarded, was *Larry P. v. Riles*.[28] Based on expert testimony the court ruled that the tests were not valid for testing black students since some of the test items were widely considered to be culturally biased. The use of such tests violated several federal laws as well as the constitutional guarantee of equal protection. The judge ordered that the test no longer be used and all children placed pursuant to its use be reevaluated without the use of tests. Erroneously placed children were to be provided individual educational plans for remediation and returned to regular classes.

Are grouping or tracking practices unconstitutional?

That depends on the basis for grouping or tracking and how educators treat the groups they formed. While there are disagreements among educators about how, when, and why to group students, grouping is not inherently illegal or unconstitutional.

However, if racial or ethnic factors somehow become important criteria in grouping, the practice may well be unconstitutional. The federal district court so ruled in Washington, D.C. in the case of *Hobson v. Hansen*[29] where students were placed in different tracks very early in their schooling, based on tests that turned out not to be valid. Evidence showed that there were no remediation or other efforts made to help students escape the low track once placed therein, and they continued there into low level vocational programs. Because of the racial and socioeconomic conditions in the District of Columbia, the students assigned to the lower tracks were poor and black whereas those assigned to the upper tracks (there were four tracks in all) were mostly affluent and white. The court ruled this arrangement to be illegal discrimination in violation of the Fourteenth Amendment.

Ability grouping (tracking), however, is not always unconstitutional. If educators create groups for advanced students, for example, and if they select students for such groups in a valid or nondiscriminatory manner, courts will not interfere with such schooling practices. As a general rule, one should be suspicious of grouping that occurs with very young children when the grouping is based on standardized tests, and particularly when such grouping tends to produce classes that are homogeneous in race, ethnicity, or apparent wealth.

What can parents do if they believe that local school policies discriminate against blacks, Hispanics or other minorities?

There are several alternatives available to parents in such situations. The most direct one is to raise their concern with local school officials and attempt a resolution at the level closest to home. If such attempts are not successful, the second alternative is to file a complaint with the state office responsible for enforcing anti-discrimination laws, though the titles of such offices vary. For example, in Massachusetts, this is called the Massachusetts Commission Against Discrimination. Depending on the size and population density of the state, there might be regional offices convenient to all parts of the state.

The third alternative is specified in the *Federal Register* in the regulations created to implement Title VI of the Civil Rights Act of 1964. (As last amended, effective March, 1983, 48 C.F.R. 6311, Feb. 11, 1983). Under these regulations, a person who believes that discriminatory practices are going on in the schools may file a written complaint with the Director of the Office of Personnel Management. The complaint shall be filed within 90 days of the alleged discrimination, unless the time for filing is extended by that office.

What will the Office of Personnel Management do after receiving a complaint?

The OPM will investigate the situation promptly, keeping confidential the identity of the complainant. If the facts warrant action, they will seek resolution through voluntary means.

If such means fail, OPM might withhold federal funds from the school district or take other action, including referring the matter to the Department of Justice for appropriate legal action.

Summary

For over thirty years, since the landmark *Brown* case, it has been an established principle of our government that segregated education violates the 14th Amendment of the Constitution. The problems of implementing this principle have turned out to be many and very controversial.

In many localities, racially mixed schooling is difficult to achieve without massive transportation of students, and busing children to desegregate the schools has emerged as the most controversial issue in education in recent decades. However, as the Supreme Court ruled in the *Swann* case and has reaffirmed in subsequent cases, busing is a legitimate means to achieve desegregation in school districts with a history of racial segregation.

It is quite possible, however, that if the current pattern of white students moving to suburban districts continues, increasing the percentage of racial minorities in the cities, desegregated schooling within city limits will be unworkable. This was the case in Detroit where a proposal was made that would achieve desegregation by busing across district lines. The Court struck down this proposal and said that the remedy must be applied only to the school district where the constitutional violations occurred. Cross-district busing for desegregation will be required only where the formation of separate districts has created or aggravated racially separate schooling.

It seems highly probable that the twin concerns of parents—neighborhood schooling and desegregation—will continue to bring cases to court into the indefinite future. On the other hand, many communities have achieved desegregated schooling through cooperative, non-legal means without recourse to the courts. Those disagreements that do reach the courts will probably be resolved by relying on the following Supreme Court principles from the *Swann* case: (1) To achieve "racial balance" mathematical ratios can be used as guides, but not as fixed quotas. (2) Attendance zones may be altered, and schools may be "paired," "clustered," or "regrouped" to eliminate dual school systems. (3) One-race schools are not necessarily un-constitutional, although the presumption is against them, and school officials have the burden of proving that assignment to them is non-discriminatory. (4) Busing is a legitimate means to desegregate schools, and its limits will be set so that the time and distance traveled will not be detrimental to the health and education of children.

Literally hundreds of decisions could be cited consistent with these principles. They have been handed down in all parts of the country, north and south, rural and urban. The ways desegregation is carried out must always be tailor-made to the unique features of the school district involved, but still must be consistent with the principles of the *Brown* case, decided over three decades ago.

In addition to issues related to desegregation, other important decisions by our courts have held that it is unconstitutional to practice racial discrimination in school discipline, and in the testing, placement, and tracking of students. Cases show that all too often a disproportionate number of black and Hispanic students have been suspended or expelled, that invalid tests have been used to place them into classes for the mentally handicapped as well as into low ability classes without appropriate remediation to help them gain the equal treatment guaranteed by the Constitution as well as federal and state laws.

Thus, it is clear that parents have often used the courts successfully to overcome illegal discrimination in schooling and to secure due process and equal treatment for their children.

Notes for Chapter 5

1. *Brown v. Board of Education,* 347 U.S. 483 (1954).

2. Ibid. p. 495.

3. *Brown v. Board of Education,* 349 U.S. 294 (1955).

4. *Swann v. Charlotte-Mecklenburg Board of Education,* 402 U.S. 1(1971).

5. Ibid. p. 9-10.

6. Ibid. p. 29.

7. Ibid.

8. *Milliken v. Bradley,* 418 U.S. 717 (1974).

9. Ibid.

10. *Little Rock School District v. Pulaski County Special School District No. 1, et al.,* 597 F.Supp. 1220 (D.C. Ark. 1984).

11. *Berry v. School District of the City of Benton Harbor,* 564 F.Supp. 617 (W.D. Mich. 1983).

12. *Green v. County School Board of New Kent Co., Va.,* 391 U.S. 430 (1968).

13. *Lee v. Johnson,* 404 U.S. 1215 (1971).

14. *Morgan v. Kerrigan,* 409 F.Supp. 1141 (D.Mass. 1975).

15. *Pasadena City Board of Education v. Spangler,* 427 U.S. 424 (1976).

16. *Crawford v. Board of Education,* 102 S.Ct. 3211 (1982).

17. *Washington v. School District No. 1,* 102 S.Ct. 3187 (1982).

18. 42 U.S.C. 1981.

19. *Runyon v. McCrary,* 427 U.S. 160 (1976).

20. *Bob Jones University v. United States,* 103 S.Ct. 2017 (1983).

21. I.R.C. of 1954, 501 (c) (3).

22. *U.S. v. Montgomery Board of Education,* 395 U.S. 225 (1969).

23. *Bradley v. Milliken,* 418 U.S. 717 (1974).

24. *Morgan v. Kerrigan,* 509 F.2d. 580 (2d. Cir. 1974).

25. *Crawford v. Board of Education in the City of Los Angeles,* 551 P.2d 28 (Cal. 1976).

26. *Hawkins v. Coleman*, 376 F.Supp. 1330 (N.D.Tex.1974).

27. *Ross v. Saltmarsh*, 500 F.Supp.935 (S.D.N.Y.1980).

28. *Larry P. v. Riles*, 495 F.Supp. 926 (N.D.Cal.1979), aff'd 52 U.S.L.W. 2456 (9th Cir., Jan. 23, 1984).

29. *Hobson v. Hansen*, 269 F.Supp.401 (D.D.C.1967), *aff'd subnom.Smuck v. Hobson*, 408 F.2d 175 (D.C. Cir.1969).

CHAPTER 6

Sex Discrimination in the Schools

May girls try out for boys' teams?

Must schools provide opportunities for interscholastic athletic competition for both male and female students?

May boys try out for girls' teams in non-contact sports?

Must schools provide identical amounts of money for the support of male and female sports?

Does Title IX forbid sex discrimination in the curriculum?

May public schools provide separate schools for boys and girls?

May different standards be used for the admission of boys and girls to school?

May schools expel pregnant students?

Are students protected against sexual harassment?

Must the school faculty and staff be sexually integrated?

How broad is the application of Title IX in an institution?

More than half the students in our public schools are female, and more than half of the teachers are women. Even so, various areas of school life have historically discriminated in favor of male students. Until quite recently schools commonly restricted certain courses to boys only, provided preferential treatment to boys' athletic activities, suspended or expelled pregnant students and treated boys and girls differently in other school-related activities. Boys, too, have been discriminated against in school, for example, when forbidden by some authorities to take cooking or sewing courses. But, by and large, they have faced far fewer problems because of their sex than girls have.

Have these policies and practices been changed or eliminated? Must boys and girls be treated identically by public schools, or can some school practices be legitimately influenced by considerations of sex? In this chapter we look at cases related to these and other issues involving sexual discrimination and stereotyping. We also discuss Title IX,[1] a federal law that has become a powerful means for eliminating sexual discrimination from the schools.

Athletic Activities

May girls try out for boys' teams?

High school interscholastic sports are highly organized in the U.S. and in most states are regulated by state-wide league rules. As in most states, Minnesota's high schools were regulated by the Minnesota State High School League, which had the following rules:

> Girls shall be prohibited from participating in the boys' interscholastic athletic program either as a member of the boys' teams or a member of the girls' team playing the boys' team. The girls' team shall not accept male members.

Despite this rule, Peggy Brenden wanted to play on her high school's boys' tennis team. She was an outstanding player, ranked number one among the 18-year-olds in her area during 1972. Since there was insufficient interest in tennis among the girls of her school, there was no girls' team and thus no interscholastic competition for Peggy. By contrast, the boys had a team, a coach, and a regular schedule of matches. School officials, citing the League rules, refused Peggy an opportunity to compete for a place on the boys' team.

Peggy and her parents went to court claiming that her civil rights and her rights to due process and equal protection had been violated. Her case was heard, together with the case of Tony St. Pierre, a 17-year-old female student at the Eisenhower High School, in another Minnesota school district, who had been denied the right to compete on the boys' cross-country running and cross-country skiing teams.[2]

The school districts maintained that the League rule was reasonable and protected the fair and orderly conduct of inter-scholastic athletic competition. Furthermore, they claimed that such competition was a privilege, not a right, and therefore could be regulated by the schools.

In deciding this case, the court acknowledged the substantial differences between boys and girls, which in general favor boys in athletic competition. On the other hand, it also recognized that Peggy and Tony were exceptional cases. So, although the court did not declare the League rules inherently uncon-stitutional, it did strike them down in their application to these two young women. In the words of the court:

> It must be emphasized in this case, however, that these physiological differences, insofar as they render the great majority of females unable to compete as effectively as males, have little relevance to Tony St. Pierre and Peggy Brenden. Because of their level of achievement in com-petitive sports, Tony and Peggy have overcome these physiological disabilities. There has been no evidence that either Peggy Brenden or Tony St. Pierre, or any other girls, would be in any way damaged from competition in boys' interscholastic athletics, nor is there any credible evidence that the boys would be damaged.[3]

A rule can be unconstitutional by itself if, for example, it is arbitrary or unreasonable or if it denies equal protection. Or it can be unconstitutional in its application. The latter was the ruling in the Minnesota case. In other words, the court found that these two exceptional women athletes were prevented from participating in interscholastic activities "on the basis of the fact of sex and sex alone." Since the school provided no alterna-tive competitive programs for them, the rules were declared un-reasonable and discriminatory, as applied to Peggy and Tony, and the girls were declared eligible to compete on the boys' teams. Moreover, the state High School League was forbidden to punish the schools on whose teams the girls would compete.

Must schools provide opportunities for interscholastic athletic competition for both male and female students?

Not necessarily. Public schools do not have to provide such activities at all. That is a policy to be decided by each state or, in the absence of state laws, by each school district. But if a school district provides such opportunities, they must be available to all on equal terms. If, for example, a school has only a boys' team for such non-contact sports as golf, tennis or swimming, girls have the right to try out for positions on the teams.

What if there are teams for boys and girls? Can a superior girl athlete try out for the boys' team if the girls' team doesn't provide enough of a challenge for her? Not in most states. In the absence of specific state laws or regulations, courts have ruled that separate teams and leagues for boys and girls are reasonable and not discriminatory. Many educators support this separation as the best way to encourage both boys and girls to participate in athletics. Although it does not benefit the exceptional female athlete, it does help the average girl. Certain states–Michigan and New York, for example–have gone further than the courts, making girls eligible for membership on boys' non-contact sports teams even in schools where girls' teams exist. Another alternative would be the establishment of both a top team based solely on ability and separate teams for boys and girls to encourage broad participation. But budgetary considerations lead most school boards to establish only two teams: boys' and girls'.

Until now, we have been talking about non-contact sports. What about contact sports such as football, basketball, baseball, or hockey? There have been fewer cases in this area, but in Pennsylvania, where the Equal Rights Amendment has been voted part of the state constitution, a court ruled that both boys and girls can try out, on an equal basis, for all athletic teams, including those in contact sports.

More than a dozen other states have added Equal Rights Amendments to their constitutions under which parents and students may pursue equal treatment in school-sponsored athletic activities. In most states, these amendments have not been litigated as yet, thus the precise application to school sports is not yet clear.

However, there have been some court cases related to girls' participation in contact sports on boys' teams. For example, two girls went to court when they successfully tried out for the boys' basketball team at the middle school level in Yellow Springs, Ohio, and the Ohio High School Athletic Association (OHSAA) prohibited coed teams in interscholastic contact sports. The 6th Circuit Court held that the rules of OHSAA were more restrictive than Title IX, the federal law, therefore schools need not follow them. In contact sports, Title IX does not prohibit girls from trying out for boys' teams, but leaves that decision to the discretion of schools. Thus, ruled the court, schools may allow girls to try out for the boys' basketball team, and the rules of OHSAA could not prevent this or exclude coed teams from league competition. Title IX, which is a federal law, takes precedence over league rules.[4]

In a related case, a federal district court upheld the right of a 13-year-old female to try out for the junior high school football team. The school offered football for boys only and volleyball for girls only, but Nicole Force wanted to play football. The school argued that 13-year-old females are more likely to get injured in coed football than 13-year-old males, and therefore the exclusion of girls was reasonable. The court was presented evidence that while in general it was true that girls at this age would be more likely to be injured, there was no evidence that this particular female could not safely play junior high school football. Thus, the court applied a stringent test and held that the school, in order to use a gender-based classification, must have a very persuasive justification for its action.

Some 13-year-old boys can't safely participate in football, yet all boys are not excluded. The exclusion of all girls reflects a historic paternalism toward girls, and that is a violation of the Equal Protection Clause of the Constitution.[5] Thus, if parents suspect that their daughters are being excluded from school athletic participation unfairly, based on sex discrimination, they may explore several areas of remedies. They may have rights under the U.S. Constitution, under Title IX, under their state's constitution, state laws, or even under local school policies.

May boys try out for girls' teams in non-contact sports?

They have no legal right to do so, although schools are not

prohibited by law from allowing such opportunities. This question arose in various communities, particularly in volleyball, when schools provided teams and interscholastic competition for girls only. Amherst Regional High School in Massachusetts, for example, allowed boys to play on the girls' team, but it took court action to force the state athletic league to allow such coed teams, under the state Equal Rights Amendment. But, in the absence of a state E.R.A., a similar lawsuit in Arizona was filed under the Equal Protection Clause of the Fourteenth Amendment of the U.S. Constitution. In this case, the Circuit Court held that the exclusion of boys from girls' teams does not violate the Constitution.

The court reasoned that in cases involving gender-based discrimination there must be an important governmental purpose, and the rule must relate to the achievement of that purpose. What is the important governmental objective here? It is to provide equal opportunities for males and females to participate in sports and to overcome historic discrimination against women in athletics. Is the exclusion of boys related to these objectives? Yes, it is, ruled the court, after examining the skills required for success in volleyball and the physiological differences between boys and girls. It is generally accepted that if everyone were allowed to try out for the same team in volleyball, boys would have an undue advantage over girls. Boys' participation would reduce the opportunities for girls. Thus, the court said that "while equality in specific sports is a worthwhile ideal, it should not be purchased at the expense of ultimate equality to participate in sports."[6]

The contrast between what happened in the Arizona case and the earlier mentioned case from Amherst, Massachusetts, is helpful to point up the difference between states that have E.R.A.'s and those that do not. While the exact meaning and consequences of the state E.R.A.'s will not be known until after many cases have been litigated under them, it is clear that they do provide some rights which courts have not granted under the Equal Protection Clause of the U.S. Constitution.

Must schools provide identical amounts of money for the support of male and female sports?

Generally, no. Historically, most of our schools and school

districts have given much larger budgetary allotments to male athletic programs than to female ones, and on the whole, male students have tended to participate more in sports than females. So most people thought it senseless for schools to provide identical resources for male and female athletics.

It is probably true that these limited opportunities and expenditures were themselves part of the reason that girls participated less in sports. But there is some evidence that this situation is changing. There are, however, no authoritative court rulings on the question of equal expenditures for female and male athletics.

The federal legislation commonly known as Title IX may prove to be the most effective means to bring about equality in budget and other allocation for athletics. It provides that:

No person in the United States shall on the basis of sex be excluded from participation, be denied the benefits of, or be subjected to discrimination under any education program or activity receiving Federal financial assistance.

Moreover, its regulations specifically refer to athletic programs and forbid discrimination in the provision of supplies, equipment, facilities and supporting services of various types. While these regulations clearly require equal treatment, they also recognize that there is not always sufficient interest among students to form teams for males and females.

In addition to Title IX, which is federal law, many states have passed legislation requiring more equitable treatment of female athletics in public schools. Parents should get to know the laws of their own states as well as the national law and the Constitution, since state laws are often more specific and helpful.[7]

Other Concerns

Does Title IX forbid sex discrimination in the curriculum?

Yes. Although we have focused our discussion on athletics, the same principles apply to other school activities. We have paid less attention to questions of sex discrimination in the curriculum and the availability of courses and programs because such practices quickly crumbled before the law. Title IX forbids sex discrimination in the curriculum, in courses and programs. Some states, such as New York and Massachusetts, have passed laws prohibiting the exclusion of students from any course of instruction by reason of sex. In states which have no such laws, suits have been brought against these practices. In every case, the suits have been quickly settled, and the practices changed.

This is not to say that all schools currently practice equal treatment of boys and girls. Tradition, ingrained customs, and habits are difficult to change. Many parents, for example, believe that girls should stay out of shop courses and boys out of cooking and sewing. There are also those who think that girls should not compete for positions on the boys' tennis or golf teams. So, even when laws and official policies support equal opportunities, the informal pressures of a school and the community often discourage equal participation by male and female students.

May public schools provide separate schools for boys and girls?

Yes, answered a Pennsylvania court, if the schools are provided on an equal basis to both male and female students.[8] The wisdom or educational value of such separation is not a legal question, the court said, and courts do not take stands for or against such arrangements, since they are basically the concern of educators and parents (and perhaps students). As long as they do not establish unfair or discriminatory treatment of either group, the courts are not likely to substitute their wisdom for that of the school and the parents.

Various commentators have noted that the doctrine of "separate but equal," which was struck down when the separation is based on race, seems to be acceptable when it is based on sex, if there are legitimate educational reasons for the separation. An equally divided Supreme Court affirmed this ruling. In other cases where the Supreme Court ruled on sex discrimination, it has not applied standards as rigorous as it has in cases of racial discrimination.

May different standards be used for the admission of boys and girls to school?

A Boston case said no. In 1970, Boston Latin School had two separate buildings. Boys Latin with a capacity of 3,000 students and Girls Latin with a capacity of 1,500. Each year, the city school department determined the necessary entry scores on the written examination for each by first checking the number of vacancies in each building. In 1970, girls had to score 133 to be admitted, while boys had to score 120. The court held this arrangement to be a violation of the Equal Protection Clause of the Fourteenth Amendment.[9] A similar decision was reached in a San Francisco case in 1974.[10] Title IX also prohibits such practices.

In a recent case, courts struck down the admission policies of the Massachusetts Maritime Academy when evidence indicated that such policies and procedures were tainted with sexual discrimination. The Academy claimed to be exempt from Title IX because it has traditionally admitted only one sex, and Title IX grants such exemptions. The lawsuit, however, was not brought under Title IX, but under the U.S. Constitution, and the Circuit Court held that such discriminatory admission policies of a public institution violate the Equal Protection Clause of the Fourteenth Amendment.[11]

May schools expel pregnant students?

In the past, most people agreed that married or pregnant students should not continue attending school, on the grounds that pregnant girls or married students disrupted school activities, that sexual relations among teenagers were immoral, and that pregnant girls and married students were physically and psychologically better off away from school.

In recent years this trend has been reversed. Although some school boards and educators would still exclude married or pregnant students from high schools, more and more believe that these students need education and that their "corruptive influence" has been grossly exaggerated. Courts have held that where a state provides public schools for teenagers, pregnant and married students have a right to attend.[12] Furthermore, Title IX regulations specify that if a school offers a separate program for pregnant students, it must be comparable to that offered for non-pregnant students, and students must be given a choice whether or not to attend such separate programs.

In an effort to discourage early marriages, some schools still bar married students from extracurricular activities, athletics, and student offices.   In 1959, a Texas court upheld such a school rule. The court made no judgment on the wisdom of the rule, but merely said that it was a matter for the Board of Education and that it would not interfere unless the school rule was arbitrary and unreasonable.[13]

On the other hand, different results were reached in more recent cases in Texas,[14] Ohio,[15] and other states. Courts now find extracurricular activities to be an important part of the school program and ask whether the student's marriage interferes with school discipline in a material and substantial way. If it does not, the court considers the rule to be arbitrary and protects the student's right to participate in the activity.

Since Title IX specifically forbids discrimination either in class or in extracurricular activities because of a student's marital status or pregnancy, there should be very few lawsuits in the future. It must be pointed out, nevertheless, that many girls still drop out of school as a result of marriage or pregnancy.

Are students protected against sexual harassment?

Yes, they are. Sexual advances toward students by teachers, administrators, or other school employees constitute immoral and unprofessional conduct for which appropriate legal action may be taken. This has always been the case in our schools, even before the term "sexual harassment" became popular. Recent federal and state laws have been enacted to protect adults from sexual harassment in the work place. Students, however, have always been protected by law against sexual advances made by school employees because students lack the legal capacity to give consent and because it is presumed that the adults are in a position of power over students.

Must the school faculty and staff be sexually integrated?

Title IX regulations forbid discrimination in employment in schools, except military schools and those religious schools where compliance would violate religious tenets. Schools that receive or benefit from federal funds must not discriminate in recruiting, hiring, promotion, tenure, job assignment or any other aspect of employment and must incorporate principles of Affirmative Action. "Affirmative Action" means that schools must make positive efforts to search for and find qualified female and minority personnel to fill job vacancies. This policy goes further than nondiscrimination. It places a responsibility on schools to increase their efforts and broaden their search for candidates who belong to the groups that are under-represented on their faculties or in leadership positions. From the perspective of parents, it could be said that there is a right to a teaching faculty and staff that are sexually nonsegregated.

How broad is the application of Title IX in an institution?

A 1984 decision by the Supreme Court severely restricted the application of Title IX and perhaps of some other civil rights laws that use similar language. The Court held, in effect, that just because some segment of the institution receives federal funds does not mean that Title IX will apply to all programs at that institution.

In the *Grove City College* case[16], some students attending a private institution, received Basic Educational Opportunity Grants (BEOG). The Court ruled that it was not the intent of Congress to apply Title IX to the entire school ". . .because one of its students received a small BEOG or because one of its departments received an earmarked federal grant." This ruling is very significant because it severely restricts the application of Title IX by making it program-specific rather than institution-wide. In other words, a school that receives federal support for its programs in departments A, B, and C, may still discriminate based on sex in departments D, E, and F. To limit the impact of *Grove City*, and to prevent its influence from spreading to other civil rights legislation, efforts have been made to pass legislation clearly stating the intent of Congress to reverse the impact of *Grove City*. Until now, such efforts have not succeeded because various issues beyond sex discrimination in education have been introduced into the legislative debate.

Summary

Court cases as well as federal and state laws have made significant gains in reducing sexually discriminatory practices during recent years. While all aspects of schooling have felt the influence of such changes, perhaps the areas of greatest significance to parents fall under three headings: (1) female students' access to sports, (2) equality in admission and in the curriculum, and (3) schooling of married or pregnant students.

Sports

Even though schools still provide more athletic activities for male than for female students, progress has been made toward equality in sports. The discrepancy might well be the function of tradition and the slow rate at which some habits change.

Schools do not have to provide inter-scholastic athletics. But if they have such teams, as a general rule they must be made available to both girls and boys on a nondiscriminatory basis. This means that in non-contact sports schools could have separate teams for boys and girls, each with proper equipment, coaching, and other support services as required by Title IX. If only boys' teams are available, girls must have opportunities to compete for positions on them. Some states have gone further and by state law or constitutional amendment have provided opportunities for girls to try out for boys' teams even when there were separate teams for boys and girls. Some states have even opened up contact sport participation to males and females alike.

Admission, Curriculum, and Counseling

In recent years public schools have tended to be coeducational, and admission policies have not been based on sex. But occasional cases have arisen. One of these, a Pennsylvania case, upheld the right of a school district to provide for separate schools for boys and girls as long as the schools were equal in quality. In a Massachusetts case, however, admission practices at Boston Latin Schools were struck down, because girls had to score higher than boys on a standardized test.

In the past, the curriculum contained many sexually segregated classes. Girls often could not take woodworking or auto shop, and boys were often excluded from cooking, sewing, and even typing. These practices are fast disappearing, and they are clearly illegal. Books and other school materials are increasingly examined to eliminate sexual stereotyping, and most counselors no longer offer vocational advice on the basis of sex alone. But when discriminatory practices continue by informal means, "friendly" advice, and subtle pressures, parents can change them more effectively than courts or legislatures.

Pregnancy and Marriage

In the past, most girls who got married or pregnant dropped out of school. School policies encouraged and often required them to do so. Some schools still have policies discouraging teenage marriages and pregnancies, though increasingly these are being challenged.

States with compulsory attendance laws specify age limits for schooling. Within those age limits, students have a right to attend school even if they marry, and the same holds true if they become pregnant.

The law is in conflict regarding the rights of married and pregnant students to participate in extracurricular activities or hold student offices. Some courts have upheld school rules that prevented married students from participating in athletics, while courts in other jurisdictions have held such rules to be arbitrary and unreasonable. Most courts are increasingly protecting the rights of married or pregnant students to full participation and completion of their schooling. But in some of these matters, the courts will respect the discretion of local school boards; therefore, it becomes very important for parent groups to make their opinions known and do what they can to influence local school policies.

Notes on Chapter 6

1. Title IX of the Education Amendments of 1972, 20 U.S.C. 1681.

2. *Brenden v. Independent School District 742*, 477 F.2d 1292 (8th Cir. 1973).

3. Ibid. p. 1233.

4. *Yellow Springs, etc. v. Ohio High School Athletic Association*, 647 F.2d 651 (6th Cir. 1981).

5. *Force v. Pierce City R-V1 School District*, 570 F.Supp. 1020 (W.D. Mo. 1983); *Lantz v. Ambach*, 620 F.Supp.663(S.D.N.Y.1985).

6. *Clark, etc. v. Arizona Interscholastic Association*, 695 F.2d 1126 (9th Cir. 1982).

7. See, for example, Ch. 622 of the Massachusetts General Laws.

8. *Vorchheimer v. School District of Philadelphia*, 532 F.2d 880 (3rd Cir. 1976).

9. *Bray v. Lee*, 377 F.Supp. 934 (D.Mass. 1972).

10. *Berkelman v. San Francisco Unified School District*, 501 F.2d 1264 (9th Cir. 1974).

11. *U.S. v. Massachusetts Maritime Academy*, 762 F.2d 142 (1st Cir. 1985).

12. See Brian E. Berwick and Carol Oppenheimer, "Marriage, Pregnancy, and the Right to Go to School," 50 Texas Law Review, 1196-1228 (1972).

13. *Kissick v. Garland Independent School District*, 330 S.W.2d 708 (Tex. 1959).

14. *Bell v. Lone Oak Independent School District*, 507 S.W.2d 636 (Tex. 1974).

15. *David v. Meek*, 344 F.Supp. 298 (N.D. Ohio 1972).

16. *Grove City College v. Bell*, 104 S.Ct. 1211 (1984).

CHAPTER 7

Student Injuries and the Right to Compensation

When can a teacher be held liable for a student's injury?

When is a teacher negligent?

Is constant supervision required?

Is supervision required after school hours?

What is the student-teacher ratio required to provide safe supervision?

When must students be warned?

How careful must schools be?

Is a careless teacher automatically liable?

Does a school's insurance cover medical expenses for injured students?

Do schools have defenses against liability?

What is "contributory negligence?"

If a student is negligent, does this always prevent recovery?

Does a student sometimes assume the risk of being injured?

Can teachers use "governmental immunity" as a defense against negligence?

Does a parental "waiver" or "release" prevent injured students from suing?

Can a parent sue on her own behalf for injuries to her child?

Can school employees be held liable for making false statements about students or parents?

Can a teacher be held liable for reporting, but failing to prove, parental abuse?

Can parents be held liable for publicly criticizing teachers or administrators?

If a parent's suit is "frivolous," could he be required to pay for the defendant's attorney's fees?

Can parents be held liable for the property damage of their children?

May schools be held liable if they fail to exclude a student or employee with AIDS?

What kinds of damages are awarded by courts?

Can school officials be held liable for violating a student's constitutional rights?

When a student's rights are violated, how will the amount of damages be determined?

Schools have a legal duty to provide students with safe facilities and adequate supervision. If a student is injured because of the negligence of a teacher or other school employee, the student may be entitled to compensation. But this does not mean that schools are responsible for damages every time a student is injured. Most injuries are accidents for which no one is legally responsible.

This chapter outlines the legal principles that courts apply to cases when parents allege that their children were injured because of the school's negligence. Lawyers refer to these principles as the "law of torts." In addition to physical injuries, the chapter considers when educators can be held liable for violating a student's constitutional rights or injuring his reputation. It also considers whether parents can be held liable for injuries caused by them or their children.

When can a teacher be held liable for a student's injury?

A teacher can be held liable for damages to an injured student if the student proves four things: (1) the teacher had a duty to be careful not to injure the student and protect her from being injured; (2) the teacher failed to use due care; (3) the teacher's carelessness caused the injury; and (4) the student sustained provable damages.

Usually, in cases of student injury, it is easy to prove that teachers have a duty to be careful toward their students and that the injuries resulted in monetary damages. Sometimes there is a question about what caused the injury. In most cases, however, the critical question is whether the teacher violated his or her duty to be careful and therefore was negligent.

When is a teacher negligent?

The *Sheehan* **Case**[1]: Margaret Sheehan was an eighth-grade pupil at St. Peter's School. One spring morning during recess, a teacher took Margaret and nineteen other girls to an athletic field where a group of eighth-grade boys were playing baseball. After directing the girls to sit on a log on the third-base line, the teacher returned to the school building. About five minutes after she left, some of the boys began to throw pebbles at the girls. Although the girls protested, the boys continued until one of the pebbles struck Margaret in the right eye, seriously injuring her.

Margaret's parents sued for damages on her behalf, claiming that the school and the teacher were negligent in failing to supervise the children's recess adequately, since the teacher was absent from the athletic area from the time she brought the girls there until after the accident.

After both sides presented their case, the judge instructed the jury: "It is the duty of the school," he said,"to use ordinary care and to protect its students from injury resulting from the conduct of other students under circumstances where such conduct would reasonably have been foreseen and could have been prevented by the use of ordinary care." But, the judge said, "there is no requirement of constant supervision of all the movements of the pupils at all times."

The jury, whose duty it was to apply the law to the facts of the case, found that it was reasonable to foresee that a student might be hurt as a result of failure to supervise the athletic area and decided that the school was negligent. The school appealed on the grounds that there was no proof that watching boys play baseball had been dangerous in the past or that supervision would have prevented the accident.

The appeals court ruled in Margaret's favor on the grounds that children have a "known proclivity to act compulsively without thought of the possibilities of danger," and that it is precisely this lack of mature judgment that makes supervision vital. "The mere presence of the hand of authority," wrote the court, "normally is effective to curb this youthful exuberance and to protect the children against their own folly."

Does this mean that a teacher is expected to anticipate every situation where one child may suddenly injure another? No. The law does not expect a teacher to prevent an unforeseen injury that could happen quickly and without warning. But this was not such a case. Here the girls protested when the pebble throwing began, and the boys continued pelting the girls for several minutes before Margaret was injured. Under these circumstances, the jury concluded that a teacher using reasonable care would have stopped the boys and prevented the injury and that the teacher was therefore negligent in leaving the athletic field unsupervised.

Is constant supervision required?

Two teachers in Chicago's Medgar Evers School organized a trip to the city's Field Museum of Natural History for about fifty students, ranging from 12 to 15 years of age.[2] When they arrived at the museum, the students were allowed to divide into smaller groups and look at the exhibits without supervision. While away from the teachers, Roberto Mancha was beaten by several boys who were not connected with the school.

Roberto's parents charged that the teachers who organized the trip were negligent in failing to supervise their students in the museum. Clearly the teachers were required to exercise reasonable care on such a trip. But the question posed by this case is whether that duty extended to foreseeing and guarding against the injury that occurred. This would depend on the likelihood of injury, the size of the burden of guarding against it, and the consequence of placing that burden upon teachers.

In this case, the court considered the risk that a 12-year-old boy would be assaulted in the museum as minimal, and the burden that would be imposed on the teachers in guarding against it heavy, since it would require constant surveillance. Such a burden would discourage teachers from providing many useful and enjoyable extracurricular activities, since a baseball game or even a game of hopscotch could suddenly break into a fight that produced serious injury.

This does not mean that teachers are never required to provide constant supervision on a field trip. On the contrary, the court indicated that such supervision would be required, for example, when students are taken to a stone quarry, a place where there is dangerous machinery, or where there is reason to believe an assault might take place. But the museum was a "great educational enterprise" for teachers and students, not a place of danger. Under these circumstances, the teachers did not have a duty to anticipate an assault or directly supervise the entire museum trip among 12-to-15-year-old students.

Similarly, a North Carolina court ruled that a teacher is not under a duty to remain in her classroom at all times while her pupils are present.[3] The case involved a sixth grade girl who was injured as a result of two classmates who were "sword fighting" with their pencils while their teacher finished lunch. Since such fighting had not occurred in the past, the court reasoned that the teacher was not negligent for failing to be with her students at the time because she could not have reasonably foreseen that an injury would occur because of her absence.

On the other hand, in a 1983 Louisiana case, the school board was held liable for an injury to Tiffany Carson, a third grade student, because of negligent supervision.[4] Tiffany's eye was injured by boys throwing apples into the girls' restroom during lunch time. The principal and teachers knew that there were frequent problems in the place where the accident occurred, but the teacher assigned to the area was not on duty at the time. Under these circumstances, the court ruled that failure to provide adequate supervision for the area led to Tiffany's injury and therefore constituted "gross negligence on the part of the school."

Is supervision required after school hours?

This depends on the circumstances. In Louisiana, a court held that a school was not liable for injuries that occurred to a student in front of the school two hours after classes were dismissed. The reason? A school usually has no responsibility to supervise a schoolyard after school hours or during vacations in the absence of school-sponsored activities.[5]

On the other hand, the situation would be different when school officials invite students back to school. Thus, another Louisiana court ruled that a school was responsible for injuries to a six-year-old student who returned to school for track practice that was negligently supervised. The school was held liable because the principal announced the practice, and teachers distributed flyers that assured parents that their children would be under "tight supervision" while on school grounds.[6]

What is the student-teacher ratio required to provide safe supervision?

The level of supervision required varies with the number, age, and maturity of the students and the danger of the activity involved. Under some circumstances, it might not be unreasonable for one teacher to supervise from 50 to 100 students. On the other hand, a court has held a school guilty of negligence for failing to provide close and continuous supervision over a "perilous" playground situation (a merry-go-round going too fast) involving one teacher and only a few fourth grade girls.[7]

When must students be warned?

In addition to providing supervision, teachers have a duty to instruct and warn students concerning the proper use of equipment and facilities, whether in class, gym, shop, or anywhere else in school. Failure to do so may constitute negligence. Thus, a physical education teacher was found negligent for allowing two boys to engage in a "slugging match" because he failed to give instructions in self-defense to any of the students.[8] Similarly, a chemistry teacher was found negligent when she failed to instruct students in the proper precautions to follow while carrying out an experiment in the production of explosive gases.[9] And a Wisconsin court found negligence in the case of a 21-year-old vocational student who was injured while operating a complicated high speed machine without being given proper instructions.[10]

How careful must schools be?

The legal principles applied in cases like these are clear: Teachers and other school employees have a duty to exercise reasonable care not to injure their students and to prevent them from being injured. "Reasonable care" is that degree of care that a reasonable teacher of ordinary prudence would exercise under the circumstances. The circumstances considered would include the age, maturity, and experience of the students and the extent of the danger involved. Whether a teacher exercised reasonable care is a factual issue, decided by the jury or the trial judge.

When circumstances are obviously dangerous, as in shop or physical education, a teacher would be expected to exercise greater care than in, for example, the mathematics class. A teacher's failure to be more careful when the dangers are greater—to provide closer supervision, clear warnings, and careful instructions—would constitute negligence.

In the case of Margaret Sheehan, it was decided that the teacher did not exercise reasonable care in leaving Margaret and her classmates at the baseball game without supervision. In the case of Roberto Mancha, however, the court did not feel that reasonable care required the teachers to provide constant supervision of all the students while they were examining the exhibits in the museum.

Is a careless teacher automatically liable?

No. Many parents believe that if a school employee is negligent, she is automatically liable for damages. The case of Wilmer Nash shows that the parents of an injured student must show more than negligence to recover—they must also show that the employee's negligence was the cause of the injury.[11]

After school one day, Wilmer, a Louisiana elementary school pupil, was waiting with a group of classmates for the school bus to take him home. While waiting, Wilmer was struck in the face with a stick carried by a little girl who was playing near him. The blow left Wilmer blind in his left eye, and his parents sued the school for failing to provide adequate supervision.

The court acknowledged that schools are required to provide supervision while pupils are waiting for the school bus. And the evidence indicated that the teachers had failed to provide any supervision at the time Wilmer was injured. But the court did not find either the school or the teachers liable. Wilmer's attorney was not able to prove that proper supervision would have prevented the injury—that, in other words, there was a causal connection between the absence of supervision and Wilmer's accident.

"How," asked the judge, "could any teacher anticipate a situation where one child, while teasing another child, would be struck in the eye with a stick by a third child?" Even if such action could have been anticipated, there was no evidence that the injury could have been prevented if a teacher had been present. "As is often the case," concluded the judge, "accidents such as this, involving school children at play, happen so quickly that unless there was direct supervision of every child (which we recognize as being impossible), the accident can be said to be almost impossible to prevent." Thus the court ruled in favor of the school because Wilmer's parents had failed to show any causal connection between the absence of supervision and the accident that occurred.

A similar case arose in New York where a student was seriously injured when he jumped for a basketball and bumped heads with another student.[12] The parents of the injured student sued the school for failure to provide proper supervision. But the court ruled that there was no "legal causal connection" between the absence of supervision and the injury. The presence of a teacher would not have stopped the boys from bumping their heads together. "That," said the court, "is one of the natural and normal possible consequences or occurrences in a game of this sort which cannot be prevented no matter how adequate the supervision."

Thus, these cases indicate that in order to hold a school employee liable for a child's injury, parents have to prove both that the employee was negligent and that there was a causal connection between the negligence and the injury.

Does a school's insurance cover medical expenses for injured students?

Not usually. Insurance policies for schools vary in their coverage. But they rarely cover medical expenses for students unless the school is negligent.

Often, schools inform parents of special medical policies that can be obtained for their children—especially for students involved in athletic activities. If parents are not told about these policies, someone on the school staff may be administratively negligent. But it is not likely that such negligence would make the school or its insurer liable for a student's medical expenses since the failure to inform the parents was not the cause of the injury.

Do schools have defenses against liability?

Yes. Parents suing for damages on behalf of their injured child may encounter defenses of "contributory negligence," "assumption of risk," or "governmental immunity." Of these contributory negligence is the most frequent and significant. Assumption of risk rarely applies except to competitive sports. And governmental immunity may protect some schools, but it is not a defense for individual teachers.

What is "contributory negligence?"

A negligent teacher might not be held liable if a student contributed to his injury by his own negligence. For example, although a school bus driver was acknowledged to be negligent in failing to repair a hole in the floor of his bus, the court held that he was not liable for damages when it was shown that the student who was injured had deliberately stuck her foot through the hole for amusement and was, therefore, contributorily negligent.[13] Similarly, a janitor who negligently unlocked a chemical supply room was held not liable for the injury suffered by a 17-year-old high school student who carelessly experimented with chemicals stolen from the unlocked room.[14] Thus, if a student fails to exercise that degree of care usually expected of a person of his age, knowledge, and experience, his contributory negligence may prevent recovery from a negligent employee.

If a student is negligent, does this always prevent recovery?

No. The younger the student, the more difficult it is to prove contributory negligence. Generally, courts will presume that students under 14 are not negligent, but with sufficient evidence this presumption can be rebutted. On the other hand, many courts presume that very young children are by definition incapable of contributory negligence. For example, in Michigan, Illinois, North Carolina, Ohio, and Wisconsin, courts hold that children under seven are incapable of contributory negligence. In other states a child will be conclusively presumed to be incapable of contributory negligence when she is under 4 or 5 years.[15] This means that even if such students contribute to their own injury by carelessness, they may be able to recover damages from a negligent school employee.

Another factor allowing negligent students to recover damages is the adoption of "comparative negligence" statutes in most states.[16] These statutes modify the common law rule prohibiting recovery by negligent plaintiffs and permit the judge or jury to compare the relative negligence of both parties. Thus, if a jury found that a student, whose injuries resulted in damages of $1,000, was responsible for 30% of his own injury, his award from the court would be proportionately decreased to $700. In 1984, for example, an injured high school cheerleader sued the school district and two drivers. Under Minnesota's comparative negligence law, the jury found the school district to be 35% liable (because of inadequate supervision) and the drivers to be responsible for 65% of the injury.[17] Despite the trend toward comparative negligence statutes, some of these laws prohibit any recovery if the negligence of the plaintiff is equal to or greater than that of the defendant.

Does a student sometimes assume the risk of being injured?

Yes. The doctrine of "assumption of risk" is a defense against liability in certain obviously dangerous activities such as competitive sports. It assumes that people who understand the danger involved in an activity and voluntarily engage in it willingly expose themselves to predictable risks. The doctrine is illustrated by an Oregon case in which a 15-year-old student was seriously injured in a football game when he was tackled by two larger players. The student charged that it was negligent for his coach to allow an inexperienced freshman to compete against older, heavier, more experienced players. The judge dismissed the case and noted "high school freshmen who go out for football are usually inexperienced," and that on every team there are some boys who are bigger and older than others.[18] Similarly, golfers assume the risk of being injured by a poorly hit drive, and baseball spectators may assume the risk of being hit by a foul ball.

On the other hand, the Oregon court wrote that it would be negligent for a coach to allow a student "to participate in a varsity football game without proper or sufficient instruction."[19] Furthermore, a Louisiana court did not protect a coach who allowed a football player suffering from severe heat stroke to remain untreated for two hours before calling a doctor.[20] Similarly, the assumption of risk defense did not protect the Philadelphia Board of Education from liability for injury to an eleven-year-old boy who lost five teeth in a school-organized floor hockey game because coaches did not require young players to use helmets, face masks, or mouth guards.[21] Thus, students do not assume the risk of improper coaching or negligence in seeking medical care.

Can teachers use "governmental immunity" as a defense against negligence?

No. "Governmental immunity" is an old common law doctrine which holds that since states are sovereign, they and their agencies cannot be sued without their consent. Some courts justify this practice reasoning that public funds raised for schooling should not be used for non-educational purposes. But, in recent years, the doctrine has been condemned by legal writers and abolished by most states.[22] In some states that maintain the doctrine, legislatures have authorized school districts to purchase liability insurance which eliminates the defense to the extent of the insurance coverage. But, even in states where governmental immunity still can be used to prevent negligence suits against school districts, students can sue individual teachers who can be held personally liable for their own negligence.

Does a parental "waiver" or "release" prevent injured students from suing?

Not usually. If a school requires parents to sign a waiver, release, or permission slip before allowing their children to go on field trips or participate in other special activities, this should not relieve teachers or schools of possible liability for negligence. Waivers may discourage some parents from suing for their child's injuries despite teacher negligence. But a teacher always has a duty to act with reasonable care, and a waiver does not change this duty. Furthermore, a release designed to exempt a person or institution in advance from liability for their negligence may be unenforceable. Thus, the Supreme Court of Montana explained that a release exempting a county from negligence was "illegal and unenforceable because it is contrary to the public policy of this state and against the public interest."[23] Even in states where waivers are not illegal, they are generally interpreted so narrowly that schools are usually unsuccessful in using them to prohibit negligence suits.[24]

Can a parent sue on her own behalf for injuries to her child?

Not usually. Typically, if a student is injured, a parent would bring suit on behalf of her son or daughter. But under special circumstances, a parent might sue on her own behalf because of her child's injuries. This was illustrated by an unusual California case in which a mother was allowed to sue a school district for emotional distress she suffered after her daughter was raped. This was allowed because the school officials negligently decided not to notify the mother after they learned of a series of sexual assaults against her daughter. The mother alleged that had she been informed of the assaults, she could have taken precautionary measures to insure her daughter's safely from the rape that occurred later. The court said that school officials should have foreseen that "covering-up" the assaults would cause the mother "more emotional distress than merely informing her of the incidents in the first place."[25]

Can school employees be held liable for making false statements about students or parents?

It depends. Citizens cannot be sued for every false statement they make—only those that are defamatory. Defamation is a statement made about another person that is not true and that injures the person's reputation. *Oral* defamation is called "slander"; *written* defamation is called "libel." A person can sue for libel without proving that the false statements damaged him financially. Defamation requires that the damaging words be communicated to a third person; derogatory words directed at the plaintiff himself are no basis for legal action. And truth is a complete defense in a defamation suit.

When school officials make statements about students or parents that are required as part of their regular duties, they have a "qualified" or "limited privilege" which may be used as a defense against charges of libel or slander. This privilege may protect a school employee against liability for making a defamatory statement when the statement is made in good faith as part of his job. But if an educator makes a defamatory statement that he knows is false, or if he maliciously intends to damage a person's reputation, the qualified privilege is forfeited. And if school officials make false and damaging statements about students or parents outside the scope of their responsibilities—for example, in gossip to a neighbor or reporter or in a letter to a newspaper or friend—their qualified privilege does not protect them. Thus a California court held that school board members who mailed a public announcement accusing two students by name of "serious violation of manners, morals, and discipline" were not immune from a libel suit.[26]

Can a teacher be held liable for reporting, but failing to prove, parental abuse?

Not if the report was made in good faith. In a Pennsylvania case, parents sued a teacher for defamation for reporting parental abuse of a student after a court dismissed a state petition concerning the matter. The court ruled against the parents because state law (1) required teachers to report "evidence of serious physical or mental injury" and (2) provided "immunity from any liability" for such actions unless they were intentionally false. Since the teacher's report of abuse was in good faith, the suit against her was dismissed even though it was incorrect and embarrassed the parents.[27]

Currently, all 50 states plus the District of Columbia have some form of child abuse and neglect statute. Although the definition varies in different states, child abuse and neglect generally include deliberate physical violence, sexual molestation, emotional injury, and negligent treatment. Every state except Vermont requires teachers to report suspected cases of child abuse and most provide criminal penalties for failure to do so. And all states grant immunity to those who in good faith erroneously report child abuse.[28]

Can parents be held liable for publicly criticizing teachers or administrators?

Not usually. Under the First Amendment, parents have a right to criticize public school teachers and administrators or to complain to the school board about their qualifications or performance. Furthermore, parents have a "qualified privilege" in criticizing school employees through appropriate channels. This means that parents will not be held liable for defamation even if their criticism is false, unless the teacher can prove "actual malice" (i.e., that "the communication was made with the knowledge that it was false or with reckless disregard of whether it was false or not").[29]

In a recent Florida case, the state supreme court ruled in favor of a parent who falsely criticized his son's teacher. The court acknowledged that a public school teacher does not totally "surrender the right to vindicate defamation." However, it also held that a parent's qualified privilege protects him in complaining to a school board about his son's instruction. In this case, the court ruled that a parent's statements that a teacher "had harassed and verbally abused" his son and was "unqualified to teach" may have been defamatory but "do not inherently demonstrate express malice." A majority of the court concluded that this criticism (together with a series of phone calls and visits to the teacher and her superiors) demonstrates "parental concern for the effectiveness of public schools which our state. . .should attempt to encourage rather than discourage."[30]

On the other hand, parents may be held liable for maliciously or intentionally spreading false information about teachers or administrators. Thus, where parents make false statements to other parents (e.g., the teacher is "insane," and "could kill my child") rather than to school officials, such defamatory remarks might not be protected.[31]

If a parent's suit is "frivolous," could he be required to pay for the defendant's attorney's fees?

Yes. In Virginia, a federal judge ruled that a parent's suit about her son's dismissal from the school band was "frivolous" and "wholly unnecessary" since state law provided a simple, less expensive way to resolve the conflict. "If the courts seriously entertain suits such as this," wrote the judge, "not only will the courts fall into disrepute, but...the Constitution will become the subject of derision."[32] Because the parent prosecuted a frivolous suit, the judge held her liable for the school's attorney's fees of $2,250.

Can parents be held liable for the property damage of their children?

Yes. Under state statutes, parents can be held financially responsible for intentional property damage done by their children in all but three states: Georgia, New Hampshire and Utah.[33] Generally these statutes are limited to civil rather than criminal liability, and they only apply to intentional and malicious actions, not to a child's careless accidents. Although most laws only apply to property damage, a few (e.g., Illinois, Minnesota, and Nebraska) also impose liability on parents for their child's intentional injury to persons.[34] While the statutes in some states limit parental liability to $500 or $1,000, other states have no limit. Generally, courts have upheld these statutes on the ground that they are a reasonable use of the state's police power "to compensate innocent victims of juvenile misconduct and to place on parents the obligation to control a minor child."[35]

May schools be held liable if they fail to exclude a student or employee with AIDS?

Not unless the school was found negligent based on the specific facts of the case. Many states and school districts now have policies to guide administrators who are confronted with this question. The concerns are serious both for students and adults who have AIDS (and are therefore especially vulnerable to other diseases) as well as for those who are in danger of getting the virus. There are constitutional issues related to privacy, equal protection, and due process involved in how schools handle this matter, and intense concern on the part of parents who fear that their children might be exposed to AIDS.

Typical policies encourage AIDS to be reported to school authorities but protect privacy by providing that only those with a need to know should have medical information about a student or employee with the disease. Generally, students with AIDS may continue regular attendance in school except those with "skin eruptions" or those who exhibit inappropriate behavior, such as biting, that endangers others. It is usually recommended that schools have students or employees with the virus examined and evaluated by a medical team to determine whether their continued attendance is likely to endanger others.

There is not yet much legal precedent on this topic to guide schools. In one highly publicized New York case, brought by concerned parents to exclude students with AIDS, a trial judge ruled that a student with AIDS could not automatically be excluded from school, since medical evidence indicated that AIDS is not transmitted through casual daily contact. The judge upheld the case-by-case judgment of medical and educational officials to permit individual students to attend classes when deemed appropriate. The state court concluded that the automatic exclusion from school of all children with AIDS would violate their rights under the Equal Protection Clause of the Constitution and under the federal Rehabilitation Act that protects handicapped persons.[36] But, in June 1986, the U.S. Department of Justice issued an opinion that gave AIDS victims very little protection as handicapped persons under federal law.[37] As a result, people with AIDS will probably turn to state law for protection against dismissal.

In short, the law on this complex topic is just developing and medical knowledge about AIDS is still incomplete. Nevertheless, schools which create reasonable policies and apply them with care on a case-by-case basis are not likely to be held liable for damages. Thus, parents and educators can work cooperatively to create and revise such policies in light of changing medical knowledge and legal precedent.

What kinds of damages are awarded by the courts?

Courts can award several kinds of damages. The most common is *compensatory* damages. The purpose of this award is to compensate injured persons for their actual losses—for their medical expenses, lost salary, court costs, and other expenses incurred as a result of the defendant's negligence. Damages can be awarded for monetary, physical, or psychological injury. *Exemplary* or *punitive* damages are awarded where defendants have shown malice, fraud, or reckless disregard for an injured student's safety or constitutional rights. The purpose is to punish the defendants for their wrongful action and deter similar action in the future. *Nominal* damages are a small, symbolic award (e.g., one dollar), where the plaintiff has been wronged but has not been able to show actual damages.

Can school officials be held liable for violating a student's constitutional rights?

Yes. In the landmark case of *Wood v. Strickland*, two Arkansas students were unlawfully suspended for three months without due process, and their parents sued the school board for damages.[38] (For more on due process, see Chapter 2.) In this decision, the U.S. Supreme Court ruled that school officials could be held liable "if they knew or reasonably should have known that the action they took within their sphere of official responsibility would violate the constitutional rights of the students affected."

What if school officials were honestly unaware of students' rights? The Court responded that an act violating a student's constitutional rights cannot be "justified by ignorance or disregard of settled, indisputable law on the part of one entrusted with supervision of students' daily lives." A school official, noted the Court, must be held to a standard of conduct based not only on good intentions "but also on knowledge of the basic, unquestioned constitutional rights of his charges."

These kinds of injuries have become known as *constitutional torts*. Based on the *Wood* case, courts have held principals, superintendents, and school board members personally liable for damages to students whose rights they violated.

When a student's rights are violated, how will the amount of damages be determined?

The Supreme Court answered this question in a case involving two Chicago students who were suspended for twenty days without due process.[39] Their lawyer introduced no evidence to show any actual damages they had suffered because of their suspension, but he argued that they should receive substantial damages simply because they had been deprived of their constitutional rights.

The Court disagreed. It ruled that when a student is deprived of his constitutional rights, the amount of damages should depend on the circumstances of the case. A student should be awarded substantial sums for two reasons: (1) as punitive damages to deter or punish school officials who intentionally deprived the student of his or her rights; or (2) as compensatory damages for actual injury, which can include "mental and emotional distress" as well as financial loss. When the violation is unintentional and no actual injury is shown, the student is only entitled to the award of a nominal sum of money.

Summary

To hold a school or its employees liable for injuring a student, parents have to prove the following:

(1) *There was a breach of duty.* Teachers have a duty to exercise reasonable care not to injure their students and to prevent injury to them. "Reasonable care" is that degree of care that a reasonable teacher of ordinary prudence would have exercised under the circumstances, which include the age, maturity, and experience of the pupils and the extent of the danger involved. When circumstances are more dangerous, as in shop or physical education, a reasonable teacher would be expected to be especially careful—to provide close supervision, clear warnings, and careful instructions. If a school employee does not use reasonable care, there is a breach of duty, and she is negligent.

(2) *The breach of duty was the cause of the injury.* It is not enough to prove that a teacher failed to exercise reasonable care. Parents must also prove that this failure caused their child's injury.

(3) *There was no contributory negligence.* This means that if a student's own negligence contributed to his injury, if he failed to exercise that degree of care usually expected of a student of his age, knowledge, and experience, his carelessness may prevent or reduce his recovery from a negligent teacher or administrator. However, the younger the student, the more difficult it is to prove contributory negligence.

Other defenses against liability include "assumption of risk" and "governmental immunity". Courts hold that students who voluntarily engage in activities such as competitive sports assume the normal risks of injury that go along with participation in these activities. In some states, the doctrine of governmental immunity prevents parents from suing school districts for negligently injuring their children. But in recent decades, most states have abolished or modified this doctrine. Moreover, a parental "waiver" allowing children to participate in special school activities generally does not prevent suits for negligence.

School employees can also be sued for libel or slander if they make false statements which injure the reputation of students or parents. Educators have a "qualified privilege" that might protect them against liability for defamatory statements made in good faith as part of their duties. But the privilege will not protect them from liability for false statements that are made maliciously or are made outside the scope of their responsibilities. Parents have a similar qualified privilege in criticizing teachers and administrators.

School officials can be held liable for damages if they take actions which violate a student's clearly established constitutional rights. Parents can be held liable for the intentional property damage of their children. But schools are not likely to be held liable for failing to exclude a student or teacher with AIDS if their decisions are based on current medical knowledge.

Courts can award several kinds of damages: *compensatory* damages for actual losses; *punitive* damages to punish defendants where there is malice or reckless disregard for a student's safety or rights; and *nominal* or *symbolic* awards where the plaintiff has been wronged, but there are no provable damages. Since the law does not provide compensation for all student injuries, parents should consider protecting their children with medical insurance.

Notes for Chapter 7

1. *Sheehan v. St. Peter's Catholic School*, 188 N.W.2d 868 (Minn. 1971).

2. *Mancha v. Field Museum of Natural History*, 283 N.E.2d 899 (Ill. 1972).

3. *James v. Charlotte-Mecklenburg Board of Education*, 300 S.E.2d 21 (N.C. App. 1983).

4. *Carson v. Orleans Parish School Board*, 432 So.2d 956 (La. App. 1983).

5. *Ulm v. Gitz*, 286 So.2d 720 (La. App. 1974).

6. *Augustus v. Joseph A. Craig Elementary School*, 459 So.2d 665 (La. App. 1984).

7. *Rollins v. Concordia Parish School Board*, 465 So.2d 213 (La. App. 1985).

8. *LaValley v. Stanford*, 70 N.Y.S.2d 460 (1947).

9. *Damgaard v. Oakland High School District*, 298 Pac. 983 (Cal. 1931).

10. *Severson v. City of Beloit*, 167 N.W.2d 258 (Wisc. 1969).

11. *Nash v. Rapides Parish School Board*, 188 So.2d 508 (La. 1966).

12. *Kaufman v. City of New York*, 214 N.Y.S.2d 767 (1961).

13. *Gilcrease v. Speight*, 6 So.2d 95 (La. 1942).

14. *Frace v. Long Beach City High School District*, 137 P.2d 60 (Cal. 1943).

15. 57 Am.Jur.2d *Negligence* 363 (1971).

16. Am.Jur.2d New Topic Service, *Comparative Negligence*, 5 (1977).

17. *Verhel v. Independent School District No. 709*, 359 N.W.2d 579 (Minn. 1984).

18. *Vendrell v. School District No. 26C Malheur County*, 376 P.2d 406 (Ore. 1962).

19. Ibid.

20. *Mogabgab v. Orleans Parish School District*, 239 So.2d 456 (La. 1970).

21. *Berman by Berman v. Philadelphia Board of Education*, 456 A.2d 545 (Pa.Super. 1983).

22. According to the Pennsylvania Supreme Court: "Whatever may have been the basis for the inception of the doctrine, it is clear that no public policy considerations presently justify its retention." *Ayala v. Philadelphia Board of Public Education*, 305 A.2d 877 (Pa. 1973).

23. *Haynes v. County of Missoula*, 517 P.2d 370 (Mont. 1973).

24. *Gross v. Sweet*, 407 N.Y.S.2d 254 (1978), 424 N.Y.S.2d 365 (1979).

25. *Phyllis P. v. Claremont Unified School District*, 228 Cal. Rptr. 776 (Cal.App.2 Dist. 1986).

26. *Elder v. Anderson*, 23 Cal.Rptr. 48 (1962).

27. *Roman v. Appleby*, 558 F.Supp. 449 (E.D.Pa. 1983).

28. "Child Abuse and Neglect: Implications for Educators," Richard

Salmon and David Alexander, 28 *Education Law Reporter* 1 (1984).

29. "Crosses Teachers Bear: The Parental Right to Criticize," M. Chester Nolte, 18 *Education Law Reporter* 1 (1984).

30. *Nodar v. Galbreath*, 462 So.2d 803 (Fla. 1984).

31. *Nolte*, op.cit., p. 3-4.

32. *Bernstein by Bernstein v. Menard*, 557 F.Supp. 92 (E.D.Va. 1983).

33. "Parental Responsibility Statutes: A Solution to Pupil Vandalism or a Cause of Home Discord," Ralph D. Mawdsley, 28 *Education Law Reporter* 1 (1985).

34. Ibid.

35. Ibid.

36. *District 27 Community School Board v. Board of Education of the City of New York*, 502 N.Y.S.2d 325 (Sup.1986).

37. Opinion of the Office of Legal Counsel, U.S. Department of Justice, interpreting Section 504 of the Rehabilitation Act of 1973, June 23, 1986.

38. *Wood v. Strickland*, 420 U.S. 308 (1975).

39. *Carey v. Piphus*, 435 U.S. 247 (1978).

CHAPTER 8

Accountability and the Curriculum

Can a school be held liable for poor instruction?

Can a school be held liable for negligent evaluation, classification or placement?

Can educators be held liable for malicious or intentional educational injury?

Do local school boards have authority to use competency tests as a requirement for graduation?

Can a state department of education require competency testing for all students?

Could student competency tests violate the Constitution?

Can handicapped students be required to pass a competency test in order to graduate?

Are teacher competency tests legal?

Do parents have the right to control school policy and curriculum?

Do parents have the right to participate in the development of school policy?

Do parents have a right to have offensive books and materials removed from the curriculum?

Can parents require schools to remove books that offend their religious beliefs?

Isn't an article that repeatedly uses vulgar words improper?

Can a school board protect students from language that some parents find genuinely offensive?

When are books obscene for students?

Can schools remove controversial books from their libraries?

Do students have a right to be excused from educational requirements that violate their religious beliefs?

Do parents have the right to demand that specific courses be added to the curriculum?

Does the Hatch Amendment give parents a right to inspect curricular materials?

Can psychological tests or treatment be given without parental consent?

Can parents file complaints under the law?

How can parents get more information about the law and its enforcement?

Parents, educators, and judges generally agree that schools should be responsible for providing a sound education. But what should be done when the education is poor? Who then should be held accountable? And how should that accountability be enforced? Some parents believe that the best way is to use the "law of torts," under which the victim of negligence can sue for money damages.* According to this theory, if schools are negligent in teaching, they should be held financially liable for damages. Another view puts the emphasis on the students—advocating the use of required competency tests for students as a way to insure that minimum standards are met. Still others argue that teachers—not students— should be tested to insure minimum professional competence in the classroom. This chapter discusses each of these approaches to accountability as well as the issue of parental control over the curriculum.

Educational Malpractice

In a series of court cases since 1973, parents have alleged

---

*For more on neglience and injuries, see Chapter 7.

three different kinds of educational malpractice: failure to provide adequate instruction; negligence in evaluating, classifying, or placing students; and willful or malicious negligence by educators. (For related issues concerning the state's duty to provide appropriate special education, see Chapter 11.)

Can a school be held liable for poor instruction?

Probably not. In California, Peter W., a high school graduate with a fifth grade reading ability, sued the San Francisco School District for failing to provide him with adequate instruction in basic skills such as reading and writing.[1] Peter claimed that the school district negligently assigned him to classes with instructors unqualified to teach and classes not geared to his reading ability, failed to keep his parents advised concerning his educational problems, and allowed him to advance through the grades even though he did not achieve the knowledge required. His lawyer argued that since schools and teachers have been held liable for failure to exercise reasonable care in situations that resulted in physical injury to students, educators also should be held liable for negligent teaching. But the California Supreme Court disagreed.

Since schools had never before been held liable for negligent teaching, this case presented a question of public policy concerning the consequence of extending liability to educational malpractice. The court noted two problems that would have to be dealt with if liability were extended in this way. First, Peter W.'s alleged injuries would be difficult, if not impossible, for the courts to measure. "Classroom methodology," wrote the judge, "affords no readily acceptable standards of care, or cause, or injury." There are many conflicting educational theories about how or what a student should be taught. And professional authorities indicate that the injury claimed in this case—the inability to read and write—is influenced "by a host of factors which affect the pupil subjectively, from outside the formal teaching process" and beyond the control of the schools. According to the court, the causes "may be physical, neurological, emotional, cultural [or] environmental." Thus the court found no objective and workable standard of care to measure the school's alleged misconduct and no way to determine a causal connection between the school's alleged negligence and the injury suffered.

Second, practical financial considerations also led to the rejection of Peter's claim. The court noted that in recent decades public schools have been charged with failure to achieve their educational objectives and with responsibility for many of society's problems. Under these circumstances, the court observed that "to hold them to an actionable 'duty of care' in the discharge of their academic functions, would expose them to the tort [negligence] claims—real or imagined—of disaffected students and parents in countless numbers." According to the court, since schools are already beset by so many problems, the ultimate consequence of permitting suits such as this "would burden them—and society—beyond calculation." On the other hand, the burden would not be too great if courts ruled that school systems found guilty of educational malpractice were simply required to provide compensatory remedial education.

Can a school be held liable for negligent evaluation, classification or placement?

The answer may depend upon the specific facts of the case. In one New York controversy, Daniel Hoffman was tested by a psychologist after he entered kindergarten and was placed in a class for the mentally retarded. The psychologist recommended that Daniel be retested within two years because of uncertainties about the boy's ability. But Daniel was not retested for over ten years, when it was discovered that he was not retarded. As a result of these events, Daniel's parents sued the schools for malpractice claiming negligent assessment, placement, and failure to retest their son. Lower courts ruled in favor of the Hoffmans, reasoning that this was not a simple failure to teach as in the *Peter W.* case, but involved "affirmative negligence"—the failure to retest Daniel as recommended. However, the New York Court of Appeals reversed and ruled in a 4-3 decision that the same policies apply to cases of "educational misfeasance and nonfeasance"* and that courts should not interfere with the professional judgment of educators concerning student placement.[2]

Nonfeasance is not doing the job; *misfeasance* is doing the job improperly.

On the other hand, in a more recent New York case, a court awarded Donald Snow $1,500,000 because he had been incorrectly categorized, confined, and treated as an imbecile and not retested until six years after a teacher had written that he was a "very bright" child and would "learn quickly."[3] The court distinguished this case from *Hoffman* on the grounds that the failure to reassess was "an act of medical malpractice on the part of the State rather than a mere error in judgment" concerning "educational progress."

Can educators be held liable for malicious or intentional educational injury?

Probably. Comments by the highest courts in Maryland and New York indicated that public educators may be held responsible for intentional negligence arising in schools. In the Maryland case, parents alleged, first, that the school negligently evaluated and misplaced their son, and second, "intentionally and maliciously furnished false information" concerning his learning disability and "altered school records to cover up their actions."[4] The court rejected the first part of the parents' claim based on negligent evaluation and placement. But it did not reject the second claim. Instead, the court wrote:

> We in no way intend to shield individual educators from liability for their intentional torts. . . .Where an individual engaged in the educational process is shown to have willfully and maliciously injured a child entrusted to his educational care, such outrageous conduct greatly outweighs any public policy considerations which would otherwise preclude liability.

Similarly, in an earlier malpractice case, the New York Court of Appeals recognized that there could be "gross violations of defined public policy" which the courts would be obliged to recognize and correct.[5]

In sum, educators may be held liable for intentional educational injury that might result from knowingly giving false or misleading information to parents about their children. However, they are not likely to be held liable for unintentional educational injury that is a result of carelessness or mistakes.

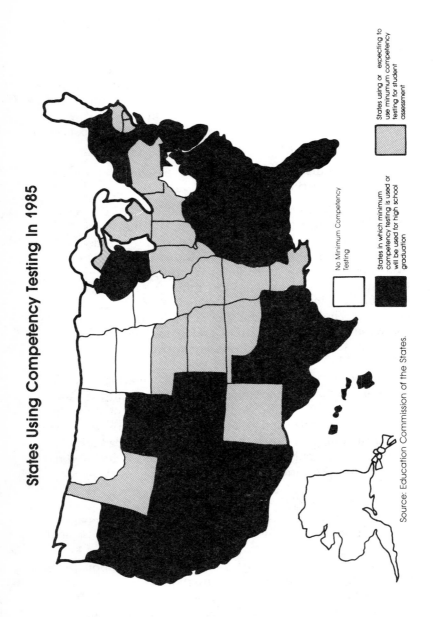

States Using Competency Testing In 1985

No Minimum Competency Testing

States in which minimum competency testing is used or will be used for high school graduation

States using or expecting to use minimum competency testing for student assessment

Source: Education Commission of the States.

Minimum Competency Tests

One result of citizen concern for accountability has been the expansion of minimum competency testing for new teachers and for students as a prerequisite for graduation or for promotion to selected grades. (See map of states using minimum competency tests, on the facing page.)

Typical statutes require that the state board of education or local school district establish standards of proficiency in basic skills such as reading, writing, and mathematics and that students be tested periodically (e.g., in the 7th, 9th, 11th, and 12th grades). Regulations often provide for parent conferences and remedial instruction for students who fail to demonstrate the prescribed level of competency. Students who fail the final competency exam are usually not awarded a diploma signifying graduation, but they may receive a certification of completion. Advocates of this approach believe that, if competency testing is implemented properly, schools will eliminate the misunderstandings that gave rise to the *Peter W.* case and give a clearer meaning to a high school diploma. Critics feel that competency testing programs may reduce creativity and flexibility in the curriculum, and that teachers may limit their instruction to the required competencies.

Do local school boards have authority to use competency tests as a requirement for graduation?

Yes. A Georgia school district established a policy that each student must demonstrate minimum skills in math and reading as a requirement for graduation with a diploma. Since neither the legislature nor the state board of education required competency tests, students challenged the local board's authority to impose such a requirement.[6] However, a state appeals court ruled in favor of the school board. It noted that state policy "specifically permits local boards to require additional credit units for graduation" and to establish "performance indicators." Therefore, the court found "no merit" in the argument that the board's additional testing requirement for graduation exceeds its authority or conflicts with state policy.

Can a state department of education require competency testing for all students?

Yes. In New York, for example, a court ruled that the adoption of graduation requirements "including basic competency exams, to establish a standard that would make a high school diploma a meaningful credential for the graduate is clearly within the power of the department of education."[7] Thus courts have held that both school districts and state education agencies have authority to make high school graduation depend on passing a minimum competency exam.

Could competency tests violate the Constitution?

Yes. In 1978, Florida required passage of a basic competency exam in order to receive a high school diploma. When black students failed in disproportionate numbers, their parents claimed that failure to award diplomas to their children based on the test would violate their constitutional rights. In 1981, a federal appeals court agreed.[8]

The first problem with the test was that the state had not determined that it covered material actually studied in the classrooms. According to Judge Fay, "If the test covers material not taught the students, it is unfair and violates the Equal Protection and Due Process Clauses of the United States Constitution."

The testing violated the Equal Protection Clause because "the immediate use of the diploma sanction" punished black students for deficiencies created by the unequal education they received in the predominantly black, inferior schools. The testing violated due process of law because it changed diploma requirements without adequate time to insure that students were taught what was on the test. Therefore, the court ordered the schools to postpone the use of the tests for awarding diplomas.

When the competency tests were again challenged in Florida in 1983, the courts ruled that the tests were no longer unconstitutional. The state proved that the test was "instructionally valid" since students had an adequate opportunity to learn the skills tested, and the disproportionate failure among seniors was no longer found to be caused "by past purposeful segregation."[9]

Thus, for parents to make a good constitutional argument, they must show that their children have a reasonable expectation of graduating from high school with a diploma, excluding the competency tests, and that this expectation was abridged without adequate notice. A competency test would also be unconstitutional if parents could prove that it covered materials not taught in the schools or that its racially discriminatory impact was due to prior segregated schooling.

Courts vary in their view of how much notice is required. In the Florida case, the trial court suggested "four to six years should intervene between the announcement of the objectives and the implementation of the diploma sanction."[10] Other courts have indicated that a two or three-year period between the announcement and the testing was sufficient to give schools and students enough time to prepare for the tests.[11]

Can handicapped students be required to pass a competency test in order to graduate?

Yes. In 1979, New York made passing a basic competency test a requirement for high school graduation. Thereafter, the Commissioner of Education objected when a local district awarded diplomas to two handicapped students who completed their individualized education programs but did not pass the basic competency tests. The district argued that to withhold their diplomas would have violated federal statutes. But a state appeals court disagreed.[12]

First, the board alleged that withholding the diplomas violated Section 504 of the Rehabilitation Act which prohibits discrimination against "qualified handicapped individuals." The court, however, ruled that the Act is violated "only when benefits are denied to an individual who is able to meet all of a program's requirements in spite of his handicap." Since the students in this case were unable to pass the competency test, their rights were not violated because they were not "qualified" handicapped individuals under the Act. Second, the court ruled that withholding diplomas from handicapped students who are unable to meet minimum competency standards does not violate the Education for All Handicapped Children Act because it did not deny them their right to a "free, appropriate public education." (For more on testing and the rights of special education students, see Chapter 11.)

Measuring Teacher Competence

Many parents feel that competency tests should be used to examine teachers, not students. Support for such tests has grown substantially during the past decade. Competency tests for teachers are used for two purposes: to select new teachers and to screen out incompetent teachers. By 1984, more than 25 states had adopted some testing requirements for new teachers, and more than 10 others were planning such tests.[13] At least three states, Texas, Arkansas, and Georgia, also use such tests to evaluate experienced teachers.[14]

Are teacher competency tests legal?

While competency tests measure subject matter knowledge, they don't measure other important characteristics of good teachers such as energy, dedication, or love of children. Nevertheless, courts have usually accepted tests as valuable assessment devices as long as they are not used in an arbitrary manner or for illegal, discriminatory purposes.[15]

Although teacher competency tests are now generally accepted for use among new teachers, there is still widespread debate about their use with experienced teachers. The director of the Educational Testing Service, whose National Teacher's Examination is used in over 25 states, refuses to allow the test to be used "as the sole determining criterion of whether a teacher should remain in the profession."[16] Many teachers argue that a standard test is the wrong way to assess the competence of in-service teachers. However, courts have generally refused to prohibit the use of such tests if they are valid and affected teachers are given adequate notice.

The Curriculum

Do parents have the right to control school policy and curriculum?

No. For most purposes, each state is in charge of its own educational system. State legislatures typically make broad pronouncements concerning educational goals and programs and then delegate to state boards of education and local districts the carrying out of these programs and goals. Usually the local school board has primary authority and responsibility for hiring and firing teachers and administrators; establishing priorities; choosing texts; and resolving educational disputes among competing groups of parents, teachers, and students. As the Supreme Court has written: "By and large, public education in our nation is committed to the control of state and local authorities. Courts do not and cannot intervene in the resolution of conflicts which arise in the daily operation of school systems and which do not directly and sharply implicate basic constitutional values."[17] Thus, if parents are dissatisfied with a school's policy, curriculum, or staff, they usually will have to try to persuade school boards or legislatures to make the changes they advocate or persuade the courts that their position is based on statutory or constitutional grounds.

Do parents have the right to participate in the development of school policy?

Federal law and local school board regulations are increasingly encouraging parents to participate in planning school policy. All parents can share their concerns and suggestions with the school board members who represent them. They also have the right to attend school board meetings. Furthermore, in some states such as Massachusetts, parents whose children are defined as educationally deprived have the right to participate in parent councils which are consulted by school officials in planning and carrying out programs that affect their children.* And the parents of handicapped children have the right to participate in the development of individual educational plans for their children.**

Do parents have a right to have offensive books and materials removed from the curriculum?

Not usually. Parents have objected to a variety of curricular materials on grounds that they violated their religious beliefs, that they were obscene and contained dirty words, that they taught prejudicial attitudes, and that they dealt with topics

---

* This subject is further discussed in Chapter 13.

** This subject is further discussed in Chapter 11.

which they did not believe should be part of the school curriculum—sex education, for example. Here are the ways some courts have dealt with these issues.

In Baltimore, a group of parents sued the Maryland Board of Education to prevent it from implementing its regulation requiring all local school systems to provide "a comprehensive program of family life and sex education in every elementary and secondary school for all students" as an integral part of the health education curriculum.[18] The parents claimed that they had "the exclusive constitutional right to teach their children about sexual matters in their own homes" and that this right should prohibit the schools from teaching about sex. The court disagreed. It held that the requirement was a reasonable public health measure, that it raised no significant constitutional questions, and that in this case the state's interest in the health of its children outweighed the parents' claim.

In a related California case, a parents' organization, Citizens for Parental Rights, brought suit to prevent the teaching of family life and sex education courses in five school districts.[19] The parents argued that the program violated their religious beliefs and would expose their children to certain subjects that were sinful. Although state law allowed parents to keep their children from participating in the program, the parents argued that there was a strong, informal pressure on the students to attend, and this pressure interfered with their religious freedom. But the court did not believe this social pressure amounted to a violation of the constitutional rights of the parents or their children. It noted that "a mere personal difference of opinion as to the curriculum which is taught in our public school system does not give rise to a constitutional right in the private citizen to control exposure to knowledge."[20]

Further, the court pointed out that if a judge prohibited the sex education program because it offended the religious beliefs of certain parents, he would be violating the First Amendment, which prohibits the state from tailoring its curriculum in accord with the principles or dogmas of any religion. Such an approach would permit any group of parents "to create chaos in the school system" by attempting to prohibit portions of the curriculum that were contrary to their beliefs.

Can parents require schools to remove books that offend their religious beliefs?

Not usually. In a controversial 1987 decision, a federal district judge, Brevard Hand, banned more than 40 textbooks from the public schools in Alabama because a group of fundamentalist Christian parents claimed that the books supported the "religion of secular humanism," offended their religious beliefs, and violated the First Amendment.*21

In a more typical federal case Cassie Grove and her mother asked that a book which offended their Christian beliefs be removed from the sophomore English curriculum. The Groves claimed that the use of *The Learning Tree* by Gordon Park violated the religion clauses of the First Amendment. But the appeals court did not agree.22 The book did not interfere with Cassie's free exercise of religion because she was given an alternative book to read and was not required to discuss the book in class. The court explained that it would be nearly impossible to eliminate everything from the curriculum that was objectionable to any religious group or inconsistent with their beliefs.

A similar case arose in Kanawha County, West Virginia, where parents argued that a series of textbooks should be removed because they contained matter that is "offensive to Christian morals" and encourages violation of both the Ten Commandments and civil law. Although the court concluded that some of the controversial materials were indeed "offensive to plaintiff's beliefs," it did not find that placing these texts in the county schools violated any of the parents' constitutional rights.23 Judge Hall observed that freedom of religion "does not guarantee that nothing about religion will be taught in the schools nor that nothing offensive to any religion will be taught." Instead, the Constitution prohibits states from encouraging or discouraging any religion, and it requires them to be neutral among different religions and between religion and non-religion. In conclusion, the judge emphasized that where no constitutional violations are involved, parents who object to texts should not go to court but should pursue their concerns

---

*On March 27, 1987, a federal appellate court temporarily suspended Judge Hand's order removing the texts from the Alabama schools while the case is being appealed.

"through board of education proceedings or ultimately at the polls on election day."

In a related New York City case, two parents asked a court to prevent the schools from using *Oliver Twist* by Charles Dickens and *The Merchant of Venice* by William Shakespeare because of their anti-Jewish bias.[24] The court refused. It wrote: "If evaluation of any literary work is permitted to be based upon a requirement that each book be free from derogatory reference to any religion, race, country, nation, or personality, endless litigation respecting many books would probably ensue. . . ." The court concluded that it would be wrong to interfere with the discretion of school officials to assign these books since the officials acted in good faith and without malice or prejudice.

Isn't an article that repeatedly uses vulgar words improper?

It depends on the article. Robert Keefe was a high school English teacher who assigned his senior class an article from *The Atlantic* entitled "The Young and the Old" which discussed dissent, protest, and revolt.[25] The article repeatedly contained the word "motherfucker." A number of parents found the word highly offensive and protested to the school board. Because of the protests, Keefe was suspended when he refused to agree never to use the word again in class. But a liberal federal court ruled that Keefe's suspension violated his constitutional rights, and in a controversial comment, it stated that the sensibilities of offended parents "are not the full measure of what is proper in education." The judge found the article in this case to be a scholarly, thoughtful, and thought-provoking piece which in no way suggested immoral conduct.

Can't a school board protect students from language that the parents of some students find genuinely offensive?

This would depend on the specific situation—the age of the students, the words used, and the purpose in which they were used. In the *Keefe* case, most high school seniors knew the word, it was used for valid educational purposes, and its use caused no classroom disruption. But the First Amendment does not protect obscenity.

When are books obscene for students?

According to current Supreme Court standards, a book is obscene if it "appeals to the prurient [or lustful] interest" of minors, describes sexual conduct in a patently offensive way, "and lacks serious literary, artistic, political, or scientific value."[26] To apply these tests, the material must be judged "as a whole" and by "contemporary community standards."

In an Ohio case, a state court ruled that Claude Brown's *Manchild in the Promised Land* and Ken Kesey's *One Flew Over the Cuckoo's Nest* violated all these standards. The books were assigned reading in two optional high school courses and were objected to by a group of parents. The court agreed with the parents that "each of these books is offensive to prevailing standards in the adult community with respect to what is suitable for juveniles." Although judges in other communities might have ruled differently, the judge in this case prohibited the school from assigning the two books as part of the curriculum; but he allowed them to be used where a parent "has knowledge of the character of the books and consents to their use."[27]

Can schools remove controversial books from their libraries?

The answer depends on the facts of the case. After obtaining a list of "objectionable" books from a conservative parents' organization, a New York school board removed ten books from their school libraries because they were allegedly "anti-American, anti-Christian, anti-Semitic, and just plain filthy."[28] But a group of parents claimed that the board's action was unconstitutional, and a majority of the Supreme Court agreed.

In the Court's opinion, Justice Brennan emphasized that students' First Amendment rights are applicable to the school library and that a board cannot ban books because of "narrowly partisan or political" reasons since "our Constitution does not permit the official suppression of ideas." If the primary reason the board removed the books was to deny students "access to ideas" with which the board disagreed, then the board's action was unconstitutional.* On the other hand, a board

---

*Similarly, the Supreme Court recently ruled that states cannot prohibit the teaching of the concept of evolution or require the teaching of "Creationism" in order to protect or advance a particular religious belief. *Edwards v. Aguillard.* Slip Opinion No. 85-1513 (June 19, 1987).

could legitimately remove books if they were educationally
unsuitable, pervasively vulgar, or inappropriate to the age,
maturity, or grade level of the students.

**Do students have a right to be excused from educational
requirements that violate their religious beliefs?**

They might. Based on Supreme Court decisions, parents
can argue that their children have a right to be excused from
school requirements that seriously interfere with the free exercise of their religion where the excuse would not seriously interfere with important state interests. It was on these grounds
that Amish children were excused from Wisconsin's compulsory school attendance laws after the eighth grade.[29] Similarly,
courts might excuse students from physical education classes[30]
or instruction in evolutionary theory for religious reasons.[31]
(For more on religion and education, see Chapter 4).

Moreover, legislatures and school districts have discretion to
exempt students from requirements that offend their beliefs.
Kansas law, for example, provides that any public school
students "shall not be required to participate in any activity
which is contrary to the religious teaching of such child. . . ."[32]
On the other hand, courts will probably not excuse students
from requirements that schools consider essential or where accommodation would be administratively impractical.[33] Thus a
federal appeals court upheld a Maryland policy of "family life
and sex education. . .for all students" despite the argument that
it violated the religious rights of the parents.[34]

Furthermore, in a recent Tennessee case, fundamentalist
Christian parents argued that the school should not require
their children to be exposed to books that offend their sincere
religious beliefs. In a widely-publicized 1986 opinion, a federal
judge agreed.[35]

The judge held that the Free Exercise of Religion Clause of
the First Amendment protects the parents' belief that they must
not expose their children to certain books used in the school's
reading program. The judge found that the school had no compelling interest in requiring all students to read the challenged
books. He also found that home schooling was authorized by
state law. Therefore, he held that the school should try to accommodate both the parents' beliefs and the state's interest.
The parents' beliefs could be protected by allowing the students

to "withdraw to a study hall or library" during the scheduled reading period at school and to study reading with a parent later at home. The state's interest in promoting literacy could be safeguarded by requiring the students to be "rated by standardized achievement tests."

Critics of this decision fear that there would be chaos if any student could opt out of any school requirement that violated her religious beliefs. But the judge indicated that these fears were unfounded since his ruling would only apply where an "accommodation could be achieved without substantially disrupting the education process."

Do parents have the right to demand that specific courses be added to the curriculum?

Generally not—except through school board procedures that allow citizens to petition the board concerning educational matters. However, Massachusetts and Rhode Island have statutes that specifically allow a certain number of parents to request new courses. For example, the Rhode Island law provides that when 20 students apply for a course in Portuguese, Italian, or Spanish, the school board shall arrange that such a course be given by a competent teacher.[36]

The Hatch Amendment

Does the Hatch Amendment give parents a right to inspect curricular materials?

The Hatch Amendment (also known as the Student Rights in Research, Experimental Programs and Testing Act) is a law that requires schools to make certain federally funded curricular materials available for parental inspection. The Amendment was originally enacted in 1978 but final regulations were not approved until 1984. This federal law requires schools to make "all instructional materials used in connection with any research or experimental program available to parents of children involved."[37] This right to review does not imply a right to revise or remove curricular materials. Although the Hatch Amendment only applies to programs funded by the U.S. Department of Education, many school districts voluntarily allow parents to review curricular materials used in their children's classes.

Can psychological tests or treatment be given without parental consent?

Not if they fall under the Hatch Amendment. This law requires schools to obtain written parental consent before their child can participate in any psychological testing or treatment funded by the Department of Education if the "primary purpose" is to reveal personal information such as political affiliation, mental problems, income, or sexual behavior and attitudes.[38]

Can parents file complaints under the law?

Yes. A parent or guardian or a student may file a complaint under the Hatch Amendment. If the written complaint contains specific allegations of fact and evidence of attempted resolution at the local level, a special office of the Department of Education will investigate the complaint and take appropriate steps to insure compliance.

How can parents get more information about the law and its enforcement?

More information about the law or about filing a complaint can be obtained by writing: Family Educational Rights and Privacy Act Office, U.S. Department of Education, 400 Maryland Ave., SW, Washington, D.C. 20202.

Summary

Although courts hold schools liable for damages if their negligence causes physical injury to students, parents have not succeeded in collecting damages from schools for negligent teaching or for negligent evaluation, classification, or placement. However, damages might be allowed if parents could prove malicious or intentional educational injury, or in cases of gross negligence amounting to medical malpractice.

Because of the difficulty in winning an educational malpractice suit, citizens have turned to legislatures and school boards to hold schools accountable. One result of these efforts has been the expansion of minimum competency tests for students and teachers. Many states use competency testing in the selection of new teachers, for grade-to-grade promotion of students and for high school graduation. Where the tests are valid and there is adequate notice, courts have upheld such testing as a prerequisite for graduation despite allegations that they discriminated against minority and handicapped students.

Parents have gone to court to force the schools to change features of the curriculum they found objectionable. They have claimed the right to prohibit courses on family life and sex education, to remove texts that offended their religious beliefs or moral values, and to prohibit books that used dirty or vulgar language. But judges generally have been unwilling to force schools to comply with these demands. Since school officials have been delegated the responsibility for making educational decisions, courts are unwilling to substitute their judgment for the judgment of professional educators in such matters—except where a valid constitutional objection is made.

If school officials violate the constitutional rights of students or parents, the courts will act to protect those rights. But if parents disagree with the educational decisions that administrators make, judges urge them to use school board procedures or political and legislative action rather than the courts to create change.

Although school boards have broad discretion in creating school policy, board members cannot use their power to censor books because of "narrowly partisan or political reasons" or to deny students "access to ideas" with which they disagree. However, a board can remove books that are pervasively vulgar or educationally unsuitable.

Under the Hatch Amendment, parents have a right to review material used in federally funded research or experimental programs and to give their consent before their child participates in federally-sponsored psychological testing. And under the First Amendment, parents may be able to have their child excused from taking courses or using books that seriously interfere with the free exercise of their religion and do not interfere with essential educational requirements.

In sum, the courts are reluctant to allow any group of parents to control the texts, courses, or curriculum for all students. But, as the next chapter will indicate, they are more sympathetic to parents who assert their right to control the education of their own children.

Notes for Chapter 8

1. *Peter W. v. San Francisco School District*, 131 Cal. Rptr. 854 (1976).

2. *Hoffman v. Board of Education*, 400 N.E.2d 317 (N.Y. 1979).

3. *Snow v. State*, 469 N.Y.S.2d 959 (A.D. 2 Dept. 1983). This decision was affirmed without opinion by the New York Court of Appeals, 475 N.Y.S.2d 1026 (1984).

4. *Hunter v. Board of Education of Montgomery County*, 439 A.2d 582 (Md. 1982).

5. *Donohue v. Copiague Union Free School District*, 391 N.E.2d 1352 (N.Y. 1979).

6. *Wells v. Banks*, 266 S.E.2d 270 (Ga. 1980).

7. *Board of Education of Northport-East Northport Union Free School District v. Ambach*, 458 N.Y.S.2d 68 (A.D. 1982).

8. *Debra P. v. Turlington*, 644 F.2d 397 (5th Cir. 1981).

9. *Debra P. v. Turlington*, 564 F.Supp. 177 (M.D. Fla. 1983).

10. *Debra P. v. Turlington*, 474 F.Supp. 244, 267 (1979).

11. "A review of the Development of and Legal Challenges to Student Competency Programs," Jeffrey T. Horner, 23 *Education Law Reporter* 1 (1985).

12. *Board of Education of Northport-East Northport Union Free School District v. Ambach*, 458 N.Y.S.2d 680 (A.D. 1982).

13. "Teacher Competency Testing: A Review of Legal Considerations," Patricia Lines, 23 *Education Law Reporter* 811 (1985).

14. "Bad Medicine?" Ezra Bowen, *Time*, March 24, 1986, p. 74.

15. "Excusal from Public School Curriculum Requirements," Patricia M. Lines, 5 *Education Law Reporter* 691,695 (1982).

16. *Time*, op. cit.

17. *Epperson v. Arkansas*, 393 U.S. 97 (1968).

18. *Cornwell v. State Board of Education*, 314 F.Supp. 340 (D. Md. 1968), 428 F.2d 471 (4th Cir. 1970). See note 33.

19. *Citizens for Parental Rights v. San Mateo County Board of Education*, 124 Cal. Rptr. 68 (1975).

20. Ibid.

21. *Smith v. School Commissioners of Mobile County, Alabama.* (1987) *Education Week* Vol. 6, No. 24, March 11, 1987.

22. *Grove v. Mead School District No. 354,* 753 F.2d 1528 (9th Cir. 1985).

23. *Williams v. Board of Education of County of Kanawha,* 388 F.Supp. 93 (S.D. W.Va. 1975).

24. *Rosenberg v. Board of Education of City of New York,* 92 N.Y.S.2d 344 (1949).

25. *Keefe v. Geanakos,* 418 F.2d 359 (1st Cir. 1969).

26. *Miller v. California,* 413 U.S. 15 (1973).

27. *Grosser v. Woollett,* 341 N.E.2d 356 (Ohio 1974).

28. *Board of Education, Island Trees Union Free School District No. 26 v. Pico,* 457 U.S. 853 (1982).

29. *Wisconsin v. Yoder,* 406 U.S. 205 (1972).

30. *Moody v. Cronin,* 484 F.Supp. 270 (C.D.Ill. 1979).

31. Lines, op. cit.

32. Ibid. p. 698.

33. Ibid. p. 694.

34. *Cornwell v. State Board of Education,* 314 F.Supp. 340 (D.Md. 1969); 428 F.2d 471 (4th Cir. 1970); *cert. denied* 400 U.S. 942 (1970). This decision was before *Wisconsin v. Yoder,* and today it is possible that an effective "free exercise" argument might persuade a court to excuse students from compulsory sex education courses that deeply offend their parents' religious beliefs — especially where the goals of the course can be achieved through home or church programs.

35. *Mozert v. Hawkins County Public Schools,* 647 F. Supp. 1194 (E.C. Tenn. 1986)

36. Rhode Island G.L. Title 16, Chapter 22-8 (1981). The Massachusetts law provides that if parents of 30 high school students request a new course, it shall be taught if it is approved by two-thirds of the school committee and there is a qualified teacher available. Massachusetts G.L. Chapter 71, 13 (1982).

37. *Federal Register,* Vol. 49, No. 174, September 6, 1984. These regulations were issued pursuant to Sections 439 (a) and (b) of the General Education Provisions Act; 20 U.S.C. 1232h (1978).

38. Ibid.

CHAPTER 9

The Right to Guide

Can states require all children to attend public schools?

Can parents exempt their children from compulsory education for religious reasons?

Can states regulate private schools?

Can states require that private schools have certified teachers?

Does a private school student have a right to attend some public school classes?

Do parents have a constitutional right to educate their children at home?

Do most states permit parents to educate their children at home?

Can home instruction qualify as a private school?

Can states regulate home schooling?

Can the regulation of schooling or home education be unconstitutional?

Can states require that home education be essentially equivalent to school instruction?

Can parents prohibit school officials from observing home instruction?

Can parents withdraw their children from specific courses?

Do parents have the right to remove their children from a school that is not safe?

What conditions are threatening enough to override compulsory educations laws?

Do parents have a right to withdraw their children from school for educational trips?

Can teachers who are parents be prohibited from sending their children to private segregated schools?

Do rules that limit a student's athletic participation violate parental rights?

Do parents have a right to change their child's teacher?

Do parents have a right to send their child to another school in the same disrict?

Do parents have a right to enroll their children in a district where they work or own property but do not reside?

May parents remove a child from school because of racial or ethnic insults?

———————————

The U.S. Supreme Court has held that parents have the right "to guide the education of their children." But the state also has a legitimate interest in the schooling of its future citizens, and it can therefore compel parents to provide their children with an adequate education. When school officials and parents disagree about what is best for youngsters, the rights of parents may collide with those of the state. This chapter considers how some of these conflicts are resolved and examines issues related to compulsory education, parental choice, and state regulation of private schools and home education. Unlike most topics in this book, the resolution of these issues usually depends on specific state statutes and local judicial interpretations.

Can states require all children to attend public schools?

No. As we pointed out in Chapter 4, parents have the right to send their children to private schools, either religious or secular. This right was established by the Supreme Court more than 60 years ago in a case involving a state statute which required all parents to send their children to public school until age 16.[1] In holding the statute unconstitutional, the Court ruled that the state may not unreasonably interfere with "the liberty of parents and guardians to direct the upbringing and education of children under their control." A "child is not the mere creature of the state," the Court said, and the state has no right "to standardize its children by forcing them to accept instruction by public teachers only."

Although states cannot compel parents to send their children to *public* schools, courts have consistently held that they can compel parents to send their children to school. This was reaffirmed in a federal case in which two Chicago parents claimed that the state compulsory education law violated their constitutional right to educate their children "as they see fit" and "in accordance with their determination of what best serves the family's interest."[2] In this case, the court ruled that the parents had failed to show any "fundamental right which has been abridged by the compulsory attendance statute." The judge pointed out that the parents' constitutional right to guide their children's education is a limited one; "it merely provides parents with an opportunity to seek a reasonable alternative to public education."

Can parents exempt their children from compulsory education for religious reasons?

Yes, but rarely. In *Wisconsin v. Yoder*, the U.S. Supreme Court recognized the rights of devout Amish parents not to send their children to school after the 8th grade. The parents showed that secondary schools, which emphasized "intellectual and scientific accomplishments, self-distinction, competitiveness, [and] worldly success," were contrary to the Amish beliefs in cooperation, piety, and a simple, agrarian lifestyle.[3] They further showed that requiring Amish children to be exposed to the influences of secondary schools would threaten the entire Amish community and its 300-year-old religious traditions. Therefore, in view of the unique circumstances of this case, the Court ruled that the state's interest in education past the 8th grade was not so compelling as to override the sincere religious way of life of the Amish community.

Despite its holding in *Yoder*, the Supreme Court recognized that generally a state has a compelling interest in compulsory education to prepare citizens "to participate effectively in our political system" and to be "self-sufficient participants in society." Thus, in a recent North Carolina case, a federal appeals court ruled against Peter Duro, who refused to send his children to school because he believed they would be "corrupted" by others who did not share his religious beliefs.[4] The court distinguished this case from *Yoder* because the Duros were not members of an established, self-sufficient religious community that requires children to be taught at home. And, unlike the Amish children who attended public schools for eight years, the Duros refused to enroll their children in any school for any length of time. Therefore, in balancing the Duros' religious beliefs against the state's interest in education, the court found "the balance in this case tips in favor of the state."

In a similar West Virginia case, a state court strongly rejected a parent's asserted religious right to ignore state education law in these words: "We find it inconceivable that in the twentieth century, the Free Exercise Clause of the First Amendment implies that children can lawfully be sequestered on a rural homestead during all of their formative years to be released upon the world only after their opportunities to acquire basic skills have been foreclosed."[5]

Can states regulate private schools?

Yes, states can establish minimum standards for private schools. The Supreme Court has written that the state has a "proper interest in the manner in which those schools perform their secular educational function."[6] The Court noted that states have power "to insist that attendance at private schools, if it is to satisfy state compulsory attendance laws, be at institutions which provide minimum hours of instruction, employ teachers of specified training, and cover prescribed subjects of instruction."

But state standards may be held unconstitutional if they go too far in controlling private education. For example, in an Ohio case parents objected to detailed "minimum standards" that regulated not only hours of instruction and teachers' qualifications but also curriculum content, teaching methods, the physical layout of the building, and educational policies.[7] The court wrote that these standards were "so pervasive and all-encompassing" that total compliance with each standard by a private school "would effectively eradicate the distinction between public and non-public education" and thereby deprive the parents of their right to direct the education of their children.

Can states require that private schools have certified teachers?

They can, according to the Supreme Court of North Dakota.[8] The case involved the Living Word Academy, a Christian school that taught all subjects from a "Biblical, God-centered perspective," and that challenged a law requiring private teachers to be certified by the state. The Academy argued that seeking certification "unduly infringed their right to free exercise of religion" since, according to their belief, "education was a religious function." However, the court ruled that in this case the state's compelling interest in minimum standards of education "out balances" the resulting strain on the Academy's religious freedom. The Academy also argued that the state could assure minimum standards without certification by having students take standardized achievement tests. The court noted that the problem with testing is that it does not discover an educational deficiency until after the school year is over. While certification may also have deficiencies, the court wrote that it was "an acceptable method" to protect standards. Finally, the Academy argued that certification would require the school to be approved by an educational system that is "inundated with the anti-religious philosophy of secular humanism." But the evidence indicated that the standards used to certify teachers have nothing to do with an anti-religious philosophy. Furthermore, religious schools have authority to insist that certified teachers use methods that further their religious beliefs, and they may incorporate religious teaching into their curriculum. The court concluded that the teacher certification law "does not unreasonably interfere with the liberty of parents in the upbringing and education of their children" or with their religious freedom guaranteed by the Constitution.

Does a private school student have a right to attend some public school classes?

Not according to a Michigan appeals court. The case involved Patricia Snyder, who attended a Christian academy, and her parents, who wanted to enroll her in a band course at the local junior high school. Although some school districts make courses available to nonpublic school students, Patricia's district did not. The court ruled that the district's policy of enrolling only full time students did not violate Patricia's consitutional rights because there were reasonable administrative, educational, and fiscal reasons to support the policy.[9] The parents' remedy, wrote the judge, "is not with the courts, but, rather, to elect a school board which will change the district's policy." (Related church/state issues are discussed in Chapter 4.)

Do parents have a constitutional right to educate their children at home?

No. In Kansas, parents who taught their children at home in violation of state education law argued that they had a "fundamental right" to educate their children in any manner they "deem most appropriate." However, the state supreme court ruled that there was no such right.[10] Since the compulsory attendance law has "a rational relationship to the legitimate state purpose of educating its children," the court ruled that the law was valid and that the parents' argument was not.

In a similar New Mexico case, Don and Paula Edgington argued that it was unconstitutional for state compulsory education laws to allow private schools but prohibit home schooling. But a state court ruled that the prohibition was reasonable since it required children to come into contact with others outside their family and to be "exposed to at least one other set of attitudes, values, morals, lifestyles and intellectual abilities."[11] Thus states can prohibit home schooling by compelling instruction in public or private schools only.

Do most states permit parents to educate their children at home?

Yes. According to a recent report published by the Education Commission of the States,* compulsory education laws in

---

*Compulsory Education Laws and Their Impact on Public and Private Education, by Patricia Lines, Education Commission of the States, LEC-84-11, March 1985.

36 states and the District of Columbia expressly permit home instruction or require simply that children be educated in lieu of school attendance (AL, AK, AZ, CA, CO, CT, DE, DC, FL, GA, HI, ID, IN, IA, LA, ME, MD, MA, MS, MO, MT, NV, NJ, NY, OH, OK, OR, PA, RI, SC, SD, UT, VT, VA, WA, WI, WV). Fourteen states have no statutory provision for home instruction. Of these, four clearly permit parents to teach their children at home (IL, KY, MI, NH,). In the ten other states, home instruction is prohibited or severely restricted. (AR, KS, MN, NC, ND, NE, NM, TN, TX, WY).

Can home instruction qualify as a private school?

Sometimes. In states where home instruction is not prohibited, some courts have ruled that parental instruction can qualify as one form of nonpublic school. Here are two examples:

In Illinois, the parents of a seven-year-old girl were convicted of violating the state's compulsory attendance law. The law exempted children attending "a private or parochial school where children are taught the branches of education taught to children of corresponding age and grade in public schools." Since the Levisens provided comparable instruction for their daughter, they contended that she was attending a "private school" within the meaning of the law. The Supreme Court of Illinois agreed.[12]

The court noted that compulsory education laws were enacted "to enforce the natural obligation of parents" to educate their children. "The object," wrote the court, "is that all children shall be educated, not that they shall be educated in any particular manner or place." Since the Levisen child was taught third-grade subjects, had regular hours of study, had third-grade proficiency and was not educationally neglected, the court ruled that the term "private school" covered the "place and nature of instruction" provided in this case. The judge concluded: "The law is not made to punish those who provide their children with instruction equal or superior to that obtainable in the public schools. It is made for the parent who fails or refuses to properly educate his child."

In a 1985 North Carolina case, Larry Delconte requested formal approval of his home as the Hallelujah School for the education of his two children. After officials wrote that his home was not a school "within the meaning of the law," Delconte went to court and won. The state supreme court did not agree that "the word 'school' because of some intrinsic meaning. . .precludes home instruction."[13] Therefore, it ruled that Delconte's home could qualify as a nonpublic school as long as it met state standards.

On the other hand, the Supreme Court of Kansas ruled differently in the case of Anna and Matthew Sawyer, who organized the Longview School in their home and enrolled their two children.[14] Mrs. Sawyer was the only teacher; her children were the only students. The state's compulsory education law allowed students to attend "substantially equivalent" private schools. But the state argued that the Longview School was not equivalent, and the court agreed. Since there was no testing, planning, or scheduling and since Mrs. Sawyer was uncertified and without teaching experience, the court found the parents' plan "though well-intentioned, [was] a thinly veiled subterfuge." The court concluded: "If such a family arrangement will serve as a substitute for school, there is no compulsory school attendance."

Can states regulate home schooling?

Yes. States that allow home education can regulate it. This was illustrated by a Maine case in which the McDonoughs refused to submit a home education plan to the local school board for approval as required. They claimed that their constitutional guarantee of personal liberty gave them a right to educate their children at home without anyone's approval. But the Supreme Court of Maine disagreed and wrote:

> For the state to allow home education without imposing some standards as to quality and duration would be, in many cases, to allow parents to deprive their children of any education whatever. . ..Furthermore, many parents even though they have a sincere desire to educate their children at home, lack the necessary training and facilities to do so.[15]

In a thorough and thoughtful Massachusetts decision, a superior court ruled that in evaluating a home education plan, school authorities should consider (1) the competency of the teachers, (2) the teaching methods, (3) whether legally required subjects are taught, (4) the number of hours and days devoted to teaching, and (5) the tests or measures used. However, the judge ruled that school authorities should not consider (1) the parents' motivation, (2) the lack of curriculum "identical" to the public schools, and (3) the "lack of group experience" or "socialization factor."[16]

Can the regulation of schooling or home education be unconstitutional?

It depends on the clarity and fairness of the regulations. Such regulations may not be too vague or ambiguous nor may they be imposed in an arbitrary manner. Recent cases from Wisconsin and Georgia illustrate these principles:

In Wisconsin, a parent organized and incorporated the Free Thinker School and enrolled his children. But the local school administrator said it was not a real private school and charged the parent with violating the state's compulsory attendance law. The evidence indicated that local officials had discretion to determine what constituted a private school, and in this case the official had no written criteria or procedure to guide his decision. Therefore, the Wisconsin Supreme Court ruled that the use of the term "private school" in the state's education law was unconstitutionally vague since it failed to provide any objective standards to parents who seek to obey it or to officials who enforce it.[17]

In a similar Georgia case, Terry and Vickie Roemhild were arrested for violating the compulsory attendance law. The parents believed that, by educating their children at home, they were providing private school education as allowed by state law. Moreover, the Roemhilds had unsuccessfully sought guidance from the state department of education about whether their home education was lawful. But the local superintendent felt it was not. Since neither state law nor the department of education defined what was meant by "private school," the state supreme court ruled that the law was unconstitutionally vague as it failed to provide the parents fair notice of how to avoid its penalties.[18] It also violated due process, since its "subjective standards pose the danger of arbitrary and discriminating enforcement."

On the other hand, the Supreme Court of Arkansas interpreted a similar compulsory education law quite differently.[19] A majority of the court ruled that a "public, private, or parochial school" is generally understood to mean "an institution to which a child is sent" and that home education does "not constitute a school within the common understanding of the word."

Can states require that home education be essentially equivalent to school instruction?

It depends on the clarity of the requirement. In a 1985 Minnesota case, Jeanne Newstrom, who taught her children at home, was convicted of violating the state's compulsory attendance law. Local officials charged that her "lack of formal educational training" automatically demonstrated that her qualifications were not essentially equivalent to "the minimum standards for public school teachers" which the law requires.[20] Newstrom argued that her "experience, knowledge, and performance" combined with her effectiveness in teaching her children were evidence of equivalent qualifications. Since judges as well as parents interpreted the term "essentially equivalent" differently, the state supreme court concluded that the law was unconstitutionally vague for the purpose of imposing criminal liability.

In a related Missouri case, two families who removed their children from public schools to educate them at home were charged with "educational neglect." Local officials claimed that the parents' teaching was not "substantially equivalent to the instruction given children of like age in the day schools" as the law required.[21] The parents argued that the law was unconstitutionally vague because it subjected them to prosecution "with insufficient direction as to what is demanded of them." In a 1985 decision, a federal court agreed. "Nowhere," wrote the court, "is substantially equivalent defined" by local officials who have an "unacceptable amount of discretion in enforcing the statute." Furthermore, no state agency has issued regulations which clarify its meaning nor has the legislature provided "minimal guidelines for law enforcement." Thus, the law "does not comply with due process requirements and is unconstitutionally vague."

On the other hand, another federal court upheld a similar Maine law and found the term "equivalent instruction" not so vague that people had to guess at its meaning.[22] Unlike the Missouri case above, numerous guidelines and regulations clarified the law, and Maine's public school requirements were described in detail. Therefore, it was much easier to understand the meaning of "equivalent instruction" as it was used in the Maine statute.[23]

Can parents prohibit school officials from observing home instruction?

Not unless the visits are so frequent that they would disrupt or discourage home instruction.

In a New York case, parents who had been visited by school officials in 1980, refused to permit another on-site evaluation of their home schooling in 1982. Since the parents supplied the officials with their educational program and curriculum, they claimed that another home inspection was "unnecessary, burdensome," and an invasion of their constitutional rights "relating to religion, privacy, and child rearing." But a state court disagreed.[24]

It is reasonable, wrote the judge, for officials to observe the "school setting" which is a "critical factor affecting the nature and quality of the education." Similarly, "it is impossible to evaluate the competency of any teacher. . .without actually observing that teacher in a classroom setting." Therefore, the court concluded that "infrequent, unobtrusive home visitation" did not violate any of the parents' rights and was a reasonable means to enable local officials to evaluate the competency and equivalency of the parents' home education.

Parental Choice

Can parents withdraw their children from specific courses?

Older decisions say yes. In an 1891 case, for example, a father demanded that his daughter be excused from studying grammar because he objected to the way it was taught.[25] The question, said the court, is who should determine what a child should study, "a teacher who has a mere temporary interest in her welfare, or her father who may reasonably be supposed to be desirous of pursuing such course as will best promote the happiness of his child?" The court ruled that the parent has "a right to make a reasonable selection from the prescribed studies for his child," and this selection must be respected by the school. According to the court, any rule compelling a child to take a course contrary to the wishes of her parents is "arbitrary and unreasonable."

It is doubtful, however, whether this "parents' right to decide" approach would be followed by judges today. Therefore, the following decisions illustrate two other approaches that might still be used by some state courts to decide when parental decisions to withdraw their children from specific courses might be upheld.

Essential for Citizenship. In a 1927 case concerning Bible reading, the Supreme Court of Colorado indicated that "children cannot be compelled to take instruction not essential to good citizenship."[26] The school board had argued that if parents object to required subjects, they should send their children to private institutions. The judges rejected this argument because it would force a parent "to surrender his rights in the public schools." The school board's "control over instruction," wrote the court, does not mean that "every child should be required to take every subject which the board puts on the list." However, the school can require "studies plainly essential to good citizenship."

How could this test be applied today? What knowledge is essential to enable children to fulfill the social and political responsibilities of citizenship? Different parents, school boards, and judges might answer this question differently. But the Deputy Attorney General of California supported the "good citizenship" standard and illustrated how it might be applied. Under this test, he wrote, "elementary mathematics could be required, although calculus could not; handwriting could be required, creative writing could not." In any event, he noted that "when the state chooses to override a parent's wish, the burden is on the state to establish that in order to function effectively as a citizen one must be versed in the subject to which the parent objects."[27]

Morality and Conscience. In 1921, a California court considered whether children of parents opposed to dancing can be compelled to participate when such activities are part of a school physical education program.[28] The authorities argued that their dance program did not violate any established religious doctrine. In response, the court commented that religious reasons were not the only basis for legitimate parental objection. It can also be a "question of morals which may concern the conscience of those who are not affiliated with any particular religious sect." Thus some judges might allow students to be excused from some courses that conflict with their moral principles. But there is no judicial consensus on this issue.

An alternative approach adopted by about half of the states is to authorize parents to excuse their child from specific courses to which they object such as sex education and family life instruction.[29]

Do parents have the right to remove their children from a school that is not safe?

They probably do. According to the Supreme Court of Pennsylvania, "a parent is justified in withdrawing his child from a school where the health and welfare of the child is threatened."[30]

What conditions are threatening enough to override compulsory education laws?

This is a matter of interpretation. In the Pennsylvania case, the court did not support the right of a group of parents to withdraw their 47 children from a school to which they had been recently assigned to improve racial balance and reduce overcrowding. Despite evidence of harassment, the court noted that these incidents only applied to 11 of the 47 students and that after the harassment, officials had taken steps to improve the safety of the school.

In a related case, Earl and Jane Ross were convicted of violating a state compulsory attendance law for failing to allow their two children to be bused to vocational training classes one day a week.[31] The parents claimed that the vocational school was unsafe, and they cited two "unpleasant experiences" to support their claim. But a state appeals court ruled that the two incidents "were not such threats to the health and safety of the Ross children as to justify the action of their parents." The court concluded that the state education law "does not authorize parents to withdraw their children from classes and activities except where the children's health and safety are positively and immediately threatened."

On the other hand, a New York court allowed parents to remove their two daughters from one elementary school and place them in another over school board objections because they had been beaten at the school to which they were assigned.[32] Similarly another New York court ruled in favor of parents who refused to send their eight-year-old daughter more than a mile over an unsafe road to the nearest bus stop. The judge held that the parents' action was based on legitimate concern for their daughter's health and safety and was not an unlawful violation of the compulsory attendance law.[33] (Concerning the fear of AIDS in school, see Chapter 7.)

Do parents have a right to withdraw their children from school for educational trips?

Not unless such trips are allowed by state or local policy. In a Pennsylvania case, John and Sherrie Hall were denied permission to remove their children for three days for an "educational trip" to Europe.[34] School policy permitted "one educational trip per school year" (not to exceed five days), and the Hall children had already been excused from school for an educational trip to Washington, D.C. a month earlier. Nevertheless, the Hall family went to Europe without permission. As a result, the school charged them with truancy, and the parents attacked the school's policy as "arbitrary and capricious." The court wrote that the parents' assertion of a "right to take their children on multiple educational trips in contravention of school district policy is without foundation in logic or law." The judge concluded that continuity of instruction through requirements which compel regular school attendance is a matter of paramount importance to which the views of individual parents must yield.

Can teachers who are parents be prohibited from sending their children to private, segregated schools?

The answer may depend on the circumstances. In the *Cook* case, a federal appeals court upheld such a prohibition.[35]

The case involved several Mississippi teachers who were not rehired when they sent their children to private, segregated academies in violation of school board policy. Evidence indicated that students in desegregated classes were "likely to perceive rejection. . .from a teacher whose own children attend a nearby, racially segregated school." Because of the importance of desegregation in this case, the court concluded that the board could restrict the teachers' freedom of association since it conflicts with their job performance.

However, in two more recent cases, federal appeals courts have given greater weight to the rights of the teachers as parents. In 1983, the same court that decided the *Cook* case, ruled that a school employee's interest in controlling the education of her child "takes precedence over the school board's interests" unless the enrollment of her son in a private school "materially and substantially interfered" with the operation of the public schools.[36] And in a 1984 Alabama case, a court ruled that two tenured teachers who wanted to send their children to a virtually all-white Christian academy should be exempt from the policy prohibiting school employees from sending their children to private schools.[37] The court explained that the "beliefs of the board members and some teachers are not sufficient justification for denying the [teachers] the right to choose and direct their children's education." The court said this controversy was different from the *Cook* case (above) in two ways: In this case, segregation was not the reason the teachers wanted to send their children to private schools; second, enrollment in the private academy is not "a serious threat to integration in the public schools."

Do rules that limit a student's athletic participation violate parental rights?

No. In a New York case, parents challenged a rule of the state high school athletic association prohibiting students' participation in non-school sports while they also participated in interscholastic competition.[38] The parents claimed that the rule unconstitutionally interfered with their right to control the upbringing of their children and to decide whether they can physically and academically participate in school and non-school sports. But the court disagreed. Since it held that the school officials have an obligation to protect the well-being of their students and since the rule prohibiting non-school sports while participating in interscholastic competition "is rationally related" to their well-being, the court refused to overturn the rule against outside competition.

Do parents have a right to change their child's teacher?

This depends on local policy. Most districts give administrators discretion to make classroom changes for educational reasons. On the other hand, there are many legitimate reasons for turning down parental requests such as class size, scheduling conflicts, and curriculum requirements. Therefore, although parents certainly may request that their child's teacher be changed, there is no constitutional right that requires schools to follow parental wishes in these matters.

Do parents have a right to send their child to another school in the same district?

This also depends on local policy. Generally, school attendance zones or districts are determined by local school officials. The assignment of students to particular schools—especially in primary grades—is usually based on administrative factors such as proximity to the schools, bus routes, school size, and student population. In many districts, parents may request that their child be assigned to a school outside their attendance zone if there is space available and if parents agree to provide transportation. However, school officials have discretion in drawing attendance zones, and courts are unlikely to overturn their decisions unless they are arbitrary, unreasonable, or promote illegal segregation. In fact, courts have ruled that the "broad discretion" given school boards to assign pupils "is not abused" even when students are required, for legitimate reasons, to attend a school more distant than one nearby their home.[39]

Do parents have a right to enroll their children in a district where they work or own property but do not reside?

No. Some public schools allow parents who live outside the district to enroll their children if they pay tuition when space is available in the appropriate grade. This, however, is a matter of local policy; it is not a legal right. And schools have discretion to restrict enrollment to children who reside in their school district.

May parents remove a child from school because of racial or ethnic insults?

Not unless the parents provide some appropriate alternative form of education. In a New York case, an American Indian mother withdrew her daughter from school after a teacher made a negative statement about Indians.[40] The teacher apologized and said she did not mean to insult Indians. The mother, however, refused to allow her daughter to return until the school agreed to add material on Indian problems to the curriculum and issue a policy statement on racism. Although the court deplored racial stereotyping, it ruled that a parent can't defy compulsory attendance laws to compel changes in the curriculum. "A child," concluded the court, "may not be used as a pawn in a battle by a parent with public school authorities"—even if her cause is just. However, if the insults were intentionally repeated after the parent's protest, the decision might have been different.

Summary

Although state compulsory education laws have been consistently upheld by the courts, parents have the right to send their children to a public or private school. And if they choose a nonpublic school, they can select a religious or non-sectarian institution. Such private schools can be regulated by the state which can set minimum standards for instruction and teacher qualifications. But these standards cannot be so detailed and pervasive that they would effectively abolish the distinction between public and private education.

Parents have no constitutional right to educate their children at home. Such education depends on state law. In some states, the law clearly allows home education if parents meet state or local standards. In others, home education is prohibited through laws that compel instruction only in public or private schools. In still others, where home education is not mentioned in the law, the right of parents to educate their children at home can be implied (e.g., from broad language permitting "equivalent instruction"). Although there is some disagreement about which states fall into each category, one recent survey indicated that parents in most states have an implied or express right to educate their children at home if they meet state standards. In judging whether home schooling is equivalent to public education, officials usually consider a variety of factors such as the parents' qualifications, goals, educational plan, curriculum materials, and hours of instruction, as well as how the student scores on standardized tests.

Early cases indicated that parents had a right to excuse their children from any course offered by the schools. Today, however, schools can generally compel students to attend courses that are deemed "basic" or "essential for good citizenship"—even over the objections of parents. But if parents can show that a course clearly violates their religious freedom, such objections will have a better chance of being respected by the courts. And several states have legislation that authorizes parents to excuse their children from specific courses such as sex education and family life instruction. Moreover, parents have the right to withdraw their children from an unsafe school where their health and welfare is seriously threatened. However, parents do not have a right to change their child's teacher or withdraw their child from school for family or educational trips.

Notes for Chapter 9

1. *Pierce v. Society of Sisters*, 268 U.S. 510 (1925).

2. *Scoma v. Chicago Board of Education*, 391 F.Supp. 452 (N.D.Ill. 1974).

3. *Wisconsin v. Yoder*, 406 U.S. 205 (1972).

4. *Duro v. District Attorney, Second Judicial District of North Carolina*, 712 F.2d 96 (4th Cir. 1983).

5. *State v. Riddle*, 285 S.E.2d 359 (W.Va. 1981).

6. *Board of Education of Central School District No. 1 v. Allen*, 392 U.S. 236 (1968).

7. *State v. Whisner*, 351 N.E.2d 750 (Ohio 1976).

8. *State v. Rivinius*, 328 N.W.2d 220 (N.D. 1982).

9. *Snyder v. Charlotte Public School District*, 333 N.W.2d 542 (Mich. App. 1983).

10. *In the Interest of Sawyer*, 672 P.2d 1093 (Kan. 1983).

11. *State v. Edgington*, 663 P.2d 374 (N.M. App. 1983).

12. *People v. Levisen*, 90 N.E.2d 213 (Ill. 1950).

13. *Delconte v. State*, 329 S.E.2d 636 (N.C. 1985).

14. *Sawyer*, op. cit.

15. *State v. McDonough*, 468 A.2d 977 (Me. 1983).

16. *Perchemlides v. Frizzle, Massachusetts Superior Court, Hampshire County*, Civil Action No. 16641, November 13, 1978.

17. *State v. Popanz*, 332 N.W.2d 750 (Wis. 1983).

18. *Roemhild v. State*, 308 S.E.2d 154 (Ga. 1983).

19. *Burrow v. State*, 669 S.W.2d 441 (Ark. 1984).

20. *State v. Newstrom*, 371 N.W.2d 525 (Minn. 1985).

21. *Ellis v. O'Hara*, 612 F.Supp. 379 (D.C. Mo. 1985).

22. *Bangor Baptist Church v. State of Maine*, 549 F.Supp. 1208 (D.Me. 1982).

23. Similarly, the Iowa Supreme Court held that "equivalent instruction" refers to public instruction which is described in sufficient detail in state regulations that its meaning is not unconstitutionally vague. *State v. Moorehead*, 308 N.W.2d 60 (Iowa 1981).

24. *Matter of Kilroy*, 467 N.Y.S.2d 318 (Fam.Ct. 1983).

25. *State ex rel. Sheibley v. School District No. 1*, 48 N.W. 393 (Neb. 1891).

26. *People ex rel. Vollmar v. Stanley*, 255 P.610 (Colo. 1927).

27. "Parental Rights and Responsibilities" Joel S. Moskowitz, 50 *Washington Law Review* 623 (1975).

28. *Hardwick v. Board of Trustees*, 205 P. 49 (Cal. 1921).

29. "Parent Rights Card," National Committee for Citizens in Education, July, 1985.

30. *Zebra v. School District of City of Pittsburgh*, 296 A.2d 748 (Pa. 1972).

31. *Commonwealth ex rel. School District of Pittsburgh v. Ross*, 330 A.2d 290 (Pa. 1975).

32. *In re Foster*, 330 N.Y.S.2d 8 (1972).

33. *In re Richards*, 2 N.Y.S.2d 608 (1938).

34. *Commonwealth v. Hall*, 455 A.2d 674 (Pa. Super. 1983).

35. *Cook v. Hudson*, 511 F.2d 744 (5th Cir. 1975); *cert. dism* 429 U.S. 165 (1976).

36. *Brantley v. Surles*, 718 F.2d 1354 (5th Cir. 1983).

37. *Stough v. Crenshaw County Board of Education*, 744 F.2d 1479 (11th Cir. 1984).

38. *Eastern New York Youth Soccer Association v. New York State High School Athletic Association*, 488 N.Y.S.2d 293 (A.D. 1985).

39. *Miller v. Lower Merion School District*, 347 A.2d 337 (Pa. 1975).

40. *Matter of Baum*, 401 N.Y.S.2d 514 (1978).

CHAPTER 10

Student Records

Why did Congress pass the Family Educational Rights and Privacy Act?

What are the main features of FERPA?

Does FERPA apply to private schools?

What education records are accessible under the Act?

How does the Act guarantee access to parents?

What student records are not accessible to parents?

May students waive their right of access?

How does FERPA restrict access to outsiders?

What are the rights of non-custodial parents to see their children's records?

Can non-custodial parents who live far from the school obtain copies of their children's records?

What are the rights of non-custodial parents to receive school notices and be informed of parent-teacher conferences?

Can parents see copies of a test their child has taken or just the results of the test?

Do parents have the right to see files on their children labeled "personal" or "confidential"?

Can a school refuse to release a student's report card for disciplinary reasons?

What general information may be shared without parental consent?

May a school allow psychologists, social workers, or lawyers who are not school employees, to review student records without parental consent?

May schools destroy student records?

Must parents be informed of their rights under FERPA?

Does the law prohibit school newspapers from publishing personal information about students?

May schools sometimes release student records without parental consent?

Do parents have a right to challenge the accuracy of their child's records?

Is it necessary for parents to hire a lawyer to represent them at a FERPA hearing?

Can a member of the school board serve as a hearing officer?

What action will be taken against schools that violate FERPA?

What have been the results of the FERPA enforcement procedures?

Can parents take their case to court if they are not satisfied with the decision of the FERPA Office?

Where can parents get more information about FERPA?

What have been the results of the Act?

In 1974, Congress passed the Family Educational Rights and Privacy Act (also known as FERPA or the Buckley Amendment) to define who may and who may not see student records. The law guarantees parents the right to have access to their child's school records. It also prohibits release of the records to outsiders without parental permission, except in case of emergency. This chapter examines the reasons for the Act, what it does and does not require, questions parents frequently ask, and what its results have been.

Why did Congress pass the Family Educational Rights and Privacy Act?

Because of past abuses in the use of student records—especially the tendency of schools to provide access to outsiders, but not to parents.

The establishment of extensive student records 50 years ago was a progressive idea. It enabled educators to have access to information about the "whole child," not just about grades and subjects studied. Over the years, as the quantity of information grew, so did the abuses. One mother was told she had no right to see records that were the basis for placing her son in a class for retarded students. A father, at a routine parent-teacher conference, discovered that his son's records contained comments that he was "strangely introspective" in the third grade, "unnaturally interested in girls" in the fifth grade, and had developed "peculiar political ideas" when he was twelve.[1] Another parent, who was told by teachers that his son needed psychological treatment, had to get a judicial order to see his son's records.[2] Yet, during the 1960s, researchers found that the CIA and the FBI had complete access to student files in 60 percent of the schools, while parents had access in only 15 percent.[3]

A few years before FERPA was passed, a national report found that parents typically had little knowledge of what was in their children's school records, or how they are used, and that most schools had no policies for regulating access to student records or procedures for allowing parents to challenge erroneous information in them. Although some school districts developed policies to control misuse of student records, they were neither uniform nor comprehensive. It was because of these problems that Congress passed FERPA.

What are the main features of FERPA?

The law contains five important features: (1) It requires school districts to establish a written policy concerning student records and to inform parents of their rights under the Act each year. (2) It guarantees parents the right to inspect and review the educational records of their children. (3) It establishes procedures through which parents may challenge the accuracy of student records. (4) It protects the confidentiality of student records by preventing disclosure of personally identifiable information to outsiders without prior parental consent. (5) It entitles parents to file complaints with the FERPA Office concerning alleged failures to comply with the Act.

The law applies to all schools receiving federal education funds. Parents may assert their child's rights of access and consent until the child becomes eighteen or begins attending a post-secondary institution; after this, these rights will "only be accorded. . .to the student."[4]* However, a college may allow parents of a "dependent student" (as defined by the Internal Revenue Code) to see their child's records.

Does FERPA apply to private schools?

The Act applies to all schools which receive funds under any federal program administered by the U.S. Department of Education. This includes funds provided to students attending the school and to schools that receive grants or contracts from the Department of Education. This means that the Act applies to all public schools and colleges and almost all private colleges and universities. But it does not apply to any parochial school. Nor does it apply to most private elementary and secondary schools since, according to the FERPA Office, most do not receive direct funding from the federal Department of Education.

What education records are accessible under the Act?

Education records include any information compiled by a school which is directly related to a current student, regardless of whether the record is handwritten, printed, on tape, film, microfilm, or microfiche.

How does the Act guarantee access to parents?

The law states that no federal funds will be made available to any school that prevents parents from exercising "the right to inspect and review the educational records of their children." This includes the right (1) to be informed about the kinds and location of education records maintained by the school and the officials responsible for them, (2) to obtain copies of records where necessary (e.g., when parents are physically unable to travel to the school to inspect the records), and (3) to receive

---

*Quotations about the Act in this Chapter are from the *Federal Regulations*, unless otherwise indicated.

an explanation or interpretation of the records if requested. Officials must comply with a parental request to inspect "within a reasonable time, but in no case more than 45 days after the request." Although a school may not deny parental access to student records, it may deny a request for a copy of such records when parents are able to personally inspect them at the school.

What student records are not accessible to parents?

FERPA does not give parents the right to review personal notes of teachers, psychologists, or administrators that are in their "sole possession" and are not shared with anyone except a temporary substitute. In addition, students at colleges do not have the right to see records of health professionals used only in connection with the treatment of a student; records of a law enforcement unit of the school used solely for law enforcement purposes; or job-related records of students employed by the school.

May students waive their right of access?

Yes. Individuals who are applicants for admission to post-secondary institutions may waive their right to inspect confidential letters of recommendation. Although institutions may not require such waivers "as a condition of admission," they may "request" them. These waivers must be signed by individual students, regardless of age, rather than by their parents. Colleges may also prohibit students from inspecting the financial statements of their parents.

How does FERPA restrict access to outsiders?

The Act generally requires that a school obtain "the written consent of the parents. . .before disclosing personally identifiable information from the records of a student." This should prevent the public posting of grades and the casual opening of student records to outsiders or their discussion at public meetings. The consent must be signed and dated and include the specific records to be disclosed and the purpose and the individual or group to whom the disclosure may be made. Schools must keep a file of all requests for access to a student's record; the file must indicate who made the request and the legitimate interests in seeking the information.

What are the rights of non-custodial parents to see their children's records?

Generally, they are the same as those of custodial parents. FERPA provides each parent with the right of access to their child's records. The Act and its regulations make no distinction based on whether a parent has custody or not. Therefore, a school district must give a non-custodial parent the same right of access as a custodial parent unless the school has been given "a legally binding instrument or a state law or court order governing such matters as divorce, separation or custody which provides to the contrary."

Can non-custodial parents, who live far from a school, obtain copies of their children's records?

Yes. According to the Act, the parent's right "to inspect and review" education records includes the "right to obtain copies of the records" where failure to provide copies would effectively prevent parents from exercising their right of access. Therefore, where parents can not personally inspect their child's records at school because of health reasons or because they live far from the school, the school is required to provide the parents with copies of the education records. Schools can charge a reasonable fee for making copies of such records unless parents cannot afford to pay.

What are the rights of non-custodial parents to receive school notices and be informed of parent-teacher conferences?

FERPA only applies to school records. It does not apply to routine notices and does not address the responsibility of schools to keep both parents equally informed. Therefore, non-custodial parents have no right under the Act to require that schools invite them to all parent-teacher conferences or mail them all notices that are sent home to custodial parents.

Can parents see copies of a test their child has taken or just the results of the test?

Parents have the right to be informed about the questions as well as the answers. Whether they have a right to see the test itself is unclear.

Parents have a right to be informed of the test questions as part of their right to a response from the school for "explanations and interpretations" of the child's record. Therefore, if test results are maintained in a student's record, it is the position of the FERPA Office that schools cannot adequately explain such results without informing parents of the questions.[5]

Some educators believe that they cannot give parents copies of copyrighted tests without violating the law. However, it can be argued that giving parents one copy of a test for a limited, educational, noncommercial purpose makes "fair use" of the material and therefore does not violate copyright law.

Do parents have the right to see files on their children labeled "personal" or "confidential"?

It depends on the specific content and use of the file, not its label. A parent's right of access applies to all of their child's education records, and labeling a record "confidential" does not block a parent's right to review and inspect such records.

Can a school refuse to release a student's report card for disciplinary reasons?

It can under some circumstances. The school cannot refuse to allow parents to see their child's grades since they are clearly part of his/her education records. Furthermore, schools must provide copies of records where failure to do so would prevent a parent from exercising her right of access. However, the Act does allow schools to describe the circumstance in which it feels it has "a legitimate cause to deny a request for a copy of such records." Thus, if the school's record policy stated that it would not release a student's report card unless all books were returned and all fees were paid, such disciplinary measures would not violate the Act. Similarly, a private school policy that prohibited the transfer of student records to another school unless tuition was paid would be lawful.

In a related case, former students sued their college for not sending out copies of their transcripts because they failed to repay their student loans. The students claimed the college violated FERPA, but a federal court disagreed. The judge ruled that the Act was for the "inspection of records by students and their parents, not for the release of records to outside parties."[6]

What general information may be shared without parental consent?

A school may disclose "directory information" from the education records of a student without requiring prior parental consent. Directory information includes such facts as a student's name, address, phone number, date and place of birth, field of study, sports activities, dates of attendance, awards received, and similar information. Before freely releasing such information, a school must try to notify parents of current students about what facts it regards as directory information and of the parents' right to refuse to permit the release of such information. It is the parents' obligation to notify the school in writing if they refuse. However, a school may release directory information about former students without first trying to notify them.

May a school allow psychologists, social workers, or lawyers who are not school employees, to review a student's records without parental consent?

No. The Act allows schools to determine what "school officials" have a "legitimate educational interest" in being able to review student records without parental consent. Such officials might include part-time consultants as well as full-time employees. But the Act does not allow psychologists, social workers, or anyone else who is not an employee of the school to have access to student records without parental consent except under special circumstances.

May schools destroy student records?

Yes, they can under FERPA. If state law does not regulate the destruction of educational records, schools may destroy some or all of a student's records at any time, except when a request has been made to inspect them.

Must parents be informed of their rights under FERPA?

Yes. Every school must give parents of all current students "annual notice" of their rights under the Act, where they can obtain copies of the school's policy for implementing and protecting these rights, and their "right to file complaints" for the school's failure to comply with the law. In addition, the Act requires that elementary and secondary schools find a way to "effectively notify parents" of students whose primary language is not English.

Does the law prohibit school newspapers from publishing personal information about students?

It depends upon the source of the information. In defending their seizure of a school newspaper that contained personal information about a student's suspension, school officials argued that FERPA prevented schools from disclosing such information about their students. However, the court ruled that the Act could not justify the seizure. Although some of the information in the newspaper would fall within the Act's protection "if the source of that information had been school records," the court wrote that the Act "cannot be deemed to extend to information which is derived from a source independent of school records."[7] Since the personal information in the student newspaper was not obtained from school records, FERPA did not require school officials to prohibit the publication of the information.

May schools sometimes release student records without parental consent?

Yes. There are several exceptions to the law which allow schools to share records without parental consent with: (1) teachers, administrators or other school officials who have "legitimate educational interests," (2) officials of another school in which the student seeks to enroll, (3) persons for whom the information is necessary "to protect the health or safety of the student or other individuals," and (4) in connection with financial aid for which a student has applied, and in a few other limited circumstances. In addition, the Act allows schools to release student records without a parent's consent "to comply with a judicial order or lawfully issued subpoena." But in this case, the school must make "a reasonable effort" to notify the parent of the order or subpoena before complying with it.

Do parents have a right to challenge the accuracy of their child's records?

Yes. If the parents of a student believe that a school record is "inaccurate or misleading or violates the privacy or other rights of the student," they may request that the school amend it. If the school refuses, it must so inform the parents and advise them of their right to a hearing.

At the hearing, parents must be given "a full and fair opportunity" to present their evidence. The school must make its decision in writing, "based solely on the evidence presented at the hearing" which must include the reasons and evidence to support its decision.

If, as a result of the hearing, the school decides the record was inaccurate or misleading, it must amend the record accordingly. But, if the school decides that the information was correct, it must inform the parents of "the right to place in the education records of the student a statement commenting upon the information. . .and/or setting forth any reasons for disagreeing with the decision" of the school. Such explanation must be maintained by the school as part of the student's record; if the contested portion of the record is disclosed to anyone, the explanation must also be disclosed.

Is it necessary for parents to hire a lawyer to represent them at a FERPA hearing?

No. The Act allows parents to represent themselves at the hearing or be assisted or represented by individuals of their choice. It also gives them the right to be represented by a lawyer at their own expense. But legal representation is not required by the Act.

Can a member of the school board serve as a hearing officer?

Yes. According to FERPA Regulations, the hearing may be conducted by "any party," including an official of the school district, "who does not have a direct interest in the outcome of the hearing." This could include a principal, teacher, superintendent, or school board member. It, of course, would exclude the person who wrote the challenged record.

Some parents feel that it is unfair to allow one school official to judge the merits of a parent's complaint against another school official. But the law assumes that hearing officers will try to be impartial and that dissatisfied parents will take advantage of their right, under the Act, to place their reasons for disagreeing with the hearing officer's decision into their child's school records.

What action will be taken against schools that violate FERPA?

Federal regulations include detailed information concerning the enforcement of the Act. A FERPA Office of the Department of Education has been established to "investigate, process and review violations and complaints." When it receives a written complaint regarding violations from a parent, the Office will notify the school involved and give it an opportunity to respond to the allegation. The Office investigates all written complaints and sends its findings to the parents and the school.

Parents usually receive a response from the FERPA Office within 20 working days after their complaint is received. If there has been a violation, the Office will indicate the steps the school must take to comply with the law. If the school does not comply, a Review Board hearing will be held. If the Board determines "that compliance cannot be secured by voluntary means," Department of Education funds to the school district will be terminated.

What have been the results of the FERPA enforcement procedures?

Thousands of complaints have been received by the FERPA Office during the past decade. Over 80% of the complaints have been resolved informally through phone calls from the Office to the school district involved. As of June, 1986, there have been 128 formal investigations.[8] No cases have yet been referred to the Review Board; thus, funds have never been terminated for noncompliance.

Can parents take their case to court if they are not satisfied with the decision of the FERPA Office?

Probably not. FERPA does not provide individual citizens with a legal right to enforce the Act through the courts. According to a federal appeals decision, "enforcement is solely in the hands of the Department of Education."[9]

Where can parents get more information about FERPA?

From their school district and the FERPA Office. Each school district is required to notify parents of enrolled students annually of their rights under the Act and where they can obtain copies of the school's student records policy. In addition,

the FERPA Office consults with parents and educators by letter or phone and will answer questions concerning the Act, its
regulations, and their interpretation and application in schools.
Furthermore, copies of the FERPA regulations and a model
policy document for elementary and secondary schools can be
obtained by writing the Family Educational Rights and Privacy
Act Office, U.S. Department of Education, Room 4512, Switzer
Building, Washington, D.C. 20202.

What have been the results of the Act?

Initially, schools were slow to comply with the statute.
Federal regulations for implementation were not published until a year and a half after the Act became law in 1974. But as
hundreds of complaints have been filed with the FERPA Office
each year, information about the Act has increased, and compliance has become more widespread.

According to some observers, two notable results of FERPA
have been the destruction of old records and the improvement
of new ones. After the law was passed, many schools across
the country conducted "massive housecleanings" of records.
Emptying school files of "undesirable material," wrote Lucy
Knight, in *American Education* magazine, "remains the single
most effective way for a school to attempt compliance with the
Buckley Amendment."[10] Second, the quality of student records
and the caliber of recommendations "has improved substantially," according to Chester Nolte. This, wrote Professor Nolte,
reflects the fact that under the Act teachers, principals, and
counselors "must adhere to absolute truth, rather than opinion,
when writing reports on individual students."[11]

Fears that teachers would be sued for libel if they wrote
anything negative in student records have been greatly
exaggerated. There is little chance of students winning libel suits
against teachers whose comments are based on firsthand obser-
vations, are accurate, and are educationally relevant. (For more
on libel, see Chapter 7.)

Two other areas of misunderstanding have regularly occurred
concerning the Act. First, many educators are still unaware that
access applies to all student records, not just to the cumulative
file. Second, many parents believe the Act gives them the right
to challenge the fairness of a student grade. Although the law

does allow parents to question whether a teacher's grade was recorded accurately, it does not allow them to challenge the reasonableness of the grade that was assigned.[12]

Summary

Abuses in the use of student records led Congress to pass the Family Educational Rights and Privacy Act in 1974. The Act has several important features. First, it guarantees custodial and non-custodial parents the right to inspect and review the educational records of their children; but this does not include teachers' personal notes about students. Second, it limits access to student records by providing that such records cannot be released to outsiders without a parent's written consent. However, such consent is not required when the records are shared with teachers and staff in the school, who have a "legitimate educational interest" in the student, or when they are released because of health or safety emergencies or pursuant to a court order or a few other specified circumstances. Third, the law gives parents the right to challenge recorded information that is "inaccurate, misleading, or otherwise in violation of privacy or other rights of students." It also gives parents the right to place an explanation in the record of any information with which they disagree. In addition, it establishes a FERPA Office in Washington, D.C., to interpret and enforce the Act. Students who apply to college may waive their right to inspect confidential letters of recommendation. And, when students become eighteen or begin attending a post-secondary institution, they take over their parents' rights under the Act. Although FERPA initially imposed additional administrative responsibilities on the schools, it has generally led to an improvement in the quality and accuracy of student records.

Notes for Chapter 10

1. Diane Divoky, "Cumulative Records: Assault on Privacy", *Learning Magazine*, September 1973, p. 9.

2. *Van Allen v. McCleary*, 211 N.Y.S.2d 501 (1961).

3. Michael Stone, "Off the Record: The Emerging Right to Control

One's School Files," 5 *N.Y.U. Review of Law and School Change* 39, 1975.

4. The text of the Act is contained in the UNITED STATES CODE Title 20 1232g. Regulations for implementing the Act can be found in the CODE OF FEDERAL REGULATIONS, Title 45, Part 99 (1979).

5. Telephone interview with Pat Ballinger, Director, Family Educational Rights and Privacy Act Office, U.S. Department of Education, June 27, 1986.

6. *Girardier v. Webster College*, 421 F.Supp. 45 (E.D.Mo. 1976), 563 F.2d 1267 (8th Cir. 1977).

7. *Frasca v. Andrews*, 463 F.Supp. 1043 (E.D.N.Y. 1979).

8. Telephone interview with Pat Ballinger, FERPA Office, June 27, 1986.

9. *Girardier v. Webster College*, 563 F.2d 1267 (8th Cir. 1977).

10. Lucy Knight, "Facts About Mr. Buckley's Amendment," *American Education*, June 1977, p. 6.

11. M. Chester Nolte, *American School Board Journal*, April 1977, p. 38.

12. Telephone interview with Pat Ballinger, FERPA Office, January 28, 1986.

CHAPTER 11

Education of Handicapped Children

What federal laws currently affect the education of handicapped children?

Why was Public Law 94-142 enacted?

Does the term "exceptional children" also refer to those who are gifted as well as those with handicaps?

What are the key provisions of P.L. 94-142

Does the law include provisions for parents' rights?

What procedural safeguards protect parents and children under this law?

Does "appropriate" education mean the "best" education?

May state laws require higher standards than the federal law?

What are "related services" required by the EHA?

Must schools provide year-round schooling for handicapped children?

Can a state limit the education of the handicapped because of lack of funds?

Will granting a diploma free a school district from further responsibility?

Are cost considerations important in determining the appropriate educational placement of a handicapped child?

May parents on their own decide to send their child to private school?

Can parents recover their attorney fees in a suit under the EHA?

May schools charge parents for special expenses for educating handicapped children?

May handicapped students be suspended for misbehavior?

May handicapped students be expelled or suspended for a long term?

How do parents learn about their rights under the EHA?

What can parents do if they disagree with their child's plan?

———————

U ntil recently most states with compulsory education
laws also provided legal ways to exclude some children
from school.   Various labels were attached to the
children who were excluded, but in general they were lumped
together under the heading of "uneducable." Throughout the
country, hundreds of thousands of children were excluded from
public schools on the basis of such laws. While in the past many
parents and educators expected very little of these children
and accepted the belief that most of them were uneducable
and untrainable, a very different view is generally held today.
According to this newer idea, all human beings can benefit from
appropriate education or training. It is now established that
with proper care, education, and training, most handicapped
children can learn enough to become largely self-sufficient, and
even the extreme cases can be trained to care for their own
bodily needs. Very few need to remain completely dependent
on the care of others.

The first case to reflect this changing view reached the courts
in 1972, when the parents of 13 retarded children, together
with the Pennsylvania Association for Retarded Children, challenged the laws in their state that kept children from school
if they were certified by school psychologists as "uneducable
and untrainable."[1] The parents claimed that the laws were unconstitutional: (a) by not giving parents a notice and proper
hearing, they violated the right to due process; (b) by assuming certain children to be uneducable without a rational basis
in fact, they denied the right to equal protection of the laws;
and (c) because the state constitution guaranteed education for
all children, the laws that excluded retarded children were arbitrary and capricious.

The Court ruled that the state cannot deny schooling to retarded children, and gave the contending parties the responsibility for working out an acceptable settlement for placing retarded children in special education to meet their needs. The agreement also included careful and elaborate provisions for due process before any child may be placed in special education classes or before any change in such placement may be made.

A federal court ruling in Washington, D.C., in the same year (1972) established the rights of other "exceptional" or "disabled" children to an appropriate education.[2] This included the emotionally disturbed, the deaf, and the blind. The District Court ruled that the constitutional right of due process must be followed before any child is identified as "exceptional" and before an educational placement is decided upon for such a child. The court further ruled that lack of funds for identifying and educating "exceptional" children could not be used as an excuse for failing to provide them with appropriate education.

The ruling included an elaborate set of procedures through which parents would be informed and involved every step of the way in working with the schools toward an appropriate educational placement of their children.

These cases, together with others in various parts of the country, made it clear that the right to education provided by the state extended to *all* children, including the handicapped. Beyond this basic right, however, other issues concerning the handicapped arose and were settled in the courts or by statutes. Among them were questions related to the proper placement of exceptional children, whether they should be placed in special classes and schools or placed together with other students, what procedures should be used to make such decisions, and what role the parents should have in these procedures.

What federal laws currently affect the education of handicapped children?

Two federal laws, enacted in 1973 and 1975, have established the right to a public school education for all handicapped children in all parts of the U.S. They are Section 504 of the Rehabilitation Act of 1973[3] and Public Law 94-142, a federal law originally known as the Education of All Handicapped Children

Act (EHA).

Section 504 of the Rehabilitation Act applies to all programs or activities receiving federal financial assistance and specifies that no "otherwise qualified individual" can be discriminated against in any federally assisted program or activity "solely by reason of his handicap." But the more specific and comprehensive federal law relevant to parents of handicapped children is the EHA. This law makes money available to states that comply with its provisions. This money is then turned over to Local Education Agencies (LEAs) if they meet the provisions of the law.

Why was Public Law 94-142 enacted?

In a preamble to the law, Congress states both its purpose and the facts on which it is based. The purposes are broad and bold: to assure that all handicapped children have available to them "a free and appropriate public education and related services designed to meet their unique needs."

Among the facts the law discussed were the number of handicapped children in the United States at the time the law was enacted in 1975—over 8,000,000—and the inadequacy of provision for their educational needs. More than a million of these children were completely excluded from public schools, and many of those in school received inadequate education due to lack of supporting services or untrained teachers. Many parents were obliged to find tutors for their handicapped children or to send them to private schools, often at great distance from home and at the parents' expense. Congress also found that, given adequate funding, teachers could be trained to provide effective special education for all children.

Does the term "exceptional children" also refer to those who are gifted as well as those with handicaps?

The Education of the Handicapped Act makes no provision for "gifted" or "exceptionally talented" children. Programs for the gifted are a responsibility of state governments. The states have differing legal approaches to special education for gifted children. Some require nothing, others mandate supportive services be available, and still others define these children as "exceptional" and provide for testing and placement in appropriate classrooms.

Forty-five states make special reference to gifted and talented children in their education laws or allocate extra money for educational programs. Seventeen states (AL, AK, AZ, FL, GA, KS, LA, NV, NJ, NM, NC, OK, PA, SD, TN, VA, WV) require services for exceptionally able children.

What are the key provisions of P.L. 94-142?

Age of Eligibility. Under the original version of the EHA, "free appropriate public education" had to be available to all handicapped children between the ages of 5 and 18, and to children aged 3-21 unless state law or practice did not allow serving 3-5-year-olds or those 18-21 years of age. In 1986, however, P.L. 99-457 extended educational services to young children. By 1991, states must have educational programs for all handicapped 3-5 year olds. In addition, federal funding will be available for early intervention services for handicapped infants and toddlers up to the age of two.*

Eligibility for Services. The EHA provides that children are eligible for services if they have one or more of the following handicapping conditions:

Hearing Impairments	Learning Disabilities
Speech Impairments	Mental Retardation
Visual Impairments	Emotional Disturbances
Physical Impairments	Chronic or Long-term
	Health Problems

Special Services Required. In addition to educational services, the EHA requires the provision of related services necessary to help the child learn: speech and language therapy, medical services for diagnosis or evaluation purposes, physical therapy, transportation, parent counseling, vocational education, and college placement services.

Individualized Educational Plan. The law provides that an

---

*The new Section 672 of the EHA defines "handicapped infants and toddlers" to mean from birth to age two, inclusive, for individuals in need of help because they are (1) experiencing developmental delays, or (2) have a diagnosed physical or mental condition which has a high probability of resulting in developmental delays.

individualized written plan must be developed for each handicapped child and reviewed annually by the child's parents and teachers, and a representative of the school district. The plan should indicate the child's present level of school performance, the educational services to be provided, and specific criteria to measure his progress. School districts must maintain records of the individualized educational plans for each child.

Least Restrictive Environment. The EHA requires that handicapped children must be educated in the "least restrictive" educational environment appropriate to their needs. In other words, as much as possible and educationally appropriate, they should be educated with children who are not handicapped. This is what is meant by "mainstreaming." Among possible programs and plans, a regular public school class with appropriate support services is preferable to special classes; special classes are preferable to special schools; special schools might be preferable to home teaching; and home teaching is preferable to no teaching at all.

Furthermore, while the Act creates a clear preference for public educational placement, private schools are proper alternatives if no appropriate public facilities are available, and public funds should be used to support the education of the handicapped child in the private school.[5] That school, of course, must meet the standards applied to state and local public schools.

While there is a general preference in the law favoring mainstreaming, this preference might be outweighed in individual cases where a more appropriate education could be achieved in a non-mainstreaming setting. Thus, the courts upheld the school district's decision to transfer a handicapped girl, over parental objections, to a nearby school district where a more qualified instructor would teach her.[6]

Does the law include provisions for parents' rights?

The following rights are required by P.L. 94-142:

Notice. Parents must receive written notice that is clear, detailed, and specific before their child is identified, evaluated or placed in any special educational program.

Evaluation. Parents have a right to a full evaluation of their child's abilities and educational needs. Parental consent must be obtained before conducting an evaluation. Parents have the right to obtain an evaluation independent of the school if they disagree with the school's test results or if they are denied an assessment by the school. They also have the right to have the child retested by the school district at least every three years.

Records and Confidentiality of Information. Parents have a right to examine all records kept on their child, and the right to challenge them if they are inaccurate or misleading. With the exception of certain individuals (school officials, for example, and teachers with legitimate education interests) no one may see a child's records unless parents give their written permission.

Educational Program. Parents have the right to participate in the conference to plan and design the individualized educational program (IEP) for their child, and the school district is obliged to make a good faith effort to include the parents. They have the right to have the child's IEP updated at least once a year.

Placement. Parental consent must be obtained before initial placement of a handicapped child in a program providing special education. Parents have a right to have their child placed in the "least restrictive environment," to be educated with non-handicapped children to the maximum extent appropriate.

What procedural safeguards protect parents and children under this law?

Language. All communications with parents must be in the primary language of the parents; testing of children must not be discriminatory in language, race, or culture.

Hearings. If at any point during the identification, evaluation, or placement, parents do not agree with the educational decisions made concerning their child, they have the right to request a hearing. The hearing, which is to be impartial and independent, is to be conducted by the State Educational Agency (SEA) or local school district, and not by the employee "involved in the education or care of the child." At any hearing, parents have the right to be represented by a lawyer or an individual trained in the problems of handicapped children, the right to present evidence, to subpoena, confront and cross-examine witnesses, and to obtain a transcript of the hearing and a written decision by the hearing officer.

Appeals. Parents may reject and appeal the decision of the local school authorities. The route of the appeal is specified by each state, and there are different models of the appeal process. The most typical model is a two-tier system where the initial appeal is conducted by local officials or their appointees, whose decision may be further appealed to the state level. There are states that use a one-tier system (e.g., CO, DC, LA, MT, TN, WI, and others) in some of which the hearing may be conducted by a state-appointed hearing officer, while in others by locally appointed officials.

Still other states have appeal processes where the initial appeal is to a state-designated official, often called a mediator, and subsequent appeals go to the state commissioner of education, superintendent of public education, or the department of education (e.g., AL, ID, IN, OK, PA, VT, etc.) Other states (e.g., MA, CT, MO, NJ) present still further variations of the appeals process. Furthermore, since such processes may change within a state through changes in state law or regulations, it is important for parents to check the appeals processes of their respective states at the time of their need.

Change in Placement. Parents must be given prior notice of any proposed change in their child's educational placement or program and a written explanation of the procedures to be followed in effecting that change. The child has a right to remain in his or her current placement until due process hearing or appeal proceedings are completed. School districts must maintain records of the individualized educational plans for each child.

Hundreds of lawsuits have been litigated since the enactment of the EHA because parents and educators often disagreed about the meaning of the language used in the law as well as about the proper application of its terms to particular situations. We present some of the key cases below as well as address the questions most commonly raised by parents.

Does "appropriate" education mean the "best" education?

This question was raised in the case of Amy Rowley, a hearing-impaired elementary school child. She was assisted by a hearing aid, speech therapy sessions three times a week, and a special tutor for an hour a day. Her parents approved her Individualized Education Plan (IEP), but also wanted a sign-

language interpreter for her even though when such an interpreter was used experimentally the year before, Amy did not
seem to need it. The school district maintained that Amy was
performing better than the average child in her classes and was
"advancing easily from grade to grade"; therefore, the extra expense for the special interpreter was not needed.

In the final analysis, the U.S. Supreme Court held that the
EHA was not violated by the denial of the services of the
sign-language interpreter. The Court ruled that the requirement
of "appropriate education" was met when Amy was receiving
"personalized instruction and related services" that enabled her
to make satisfactory progress at or above grade level. Congress,
in the opinion of the Court, did not intend to require that
schools provide the "best" education; as long as the child's
education was "adequate" and the procedural requirements of
the EHA were followed, the law was satisfied. In short, the
EHA provides for a "basic floor of opportunity" and does not
require that a child receive optimal education.[7]

Rowley has made an impact on lower courts. For example,
parents of a severely handicapped child filed suit to keep their
child in a 24-hour residential care and educational program.
The federal district court originally ordered school officials to
provide such residential care and education for this child, but
after Rowley, it reversed itself and ruled that a day program
would suffice to advance the child's educational needs even
though the more comprehensive residential program would be
better. The circuit court upheld this decision.[8] Other cases,
however, have reached conclusions under state laws that
provide for higher standards than the Rowley case. Some of
these are discussed in the following section.

May state laws require higher standards than the federal law?

Yes, they may and, where they do, school districts must meet
the higher standards. The laws of New Jersey, for example, require that public school districts must provide a special education program and related services according to how a student
can "best" achieve in school. Since EHA only provides access
to a "free appropriate education," New Jersey's standards are
higher. Based on the distinction between these two standards,
a federal district court decided that placement in a residential

school would be more beneficial to a severely handicapped child than placement in a regular day program of a public school.[9] Similarly, a Massachusetts case held that since the state law set higher standards than the federal law, the higher of the two standards must be followed. In this case, a student with Downs Syndrome could have been educated locally, pursuant to an IEP. However, his uncontrollable, sexually aggressive behavior in and out of the classroom required around-the-clock supervision. Therefore, under the higher state standards, the court ruled that a residential program would be the appropriate one for this student.[10]

What are "related services" required by the EHA?

The Rowley case was based on the Supreme Court's interpretation of the meaning of "related services" required by the EHA. The Act defines related services as: "transportation, and such developmental, corrective, and other services (including speech pathology and audiology, and medical and counseling services, except that such medical services shall be for diagnostic and evaluative purposes only) as may be required to assist the handicapped child to benefit from special education, and includes the early identification and assessment of handicapping conditions in children."[11]

The ambiguity of the phrase "medical services" and the high cost of some services required to educate certain types of students led to a large number of lawsuits. One interesting case involved an eight-year-old girl, Amber Tatro, who was born with spina bifida.[12] She suffered from orthopedic and speech impairment and a bladder condition that required catheterization every 3-4 hours. Is this periodic catheterization an excluded medical service or a "related service" schools must perform? The IEP was quite comprehensive, but excluded the "clean, intermittent catheterization" (CIC) that Amber needed. While CIC is a simple procedure that can be learned in about an hour, and requires no more than five minutes to administer, the district court ruled that it was not a related service. On appeal this was overruled, and ultimately, the Supreme Court held that CIC is not significantly different from other related services, such as dispensing necessary medicine or administering emergency injections following medical authorization. We can expect further lawsuits on the question of related services as we attempt to define which medical services must be provided and which excluded.

A 1983 case in New Jersey, for example, held that psychotherapy can be a related service. The appeals court noted that, since Congress authorized psychological and counseling services under the EHA, it must have intended to include psychotherapy as well, particularly when such help was provided by qualified counselors, psychologists, and social workers.[13] It is probable that if the psychotherapy could be provided only by a psychiatrist, it would be excluded as a medical service.

Must schools provide year-round schooling for handicapped children?

Certain handicapped children suffer educational setbacks during the summer breaks that accompany traditional school calendars. Several lawsuits have been filed to provide for year-round schooling in an attempt to avoid such regression. Lower federal courts have ruled that school policies limiting attendance to approximately 180 days may violate the requirements of the EHA that individually tailored educational plans be provided each handicapped child.[14] However, the Supreme Court overturned such a ruling without comment.[15] This action casts some doubt on the holding of the lower court concerning year-round schooling for the handicapped, although the 5th Circuit in 1986 again upheld the requirement that full summer services be provided for a handicapped child who would have experienced substantial regression during the summer months.[16]

Can a state limit the education of the handicapped because of lack of funds?

No, it can not. Historically, states used to do so, claiming that there was hardly enough money to educate "normal" children. Such discrimination against the handicapped is unconstitutional, and it also violates the EHA. The state of Oregon passed a law that provided that the education of handicapped children was "subject to the availability of funds" and subject to the district receiving reimbursement for their costs. This was struck down by a federal court which held that the state had a responsibility to provide funding for educating handicapped children.[17]

Will granting a diploma free a school district from further responsibility?

Not necessarily. A school district cannot rid itself of all obligation merely by granting a diploma to a handicapped student. In an Illinois case, the court revoked the diploma and reinstated the student in school after determining that intensive psychotherapy should have been provided by the school, but was not.[18] A similar situation arose in Massachusetts, when a diploma was granted by a hospital school, terminating the student's eligibility for further special education. The court, however, held that "the graduation was procedurally and substantively defective." The parents were not notified or otherwise informed that graduation would terminate their son's eligibility for further educational services, or of their right to challenge the IEP. Evidence showed that the boy was unable to function either independently or in a sheltered workshop. Thus the court found that both federal and state laws were violated.[19]

Are cost considerations important in determining the appropriate educational placement of a handicapped child?

Cost considerations may enter only when choosing among options, all of which offer an "appropriate" education.[20]

May parents on their own decide to send their child to private school?

Yes, they may, but they might have to pay for it. When parents disagree with the placement of their child pursuant to an IEP, it is safest to exhaust their administrative remedies, that is, go through the appeal process, without moving the child. If they decide to change the child's placement on their own, in many instances they will do so at their own expense. Exceptions to this rule may occur when school officials acted in bad faith or denied due process to the parents, or when a court agrees with the placement and decision made by the parents. Courts have a great deal of discretion whether or not to order such reimbursement. In a 1985 case that arose in Massachusetts, the Supreme Court ruled that parents may be reimbursed for the cost of private schooling even if they place their handicapped child there unilaterally, in disagreement with public school officials, if such placement is deemed to be the proper one through appeal procedures set forth in the law. The Court reasoned that without this provision, children of poor parents might have to spend years in inappropriate placement awaiting the outcome of the case. Parents, however, take a risk of not being reimbursed when they unilaterally move children to a private school. [21]

In a District of Columbia case, the court held that parents may receive reimbursement and their expenses for attorney fees where school officials did not follow the IEP or otherwise violated the due process rights of parents. In this case, parents paid tuition elsewhere in face of the wrongful actions of the school officials. [22] Also in the District of Columbia, a federal court ordered the reimbursement of the cost of private schooling when a child who had hearing disabilities and was emotionally disturbed had to spend at least a fourth of his time in regular classes in a large public high school. The court thought such placement to be inappropriate and ordered cost reimbursement even though the parents acted without permission from the school authorities. [23]

Despite the cases cited above, parents take a risk when they act on their own and place their child into a private school or other institution. In some instances they will not be reimbursed for costs incurred. Furthermore, a state may not cut off funds it has been paying to a private school during due process procedures, while attempts are being made to determine a possible new placement for the student. That would violate the "status quo" ("stay put") provision of the EHA which requires the child to be maintained in the current placement pending completion of the due process procedures. [24]

Can parents recover their attorney fees in a suit under the EHA?

Until 1986, they could not because the original version of the EHA did not provide for an award of attorney fees. Questions have arisen about the possibility of bringing suit under Section 504 of the Rehabilitation Act of 1973 or under 42 U.S.C.A. 1983, a general civil rights law, each of which allows for the recovery of attorney fees. Courts have held, however, that parents must proceed under the EHA, the most specific comprehensive special education law and can't go directly into the federal court under the other two laws mentioned above. Thus, they can't circumvent the procedural requirements of the EHA.[25] However, P.L. 99-372 amended the EHA in 1986 to allow courts to award attorney fees to parents who win lawsuits involving the education of handicapped children.

May schools charge parents for special expenses for educating handicapped children?

No, they may not. A suit was filed by parents whose handicapped children were placed in a private facility on the basis of a developmental disability and were charged up to $100 per month for the child's living expenses. They brought a class action suit, alleging that the state violated the EHA by this requirement. The courts agreed with the parents, ordered reimbursement and enjoined the state from requiring such payment.[26]

May handicapped students be suspended for misbehavior?

Yes, they may be, for a short period of time. While the EHA is silent on disciplining handicapped students, school officials may deal with disruptions and emergencies according to the school rules governing student conduct. This is the case for short-term suspensions or in-school detentions. Such short-term suspensions do not constitute a change in placement that would necessitate a new look at the IEP and full blown due process. For example, when an 11th grade learning-disabled boy used abusive language objecting to a detention, he was suspended for five days. The court upheld the suspension, holding that his special education was not terminated, merely disrupted for five days because of a "flagrant offense."[27] Thus, in ordinary discipline situations, including short suspension when the student's misbehavior is unrelated to his handicap, handicapped students may be disciplined as non-handicapped students. (See Chapter 2.)

May handicapped students be expelled or suspended for a long term?

Long-term suspensions or expulsion might constitute a change in placement under the EHA, therefore special protections come into play to ensure that the handicapped child continues to receive "a free and appropriate education." Before handicapped students are disciplined for misbehavior, school officials must ascertain that their misbehavior is not the result of their handicapping condition.[28] A handicapped child may not be expelled or suspended for a long term or for an indefinite period if his disruptive behavior is a manifestation of his handicap. Furthermore, if expulsion or long-term suspension does take place, educational services must not stop completely. As a minimum, there must be provisions for educating the student at home.[29] Thus, disruptive handicapped children, whose disruptive behavior is not a function of their handicap, may be expelled from school. However, because expulsion or long-term suspension are changes in placement, the procedural safeguards guaranteed by the EHA must be followed.[30]

Violent and disruptive students' placements may be changed by school officials without awaiting the final outcome of an appeals process. As a general rule, the EHA provides for the maintenance of students in their current placement during the appeals process. However, schools have the discretion to change the placement if a student's behavior threatens to disrupt a safe school environment.[31] This result was also reached in a Florida case where a student with a special hearing disability was involuntarily transferred from a high school to an alternative learning center because of violent behavior that threatened both students and school officials. The appeals court noted that the EHA does not deprive school boards of their traditional authority or responsibility to ensure safety in schools.[32]

How do parents learn about their rights under the EHA?

Before a child is identified as handicapped, schools must go through a careful and comprehensive process of evaluating him. Parental consent is required for this evaluation, and parents should be informed of their right to full participation and their right to due process and appeal before any evaluation or assessment takes place. The IEP is created pursuant to the evaluation process, and it cannot be put into effect without parental consent. Furthermore, the law requires periodic review of the IEP with alterations as deemed appropriate.

What can parents do who disagree with their child's plan?

Parents who disagree with the IEP do not have to accept it. They may reject the plan or postpone its acceptance or rejection

pending the outcome of an independent evaluation. If parents
do not agree with the independent evaluation, they have a right
to appeal. This appeal is usually to a regional office of the state
department of education which may try to mediate the disagreement or assign it to an arbitrator, an impartial hearing officer.
This hearing officer should not be an employee of the local
school board nor should s/he have been involved in the for-
mulation of state policies for the handicapped.[33] If parents are
still dissatisfied with the recommendation made by the highest
office in this chain of administrative appeals, they may go to
court. The entire process prior to going to court is part of the
due process provided by law and must be followed all the way
before courts will hear the case.

The EHA contains many other provisions, such as those related to formulas for allocating funds to states and to local
school districts. But the major provisions of the law, those
which directly affect the rights of parents and of children, are
the ones presented above.

Summary

As difficult and expensive as it is to provide educational programs of sound quality for children without handicaps, it is
even more difficult and expensive to educate those with handicapping conditions.

Yet courts have held that if a state provides public education for all of its children, it must do so without discriminating
against the handicapped. This concept has been given powerful
impetus by the passage of the federal Education for All Handicapped Children Act of 1975, currently known as the Education
of the Handicapped Act, EHA.

According to the terms of this law, the federal government
will make significant funds available to states to be used for
special education. The states in turn will channel these funds
to local schools. But the states and local schools must satisfy the
federal guidelines. Thus, local control and responsibility will be
retained, yet federal standards and aid will help provide more
appropriate schooling for handicapped children.

The law lists the right that parents have to participate in the
diagnosis, placement, education, and periodic re-evaluation of
their children, and lists similar rights for children. It points the

way to a comprehensive approach to provide individualized educational programs, at public expense, for all handicapped children, in the least restrictive educational environment. It has been hailed by parents and educators alike as a major new development, perhaps one that can become a model for the education of all children.

Many lawsuits have been filed due to disagreements over the proper meaning and application of the EHA and because of the large costs involved. We can expect many more lawsuits in this area. Currently, we know that the EHA is satisfied if the handicapped child has an IEP, if due process has been followed and the child is making adequate progress in school. The federal law does not require the optimal education for each child, although some state laws do provide for higher standards, in which case these higher standards must be met.

Support services of various kinds must be provided by the schools, as specified by law, though medical services are provided only for diagnosis and evaluation but not for treatment. The precise line separating medical services from non-medical related services is difficult to draw, and we can expect more controversy over this distinction. The Supreme Court has upheld the provision of clear intermittent catheterization as a related service, while lower courts have ruled that psychotherapy provided by counselors, psychologists, or social workers could be a related service but when provided by a psychiatrist, it may well be an excluded medical service.

States may not deny or restrict the education of the handicapped due to lack of funds, may not attach special fees or charges, nor try to avoid further services by granting them diplomas before they are fully ready for it. On the other hand, parents who unilaterally send their children to private schools or who change the student's placement before the appeals process is completed will take a chance of not being reimbursed for their expenses.

Schools may discipline handicapped students for minor misbehavior the same way as other students. Even short-term suspensions are proper as for other students when the disruptive behavior is not caused by the handicapping condition. Long-term and indefinite suspension or expulsion is more complicated. They may also be applied to the handicapped student; but, since they constitute a change in placement, due process must be followed, and some form of education must continue to be provided.

Clearly, significant strides have been made under the law to provide individually tailored, appropriate education for the nation's handicapped children. It is also clear that we still have a way to go to fully implement the spirit of the law, which is nothing more than our expression of respect for the educational potential of all our children.

Notes for Chapter 11

1. *Pennsylvania Association for Retarded Children v. Commonwealth of Pennsylvania*, 343 F. Supp. 279 (E.D. Pa. 1972).

2. *Mills v. Board of Education of the District of Columbia*, 348 F.Supp. 866 (D.D.C. 1972).

3. 29 U.S.C. 794 (1982).

4. 20 U.S.C. 1400 et. seq. (1982).

5. *Mark A. v. Great Wood Area Educ. Agency*, 795 F. 2d 52 (8th Cir. 1986).

6. *Wilson v. Marana Unified School District No. 6 of Pima City*, 735 F.2d 1178 (9th Cir. 1984).

7. *Board of Education v. Rowley*, 458 U.S. 176 (1982).

8. *Matthews v. Davis*, 742 F.2d 825 (4th Cir. 1984).

9. *Geis v. Board of Education of Parsippany-Troy Hills*, 599 F.Supp. 269 (D.N.J. 1984).

10. *David v. Dartmouth School Committee*, 615 F.Supp. 639 (D.Mass. 1984).

11. 20 U.S.C. 1401 (17) 1982.

12. *Irving Independent School District v. Tatro*, 468 U.S. 883 (1984).

13. *T.G. & P.G. v. Board of Education*, 576 F.Supp. 420 (D.N.J. 1983), *aff'd. mem.* 738 F.2d 425 (3rd Cir. 1984), *cert. denied*, 105 S.Ct. 592 (1984).

14. *Battle v. Pennsylvania*, 629 F.2d 269 (3rd Cir. 1980).

15. *Georgia Association of Retarded Citizens v. McDaniel*, 511 F.Supp. 1263 (N.D.Ga. 1981), *aff'd*, 715 F.2d 1565 (11th Cir. 1983), *vacated*, 52 U.S.L.W. 3932 (1984).

16. *Alamo Heights Indep. School Dist. v State Board of Educ.*, 790 F 2nd 1153 (5th Cir. 1986).

17. *Kerr Center Parents Association v. Charles*, 572 F.Supp. 448 (D.Or. 1983).

18. *May M. v. Thompson*, 585 F.Supp. 317 (N.D.Ill. 1984).

19. *Stock v. Massachusetts Hospital School*, 467 N.E. 2d 448 (Mass. 1984).

20. *Clevenger v. Oak Ridge School Board*, 744 F.2d 514 (6th Cir. 1984).

21. *Burlington School Committee v. Department of Education, Commonwealth of Massachusetts*, 105 S.Ct. 1996 (1985).

22. *Parker v. District of Columbia*, 588 F.Supp. 518 (D.D.C. 1983).

23. *McKenzie v. Smith*, 771 F.2d. 1527 (D.C.Cir. 1985).

24. *Grymes v. Madden*, 672 F.2d 321 (3rd Cir. 1982).

25. *Austin v. Brown Local School District*, 746 F.2d 1161 (6th Cir. 1984); *Georgia Association of Retarded Citizens v. McDaniel*, 740 F.2d 902 (11th Cir. 1984); *Smith v. Robinson*, 52 U.S.L.W. 5179 (July 5, 1984).

26. *Parks v. Povkovic*, 753 F.2d 1397 (7th Cir. 1985).

27. *Board of Education v. Illinois State Board of Education*, 531 F.Supp. 148 (C.D. Ill. 1982).

28. *Kaelin v. Grubbs*, 682 F.2d 595 (6th Cir. 1982).

29. *S-1 v. Turlington*, 635 F.2d 342 (1981); *cert. denied*, 454 U.S. 1030 (1981).

30. *Doer v. Maher*, 793 F. 2d 1470 (9th Cir 1986.); but see *Stuart v. Nappi*, 443 F. Supp. 1235 (D. Conn. 1978).

31. *Jackson v. Franklin County School Board*, 765 F.2d 535 (5th Cir. 1985).

32. *Victoria L. v. District School Board of Lee County, Florida*, 741 F.2d 369 (11th Cir. 1984).

33. *Mayson v. Teague*, 749 F.2d 652 (11th Cir. 1984).

CHAPTER 12

Personal Appearance

Is grooming a constitutional right?

What other reasons support grooming as a constitutional right?

Can students challenge grooming regulations without their parent's support?

Why are grooming regulations upheld?

Why doesn't the Supreme Court resolve this conflict?

What is the law in my state?

Are school dress codes ever illegal?

Will courts rule the same way in clothing cases as in hair controversies?

S hould parents have the right to allow their children to choose their own dress and hair style? Or should public schools be able to limit that right? Should the Constitution protect student grooming and clothing just as it protects freedom of expression? Or is the conflict over personal appearance a less significant issue?

The judicial response to these questions has been extraordinary. Controversies over grooming—particularly hair length—have provoked widespread disagreement not only among state and federal courts but among judges on the same court. The U.S. courts of appeals have issued conflicting rulings about the constitutionality of hair regulations, and the Supreme Court has declined to perform its usual role of resolving such differences. Therefore, this chapter will discuss and explain the

conflicting judicial approaches to the regulation of grooming
in the public schools. In addition, it will discuss two related
questions. Should students be able to choose their own dress
style? Do schools have the right to limit that choice?

Is grooming a constitutional right?

The *Carpenter* Case[1]: Indiana's Wawasee High School dress
code was devised "to insure the best possible overall appearance" of the student body and was carefully developed by a
committee of students, teachers, and administrators. It was
adopted by a vote of the students, and they and their parents
were clearly notified of its provisions. Nevertheless, Greg Carpenter, with his parents' consent, chose to violate the code's
"long hair provision." For this Greg was punished as the code
provided—by being separated from his classmates and deprived
of classroom participation until he cut his hair. As a result,
Greg's father sued on his behalf to prohibit enforcement of the
code's hair length provisions. And the Seventh Circuit Court of
Appeals ruled in his favor, holding that "the right to wear one's
hair at any length or in any desired manner is an ingredient of
personal freedom protected by the United States Constitution."
To limit that right, a school would have to bear a "substantial
burden of justification."

Here the board presented no evidence that Greg's hair disturbed classroom decorum or distracted other students, or that
the hair provision was related to safety or health. To justify
its interference with Greg's constitutional rights, the court said,
the school must show a reasonable relationship between the
code and some educational purpose, such as avoiding substantial disruption. Since such a relationship was not shown, the
court concluded that the democratic process by which the code
was adopted did not justify the denial of Greg's constitutional
right to wear his hair as he chose. The U.S. Constitution, said
the court, cannot be amended by majority vote of any school or
community.*

---

*In an interesting dissenting opinion, Judge Stevens observed: "In the
process of requiring the young to conform to the manners of their
elders, parents and teachers are necessarily partners. If they agree that
a child should be compelled to observe a given form of tradition, no

What other reasons support grooming as a constitutional right?

Other federal appeals courts have given other reasons for supporting the concept of grooming as a constitutional right:

(1) In holding unconstitutional a Marlboro, Massachusetts, school policy forbidding "unusually long hair," the First Circuit Court of Appeals wrote that it saw "no inherent reason why decency, decorum or good conduct" requires a boy to wear his hair short. Nor, it concluded, does "compelled conformity to conventional standards of appearance seem a justifiable part of the educational process"[2]

(2) In striking down a St. Charles, Missouri, restriction on long hair, one of the judges on the Eighth Circuit Court wrote:

> The gamut of rationalizations for justifying this restriction fails in light of reasoned analysis. . .I am satisfied a comprehensive school restriction on male student hair styles accomplishes little more than to project the prejudices and personal distastes of certain adults in authority on to the impressionable young students.[3]

(3) In a North Carolina case, Joe Massie was suspended because he refused to conform to grooming guidelines and because his hair length "evoked considerable jest, disgust, and amusement."[4] In its decision, the Fourth Circuit Court noted that the disruptions were minor and probably could have been prevented. The Court observed that the school administration had made no effort to teach students that "there is little merit in conformity for the sake of conformity" and that a student may exercise a right any way he chooses so long as he does not "run afoul of considerations of safety, cleanliness and decency." The Court concluded that faculty leadership in "promoting and enforcing an attitude of tolerance rather than one of suppression or derision would obviate the relatively minor disruptions which have occurred."

---

matter how irrational it may be, the child has no legitimate recourse but to obey. . . .It is only when the parent supports a child's attempt to accelerate a change in customs that a meaningful (legal) conflict arises."

Can students challenge grooming regulations without their parent's support?

Although minors rarely take legal action without the approval and support of their parents or guardians, a Michigan appeals court ruled that a 16-year-old student could sue his school district against his parents' wishes. The student was suspended because of his hair length, and he was represented by a Legal Services Attorney, appointed by the court under Michigan Court Rules which allow minors over the age of 14 and their representatives to bring suit without parent approval.[5]

Why are grooming regulations upheld?

The following cases are examples of judicial reasoning which uphold the school's right to regulate student grooming.

The *Zeller* Case: When Brent Zeller was excluded from a high school soccer team in Pennsylvania for noncompliance with athletic code hair regulations, his parents sued the school for violating their son's constitutional rights. But the Third Circuit ruled against Brent and his parents.[6]

The court declined to overturn the school regulations because it did not believe that federal courts are the right place to interpret "the conflicting ideals of student liberty and school regulation in the context of students' hair." On the contrary, the court said, in matters such as this, "the wisdom and experience of school authorities must be deemed superior and preferable to the federal judiciary's." Because our system of public education necessarily relies on the discretion and judgment of school administrators, federal courts should not attempt to correct errors "in the exercise of that discretion" unless specific constitutional rights are violated. In this case, the court concluded that Zeller's complaint about the school hair regulations did "not rise to the dignity of a protectable constitutional right."

The *Olff* Case: Because 15-year-old Robert Olff violated his California school's "Good Grooming Policy," he was not allowed to enroll. As a result, Olff's mother asked the Ninth Circuit Court to declare the policy unconstitutional because it violated her son's "right of privacy." The court refused.[7] "The conduct to be regulated here," wrote the court, "is not conduct found in the privacy of the home but in public educational institutions where individual liberties cannot be left completely uncontrolled to clash with similarly asserted liberties of several thousand others." The court emphasized that this was not a question of preference "for or against certain male hair styles, but a question of the right of school authorities to develop a dress code in accord with their professional judgment."

The *Karr* Case: The Fifth Circuit rejected the notion that hair regulations interfere with fundamental constitutional rights.[8] Even if these regulations interfere with a student's liberty, the interference is a "temporary and relatively inconsequential one." Furthermore, the court was disturbed by "the burden which has been placed on the federal courts" by suits such as this which took four full days of testimony, when many more important cases were kept waiting. Because of this burden and because these cases do not raise issues of "fundamental" liberty, the court announced that in the future, school grooming regulations should be presumed valid in all district courts in the circuit.

Why doesn't the Supreme Court resolve this conflict?

When federal circuit courts differ in their interpretation of the Constitution, the Supreme Court usually reviews the question, renders a decision, and thus establishes a "uniform law of the land." But despite the sharp differences of opinion among federal courts concerning student grooming, the Supreme Court has on at least nine occasions declined to review the decisions on this issue. This is because most justices of the Court apparently do not believe the cases raise important constitutional questions of national significance.

In rejecting an urgent appeal to the Supreme Court in one of the grooming cases, Justice Black wrote: "The only thing about this that borders on the serious to me is the idea that anyone should think the Federal Constitution imposes on the United States courts the burden of supervising the length of hair that public school students should wear."[9] As long as the Supreme Court refuses to hear these cases, the law will continue to vary throughout the United States.

What is the law in my state?

Federal appeals courts have decided that grooming is a constitutional right in the First Circuit (ME, MA, NH, RI), the

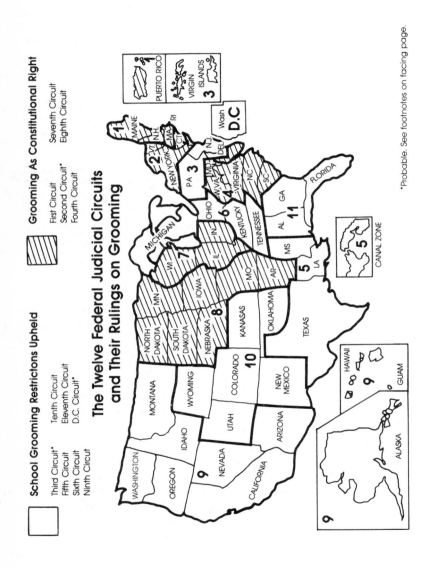

The Twelve Federal Judicial Circuits
and Their Rulings on Grooming

School Grooming Restrictions Upheld

Third Circuit*
Fifth Circuit
Sixth Circuit
Ninth Circuit

Tenth Circuit
Eleventh Circuit
D.C. Circuit*

Grooming As Constitutional Right

First Circuit
Second Circuit*
Fourth Circuit

Seventh Circuit
Eighth Circuit

*Probable. See footnotes on facing page.

Fourth Circuit (MD, NC, SC, VA, WV), the Seventh Circuit (IL, IN, WI), the Eighth Circuit (AR, IA, MN, MO, NE, ND, SD), and probably the Second Circuit (CT, NY, VT).* This means that parents who live in these circuits can go to court to challenge school grooming codes which restrict their child's hair length or style. In these states, grooming restrictions will be examined by the courts and can be declared unconstitutional unless school officials present convincing evidence that they are fair, reasonable, and necessary to carry out a legitimate educational purpose.

The law is different in the Fifth Circuit (LA, MS, TX), the Sixth Circuit (KY, MI, OH, TN), the Ninth Circuit (AK, AZ, CA, HI, ID, MT, NV, OR, WA), the Tenth Circuit (CO, KS, NM, OK, WY, UT), the Eleventh Circuit (AL, FL, GA), and probably the Third Circuit (DE, NJ, PA), and the District of Columbia Circuit.**

In these states, the circuit courts of appeals have decided that grooming is not a significant constitutional issue and that the federal courts should not judge the wisdom of codes regulating hair length or style. This does not necessarily mean that parents have no legal remedy if a child is disciplined for violating school grooming regulations. It only means that the federal courts will probably not consider the case. Restrictions can still be challenged in state courts. And even if state courts uphold school grooming regulations, this only means that they are permitted, not required, in a school district.

---

* In 1973, the Second Circuit ruled[10] that hair length regulations raised "a substantial Constitutional issue." Although the U.S. Supreme Court overruled that decision as it applied to a policeman,[11] the ruling probably would stand if it were applied to students.

**Although a decision of the Third Circuit[12] held that civilian employees of the National Guard could challenge the Guard's hair length regulations, the Court clearly ruled in 1975[13] that "the federal courts should not intrude" in the area of school regulation of student hair length and that it would no longer consider school grooming cases. The D.C. Court of Appeals has not ruled directly on the issue of school grooming regulations, but it indicated in a related case[14] that it agreed with the U.S. Supreme Court and "sees no federal question in this area."

Are school dress codes ever illegal?

Yes. Although schools clearly have the right to regulate student clothing, not all dress codes are legal. In New Hampshire, for example, a federal court held that a rule against dungarees was unconstitutional since the prohibition was not reasonably related to the school's responsibility or curriculum.[15] Although the court indicated that the freedom to wear the clothes of one's choice is a protected liberty under the Fourteenth Amendment, it did not hold that students could wear anything they wanted to school. As the judge observed, a school "can, and must, for its own preservation exclude persons who are unsanitary, obscenely or scantily clad."

Similarly, a New York court annulled a high school's prohibition against girls wearing slacks because the rule enforced "style or taste and not safety, order, or discipline."[16] The court ruled that a board's regulation of dress was valid only to the extent necessary "to protect the safety of the wearer. . .or to control disturbance or distraction which interferes with the education of other students." And in Arkansas a judge held unconstitutional that part of a school dress code which prohibited all long dresses, frayed trousers, and tie-dyed clothing, and required that all boys wear socks. These rules, said the court, were arbitrary, unnecessary, or overly broad.[17] On the other hand, the judge indicated that the following dress code provisions would be held valid: prohibitions against girls wearing "excessively tight skirts or pants" or dresses more than six inches above the knee (to prevent immodest clothing), prohibitions on boys wearing shirt tails outside their pants in shop (for safety reasons), or any student from wearing clothing displaying obscene pictures "or profane slogans or emblems."

Will courts rule the same way in clothing cases as in hair controversies?

Sometimes. Those courts that do not protect a student's choice of hair style will probably not protect his choice of clothing. But not all courts that *do* protect hair style also protect student freedom in matters of dress. This is because some courts distinguish hair from clothing and indicate that restrictions on hair style are more serious invasions of individual freedom than clothing regulations. According to one judge: "the cut of one's hair style is more fundamental to personal appearance than the type of clothes he wears. Garments can be changed at will whereas hair, once it is cut, has to remain constant for substantial periods of time."[18] Thus some courts that recognize choice of hair style as a constitutional right do not protect choice of clothing style, and most give schools much wider discretion to regulate clothing in the interests of health, safety, order or discipline.

Summary

Grooming

Nine out of the twelve U.S. Circuit Courts of Appeals have clearly ruled on the constitutional right of students to choose the length of their hair.* As the map on page 206 indicates, four circuits hold that grooming is a constitutional right that should be protected by the federal courts and five circuits do not. The arguments used on each side are varied and vigorous, and no final decision establishing a uniform law has been reached, since the Supreme Court has refused to rule on the issue.

Upholding Student Rights. These are some of the arguments used to support a student's right to wear his hair as he wishes: A student's hair style is part of the personal liberty assured to citizens by the Due Process Clause of the Fourteenth Amendment; the "freedom to govern one's personal appearance" is retained by individual citizens under the Ninth Amendment, and it is part of the freedom of expression protected by the First Amendment. In addition, judges have written that hair regulations bear no reasonable relation to a legitimate educational objective; they teach conformity for its own sake; and they are not necessary for health or safety. Their enforcement projects the prejudices of certain adults in authority and causes more disruption than does the presence of long-haired students. If such students cause others to be disruptive, school officials should teach the disrupters tolerance

---

*For an indication of how three other circuits *probably* would rule on this issue see footnotes on page 207.

and not suppress diversity. It is dangerous to say the problem is best left to local authorities; such a rationale could support any prohibition of parent or student rights.

Upholding School Rules. Among the reasons courts give for upholding school grooming regulations are these: The regulations seek to accomplish "legitimate objectives" and have "a real and reasonable connection" with the maintenance of school discipline; the Constitution does not protect grooming, but even if it does, it is one of the "lesser liberties" and not a fundamental right. Judges have said that the purpose of these regulations is to eliminate distracting extremes in hair style, to avoid possible conflicts, and to eliminate potential health and safety hazards. Even if some codes restrict student freedom, their effect is temporary and "relatively inconsequential" and still leaves students a wide range of choice in grooming. School officials should have discretion and authority to develop dress codes without having to justify their professional judgment in court.

Finally, all school regulations restricting student liberty cannot be litigated, for the judicial process is administratively unable to deal with the infringement of every minor right.

Clothing

All courts recognize that schools have authority to regulate students' clothing. But not all dress codes are constitutional. Thus a few courts have ruled that absolute prohibitions against boys wearing dungarees or girls wearing slacks or long dresses are illegal because they are not reasonably related to the school's responsibility or its curriculum. Even these courts, however, recognize the validity of school regulations prohibiting certain kinds of clothing because of health or safety or to prevent disturbance or distraction.

Today some readers may find it difficult to understand why so many students, parents and school officials were concerned with the issue of hair length in the past. But the questions raised by these controversies involve far more than grooming; they concern such fundamental legal and educational issues as: When can school officials restrict students' freedom? Should nonconformity be prohibited or guarded in our schools? Should courts protect individual choices or just "fundamental" freedoms?

In the coming years, hair length may no longer be the symbol that triggers this larger debate. But the basic issues will be with us as long as parents and educators continue to struggle with the problems of freedom and conformity in the public schools.

Notes for Chapter 12

1. *Arnold v. Carpenter,* 459 F.2d 939 (7th Cir. 1972).

2. *Richards v. Thurston,* 424 F.2d 1281 (1st Cir. 1970).

3. *Bishop v. Colaw,* 450 F.2d 1069 (8th Cir. 1971).

4. *Massie v. Henry,* 455 F.2d 779 (4th Cir. 1972).

5. *Buckholz v. Leveille,* 194 N.W.2d 427 (Mich. 1972).

6. *Zeller v. Donegal School District Board of Education,* 517 F.2d 600 (3rd Cir. 1975).

7. *King v. Saddleback,* 445 F.2d 932 (9th Cir. 1971).

8. *Karr v. Schmidt,* 460 F.2d 609 (5th Cir. 1972).

9. *Karr v. Schmidt,* 401 U.S. 1201 (1971).

10. *Dwen v. Barry,* 483 F.2d 1126 (2d Cir. 1973).

11. *Kelley v. Johnson,* 425 U.S. 238 (1976).

12. *Syrek v. Pennsylvania,* 537 F.2d 66 (3rd Cir. 1976).

13. *Zeller v. Donegal,* op. cit.

14. *Fagan v. National Cash Register Co.,* 481 F.2d 1115 (D.C. Cir. 1973).

15. *Bannister v. Paradis,* 316 F.Supp. 185 (D. N.H. 1970).

16. *Scott v. Board of Education,* Hicksville, 305 N.Y.S.2d 601 (1969).

17. *Wallace v. Ford,* 346 F.Supp. 156 (E.D. Ark. 1972).

18. *Dunham v. Pulsifer,* 312 F.Supp. 411, 419 (D. Vt. 1970).

CHAPTER 13

Other Rights and Issues

Do children from low-income families receive special help from the federal government?

What rights are parents provided in Title I/Chapter 1 programs?

What are the rights of parents of students who speak little or no English?

Does federal law require bilingual education?

Why do some schools have more money than others?

Do such large inequalities violate the Equal Protection Clause of the Constitution?

If parents cannot achieve equal funding for schools under the national Constitution, can they do so under state constitutions and statutes?

What is the way to equity in school finance?

Are public schools completely free?

Are school board meetings open to parents?

Are the minutes of the school board available to parents?

Do parents have a right to notice of board meetings?

May a school board go into a closed session during its meeting?

What if board members violate open meeting laws?

Do parents have the right to see the budget and other documents the school administrators prepare for the board?

How can parents remove a board member?

May parent groups use school facilities?

Can religious groups use schools?

Do parents have the right to object to tracking systems in the schools?

Does that mean tracking is always unconstitutional?

May parents object to psychological testing in the schools?

T his chapter discusses a number of topics that concern parents, not all of which are related to one another. Among them are: a statute that provides important rights to parents whose children do not speak English, or speak only limited English, and a statute that relates to poor parents and their children. The chapter also examines such topics as the financing of public schools; the meaning of "free" education; tracking and testing of students; the openness of school board meetings; and the use of school facilities by parent groups.

Special Needs Children

Do children from low-income families receive special help from the federal government?

Yes they do. The current law is a modification of Title I of the Elementary and Secondary Education Act of 1965, which provided federal funds to state and local education agencies to provide compensatory education services to educationally disadvantaged children attending public and private schools. Eligible children include those from low-income families, from migrant worker families, and neglected or delinquent children.

Title I was first developed as part of President Lyndon Johnson's War on Poverty. Under Title I, many billions of dollars have been allocated to state and local educational agencies with particular concern for educationally disadvantaged children residing in areas with high concentrations of children from low-income families. Educational deprivation (not economic deprivation) was the central concern of Congress, and Title I regulations defined this to mean "(1) children who have need for special educational assistance in order that their level of educational attainment may be raised to that appropriate for children of their age, and (2) children who are handicapped." From its inception, Title I has involved parents, along with teachers and school board members, in both the planning and evaluation of programs. This was the requirement of "constituent involvement."

Under the Educational Consolidation and Improvement Act of 1981 (ECIA) which amended many federal education programs, Title I became Chapter 1. Small changes have been made in the legislation, but the intent of the program continues as originally enacted.

What rights are parents provided in Title I/Chapter 1 programs?

Since the original ESEA law was enacted in 1965, the provisions for parent involvement have undergone changes as the law has been amended. Direct parent involvement became an explicit part of the law in 1970, when parent councils serving the school system were required. The 1974 amendments required both district and school-level Parent Advisory Councils, with parents as a majority of the membership.

The 1981 legislation resulted in a significant reduction in the requirement for parent involvement. Parent councils were no longer required; district officials were directed to consult with parents, but the process for doing this was left undefined.

However, some states continued to create state and local parent councils to advise them on program implementation, and the federal law allows for such groups even though it does not require them. Massachusetts, for example, through its Department of Education and its regional offices has continued with the same provisions for parent advisory councils as existed under the earlier law (Title I). Their experience is that parent councils are very helpful to the schools and lead to more extensive parent participation in the schooling of children. Some other states are continuing the same pattern as Massachusetts.

Federal Regulations issued by the Department of Education in May 1986 reinstated a stronger policy mandating parent involvement. Each local educational agency must develop written policies, developed with parent involvement, to ensure that parents of the children being served have an adequate opportunity to participate in the design and implementation of the Chapter 1 project.

Do states have the authority to enact statutes to create and/or require parent advisory groups to participate in educational decision making?

Yes. Some states have enacted laws which encourage or require parent groups, which may have a broad range of responsibilities, from an advisory role to joint decision making authority. Community advisory groups may be called by various names, such as Parent Advisory Councils in Massachusetts, School Site Councils in California, and School Improvement Councils in South Carolina.

What are the rights of parents of students who speak little or no English?

Since their children must attend school, how can they learn if the language of instruction is English while the language spoken at home is not?

Until recently, children who spoke a language other than English had to sink or swim in school programs, since most states had laws requiring that English be the language of instruction. In recent years, several language minorities have challenged these laws as establishing an unfair requirement, and court fights as well as legislative efforts have been mounted for bilingual education. A major step in this direction was taken with the passage of the Bilingual Education Act of 1974.[1]

This statute was designed to meet the "special educational needs of large numbers of children of limited English speaking ability in the United States." It provides federal funds to states and local educational agencies for planning and developing bilingual programs and bilingual teacher education, as well as for early childhood and adult education, programs for dropouts, vocational programs, and courses in the history and culture of the language minority being served.

The law also provides funds for supplemental community activities, for fellowships and for program planning. It provides for classes in the students' own language and for classes in English-as-a-second-language, but it stipulates that the children served by these classes shall attend the regular classes in such courses as music, art, and physical education, where language skill is not a major requirement for success. The law also gives parents important responsibility in planning programs, and requires that the students concerned be included in program planning and development in secondary schools.

The Bilingual Education Act of 1985 authorized a continuation of the programs for limited-English-speaking students.[2] This act continues to recognize that there are a large and growing number of limited-English-proficient (LEP) children and an obligation on the part of the federal government to help these children acquire proficiency in English. The law expresses respect for the language and culture of the children and their parents. While the programs under this law should be designed to "enable students to achieve full competence in English," they may also "provide for the development of student competence in a second language."

A significant new provision in the 1985 law is that all school districts that operate programs under this act inform the parents or guardians of LEP students of the reasons why their children were designated as needing bilingual education services. Parents and guardians must also be told about alternative instructional programs available, if any, and about the nature of both the bilingual and alternative programs. Finally, parents must be informed of their right to decline enrollment of their child in either bilingual or alternative programs and thus keep the child in mainstream classrooms.

It was under Title VI of the Civil Rights Act of 1964 that one of the best known cases in bilingual education was brought to court. The *Lau* case[3] in San Francisco, California, was brought on behalf of Chinese-speaking students who were at a disadvantage in classes where English was the language of instruction. Ruling in favor of the parents and children, the Supreme Court placed an affirmative obligation on schools to provide a meaningful educational program for non-English-speaking students. Clearly, if students can't speak, read, or write English, they are effectively excluded from an educational process conducted in English.

Similar results were reached by the 10th Circuit Court in a case brought on behalf of Spanish-surnamed students in Portales, New Mexico.[4] In this case, the evidence showed that many of these students spoke only Spanish at home and were growing up in a "culture totally alien to the environment thrust upon them in the Portales school system." The language discrepancy between the home and the school was resulting in low school achievement and a high dropout rate. The court ordered that a bilingual program be instituted.

Does federal law require bilingual education?

No, it does not. The law can be satisfied by a variety of programs that help remedy the English language deficiency of students. English-as-a-second-language (ESL) or bilingual education programs are common, but other alternatives which are based on sound educational theory and supported by research will satisfy the courts. The selection of a program is for educators, not judges, to decide.

Furthermore, the federal law intends that students with limited English proficiency learn English rather than be maintained in their native non-English tongue. Thus, the law provides for transitional bilingual education. Local school districts have the option, of course, to offer not only transitional bilingual education, but also programs for language maintenance as well as courses about the culture of the students' ethnic group.

In addition to federal statutes and courts cases, several states also have laws providing for bilingual education in their public schools. Among them are Massachusetts, Texas, Illinois, California, and Washington. These state laws make more specific, and at times expand, rights granted by federal laws.

Equity and Finance

Why do some schools have more money than others?

Most of the money that supports the public schools comes from local property taxes. Some school districts have substantial budgets because the taxes that support them come from industries, businesses and expensive private homes. Others have to rely primarily on the taxes levied against low- or moderate-income homes. The result is enormous differences in the financing of schools.

Do such large inequalities violate the Equal Protection Clause of the Constitution?

Some parents in Texas raised this question, on which the Supreme Court ruled in 1973 in the *Rodriguez* case.[5] The facts showed that Texas, like virtually every other state, contained both rich schools and poor schools and that the wealthy schools spent more money per pupil even though the property taxes were less burdensome than those paid in poor districts. The Court decided, nevertheless, that the Texas system of school finance did not violate the Constitution.

The U.S. Constitution contains no references to education, the Court pointed out. It is, therefore, not a fundamental federal right, and the remedy for inequitable school financing must be sought under state constitutions and laws. In its ruling the Court did not minimize the importance of education; but it placed responsibility for its financing on the states, noting that "the need is apparent for reform in tax systems which may well have relied too long and too heavily on the local property tax."

If parents cannot achieve equal funding for schools under the national Constitution, can they do so under state constitutions and statutes?

That depends on the laws of their respective states. While all states are responsible for their public schools, all but Hawaii have delegated authority to local districts for school financing and management, and although these districts must meet the requirements of state laws, they nevertheless have substantial control over the schools. A number of states, recognizing the great disparities in school district wealth, have developed some type of equalization formula. But most of these attempts have not yet succeeded in equalizing school expenditures. Since most citizens value local control, they are reluctant to vote for statewide legislation which tells school districts just how much they may spend for education.

In addition to state legislative efforts, suits have been brought under state constitutions to achieve equalization. In New Jersey[6], California[7], Washington[8], Arkansas[9], and Connecticut[10], such suits have been successful. In Arizona[11], Idaho[12], Oregon[13], Ohio[14], and Maryland[15], however, the courts have ruled against equalization efforts. There are two reasons for this disagreement among the courts: first, the specific wording in state constitutions differs; second, constitutional provisions are often vague and abstract, making it possible for different judges to have different interpretations.

What is the way to equity in school finance?

While some knowledgeable people argue for the usefulness of lawsuits as prods to legislative action, others urge that solutions should be sought through legislation rather than judicial action. Furthermore, an increasing number of people question whether complete equality in school financing is a desirable social policy. If we are to maintain local control of our schools, we may need to preserve the right of local districts to spend more money than the average on each child if they so choose. Through carefully drafted and properly administered laws, large discrepancies can be eliminated and substantial fairness accomplished in school financing. On the other hand, state-imposed uniformity in school finance may insure equality at the cost of destroying educational freedom. A state could decide, for example, that it will allocate $2,000 per year per child in its schools. This would provide for equality in school finance. But what if the parents in school district A wanted to pay extra taxes to provide special teachers in art and instrumental music and thus spend $2,200 per year per child? If parents are prevented from doing so, their liberty is curtailed; if they are allowed to proceed, equality suffers. Some commentators believe that "equality at the cost of liberty can lead only to intellectual bankruptcy."[16] In all probability, efforts to achieve a proper balance between equality and liberty will continue in the courts and legislatures for some time.

Are public schools completely free?

Yes and no. Public schools are free in the sense that no fees can be charged for admission, attendance, and basic instruction. However, states vary on the provision of texts, instructional supplies, athletic equipment and uniforms, transportation of pupils, cost of transcripts, and other incidental fees.

Each state's constitution and statutes must be interpreted to determine what is and is not included in free schooling in that state. A case in Colorado, for example, held that its state constitution does not mandate the provision of free books in the public schools for children of non-indigent parents.[17] Similar results were reached by courts in Arizona, Illinois, Indiana, and Wisconsin, while courts ruled the other way in Idaho,

Michigan, and Montana. Since a Colorado statute exists which requires school boards to provide books for children of indigent parents, the court concluded that the schools are not required to furnish free books for all pupils.

Most state constitutions provide for a "uniform system of free public education," a "system of free and common schools" or some similarly expressed system of public education. The Colorado case is but one example of disagreements over the interpretation of such provisions. For example, a New Mexico court ruled in 1976 that "a uniform system of free public schools" means that only required courses must be free, and that a fee may be charged for the others.[18] Some courts have upheld the power of schools to charge a reasonable fee for participation in extracurricular activities, but have exempted from that fee students who do not participate.[19]

The Supreme Court of North Dakota decided a case in 1978 concerning the provision of free textbooks in the elementary schools. The court examined all prior holdings within the state as well as the state constitution to determine the intent of the framers of the constitution when they provided a "uniform system of free public schools throughout the state." While concluding that this language did include free textbooks at the elementary level, it said nothing about other fees a school might charge.[20] In a related case two years later, the Supreme Court of North Carolina upheld the charge of "modest, reasonable fees" for supplementary materials and supplies for use by students whose parents were able to pay.[21] The local school boards were required by the court to inform parents of the procedures used for a confidential application for a waiver or reduction of fees.

Courts in different states have also reached different conclusions on whether or not public schools can charge fees for attendance in summer school. For example, the appeals court in South Carolina upheld such a fee based on the interpretation of its state constitution.[22] One of the most sweeping statements came from the Supreme Court of California which held in 1984 that under the state constitution all educational activities must be free, whether academic, non-academic, extracurricular, credit or non-credit.[23]

Thus, there is wide variation among the states in the provision of free schooling. Some school districts charge for pupil transportation, for field trips, athletic activities and even lab fees in chemistry classes. Some school districts charge no fees at all. Parents must check the laws of their state to determine the legality of fees charged by public schools in our "free" system of schooling.

School Boards and School Facilities

Are school board meetings open to parents?

Yes, they are. Many states have statutes (sunshine laws), that require school board meetings to be open to the public. But even in states which have no such statutes, courts would require them to be open. Sunshine laws vary from state to state; therefore, it is important for parents to get to know the law of their states. The typical law, however, requires that the school board conduct both its deliberations and its vote in public. Exceptions are sensitive matters that should not be discussed in public because they might hurt someone or harm the public interest. Examples of such sensitive matters might include the discussion of collective bargaining strategy, the purchase or lease of real property, or the discussion of the mental health of an individual.[24]

Are the minutes of the school board available to parents?

Yes they are, except for the minutes taken in executive session. School boards act through their minutes, and they are to keep accurate minutes as a way of informing the citizens and future boards of their deliberations and actions. Some state laws give specific directions for board minutes, but in most states, boards are only expected to keep minutes in some reasonable form that will make them useful to the community and to future board members.

Do parents have a right to notice of board meetings?

Yes, they do. To have a proper meeting, the board members must know the meeting time and place in advance. This, of course, is known for the regularly scheduled meetings, but special notices must be given to each board member for special meetings. In addition, state laws generally specify what kind of public notice must be given, where posted, and how far in advance of the meeting. The place of the meeting should be within the boundaries of the particular school district under the jurisdiction of the board. School boards must have good reason to change the time and place of a meeting and may do so only if proper notice is given for the new meeting.

May a school board go into a closed session during its meeting?

Yes, it may go into executive session in order to discuss any of the items specified by the state law. However, where state law specifies that board actions will be taken in public, it will have to act in an open meeting reconvened after the executive session (closed session). Such interruptions of open meetings to discuss the termination of teachers' contracts in a Michigan community were upheld when the final action was taken in public.[25] Other cases have ruled similarly in controversies involving teachers' contracts as well as land acquisition.

What if board members violate open meeting laws?

State statutes generally provide a method of preventing the recurrence of such violations and for setting aside actions taken at the improper meeting. For example, the Massachusetts laws provide that at the request of three registered voters the attorney general or the local district attorney may request a judge of the Superior Court or of the Supreme Judicial Court to issue an order requiring compliance with the law in the future. Futhermore, the order may invalidate any action taken at the improper meeting if the complaint is filed within 21 days of the date when such action was made public.[26]

Do parents have the right to see the budget and other documents the school administrators prepare for the board?

Since the minutes of the school board are a public record, when the recommendations of administrators become part of the minutes of the board, parents have a right to see them. This is the general principle that applies to budgets, curricula, or other recommendations, with the exception of those highly sensitive materials recognized by the law as reserved for executive sessions.

How can parents remove a board member?

Each state has its own laws governing the election or appointment of members of school boards. These laws generally also specify the terms of service, the filling of vacancies, as well as possible ways of removing members from office. The most common means parents use to remove someone is by not re-electing him/her. However, recall petitions are possible, which may lead to recall elections. Local laws must be carefully followed in such action to be sure that proper signatures are gathered on a clearly stated petition. For that purpose, a close examination of the legal requirements of the particular state is necessary, otherwise a lot of effort might be wasted.

May parent groups use school facilities?

The use of school facilities is under the control of the local school board. In the absence of state legislation on the matter, the board, in its discretion, may deny the use of school buildings to all outside groups, including parent groups. Most school boards do not have such a blanket prohibition but allow various groups to use school facilities after regular school hours. If such use is permitted by the board, it may not exclude a parent group even if that group is controversial or the particular meeting will have a controversial topic or speaker.

The strongest case for parental use of school facilities is where the activity is somehow school-connected. However, courts have allowed the use of school buildings by parents even if the activity is not school-connected, as long as there is no interference with the programs of the school, nor damage to the facilities. While in most states the school board has virtually complete power over the use of school buildings, some states, such as California, provide for wide non-school use by the public. The California statute establishes a "civic center" at every public school in the state and provides for the free use of buildings and grounds for community groups to meet and discuss whatever "appertains to the educational, political, economic, artistic and moral interests of the citizens." The local school board still has the power to adopt reasonable rules to carry out this law and to see to it that community use of school facilities does not interfere with the daily programs of the schools.

In the absence of such state laws, school boards retain substantial authority over the use of school facilities as long as they act fairly and without discrimination. Their authority is illustrated in a conflict that arose in Arkansas, where a group of parents wanted to rent the school gymnasium to hold dances for high school students. When the school board denied their request, they went to court claiming their First Amendment right to freedom of expression was denied. The federal courts ruled against the parents and held that, (1) recreational dancing might be a type of expression, but it is not "speech" protected by the First Amendment, and (2) even if such dancing were "speech," the past practice of this school board did not turn the school gymnasium into a public forum.[27]

Can religious groups use schools?

School facilities may be used by religious groups along with others. Where a board allows the school to be used as a "forum" either by explicit policy, or by the fact that it has been used as such, all legal activities must have equal access to them. The free speech guarantees of the First Amendment apply to religious groups as well as to secular ones. A Kansas case, for example, held that once the school has become a public forum, a church group could not be excluded because of the religious content of its speech.[28]

Whether or not a school building could be leased for religious use on a long-term basis is questionable. Concerned that such long-term use might violate the Establishment Clause of the First Amendment,* school boards have shied away from long-term leases, and state courts have set a one-year limit on such leases and required that the rental fee be at the fair market value. One state appeals court, however, stated that such restrictions are not required either by the Constitution or by state law.[29] This case involved the rental of a state university stadium for a number of religious services. In a related case, the temporary rental of school buildings for religious purposes was upheld on terms comparable to non-religious community groups, where the groups paid for the heating, cleaning and maintenance expenses.[30]

*See Appendix A, page 235.

Tracking, Testing and Classification

Do parents have the right to object to tracking systems in the schools?

Yes, they do, ruled a federal court in Washington, D.C.[31], if it is shown that the tracking is based on socioeconomic or racial discrimination. In the Washington case, students were placed in a track at the beginning of their school careers, and remained more or less locked into it for the rest of their schooling. Children who came from poor homes and from black families tended to be placed in the lower tracks and to remain there. Since Washington had a history of segregated and discriminatory schooling, the track system perpetuated separate and unequal education. The court, therefore, declared it a violation of the Equal Protection and Due Process Clauses of the Constitution.

Does that mean tracking is always unconstitutional?

No, it does not. If schools are very careful in forming tracks, if they keep them open and flexible so that students are not rigidly locked into one particular track early in their schooling, and if tracking is not based on racial, ethnic, socioeconomic or other illegitimate criteria, the courts will not object to them. (See Chapter 5 for further information on this topic.)

May parents object to psychological testing in the schools?

The answer depends on the kind of testing, its purposes, and the way the test results are used. If, for example, the use of I.Q. tests places a disproportionate number of minority children in classes for the learning disabled, the burden is on the school district to show that the tests are valid, and there is a rational relationship between the way students are classified and a valid educational purpose.[32] On the other hand, if the tests are valid, are fairly administered, are not culturally biased, and if they are administered in the students' own language, courts will uphold the schools' right to use them.[33] However, parental consent must be obtained if the psychological testing is funded by the U.S. Department of Education and its purpose is to reveal personal information.*

Some parents have objected to the use of psychological tests that probe the attitudes and values of students, their emotional well-being, and their relationships with members of their families. Parents have the right to have such tests and their uses explained to them, and if not satisfied, they may prevent the use of such tests with their children.

Summary

Chapter 1 of the Education Consolidation and Improvement Act of 1981 superseded the earlier Title I programs, and grants money to every state to meet the education needs of children from poor families. Local school districts must develop written policies to insure that parents have an opportunity to be involved in the planning, implementation, and evaluation of Chapter 1 programs. The Bilingual Education Act is another federal law that provides additional rights for parents. It attempts to meet the special needs of children with limited ability to speak English and provides a variety of educational programs designed to involve them and their parents.

Although the Supreme Court has ruled that the unequal financing of public schools does not violate the U.S. Constitution, parents may still challenge this practice in state legislatures or local courts. Some state courts have held unequal financing illegal while others have not found this practice unconstitutional. State provisions for "free" public education have generally meant that no fees can be charged for admission, attendance, and required courses. But states differ concerning whether public schools can charge for books, elective courses, laboratory fees, and extracurricular activities.

Statutes in every state provide that meetings of public bodies such as school boards be open; but many of these laws also specify that certain sensitive matters may be discussed in closed sessions. However, after discussion, the formal action must take place in public. Because of the wide variation in state law,

---

*For more on the federal Hatch Amendment, see Chapter 8.

parents should consult the laws of their own state concerning the rules that govern meetings of school boards.

Parents may object to tracking, or other classifications of their children based on racial or socioeconomic discrimination. However, when such classifications are based on legitimate educational criteria, they are permissible.

A school board has no legal obligation to make its facilities available to any outside group. But if it does allow some organizations to use its buildings, it must make them equally available to all and cannot prohibit their use by a group because it considers the group's actions unsupportive of the public schools.

Notes for Chapter 13

1. 20 U.S.C.A. 880b. The 1974 statute builds on the Bilingual Act of 1968.

2. 20 U.S.C.A. 3221 (1985).

3. *Lau v. Nichols,* 414 U.S. 563 (1974).

4. *Serna v. Portales Municipal Schools,* 499 F.2d 1147 (10th Cir. 1974).

5. *San Antonio Independent School District v. Rodriguez,* 411 U.S. 1 (1973).

6. *Robinson v. Cahill,* 303 A.2d 273 (N.J. 1973).

7. *Serrano v. Priest. 557 P.2d 929 (Cal. 1976).*

8. *Seattle School District No. 1 of King County v. State,* 585 P.2d 71 (Wash. 1978).

9. *Dupree v. Alma School District No. 30 of Crawford County,* 651 S.W.2d 90 (Ark. 1983).

10. *Hopton v. Meskill,* 332 A.2d 113 (Conn. 1974).

11. *Shofstall v. Hollins,* 515 P.2d 590 (Ariz. 1973).

12. *Thompson v. Engelking,* 537 P.2d 635 (Idaho 1975).

13. *Olsen v. State,* 554 P.2d 139 (Ore. 1976).

14. *Board of Education of City School District of Cincinnati v. Walters,* 390 N.E.2d 813 (Ohio 1979).

15. *Hornbeck v. Somerset County Board of Education,* 458 A.2d 758 (Md. 1983).

16. Nathan S. Kline, M.D., Columbia U., Bergman lecture, Feb. 9, 1976, in Westhampton, New York.

17. *Marshall v. School District Re #3 Morgan County, Colorado*, 553 P.2d 784 (Colo. 1976).

18. *Norton v. Board of Education of School District No. 16*, 553 P.2d 1277 (N.M. 1976).

19. *Paulson v. Minidoka County School District No. 331*, 463 P.2d 935 (Idaho 1970).

20. *Cardiff v. Bismarck Public School District*, 263 N.W. 2d 105 (N.D. 1978).

21. *Sneed v. Greensboro City Board of Education*, 264 S.E. 2d 106 (N.C. 1980).

22. *Washington v. Salsbury*, 306 S.E.wd 600 (S.C. 1983).

23. *Hartzell v. Connell*, 679 P.2d 35 (Cal. 1984).

24. See, for example, the laws related to open meetings of school committees in Massachusetts, Chapter 39 of the General Laws of Massachusetts, S.23B, 1984.

25. *Dryden v. Marcelluse Community Schools*, 257 N.W.2d 79 (Mich. 1977).

26. Chapter 39 of the General Laws of Massachusetts, S.23B, 1984.

27. *Jarman v. Williams*, 753 F.2d 76 (Ark. 1985).

28. *Country Hills Christian Church v. Unified School District Number 512*, 560 F.Supp. 1207 (D.Kan. 1983).

29. *Pratt v. Arizona Board of Regents*, 520 P.2d 514 (1974).

30. *Resnick v. East Brunswick Township Board of Education*, 389 A.2d 944 (N.J. 1978).

31. *Hobson v. Hansen*, 269 F.Supp. 401 (D.D.C. 1967).

32. *Larry P. v. Riles*, 343 F.Supp. 1306 (N.D. Calif. 1972).

33. *Murray et al. v. West Baton Rouge Parish School Board et al.*, 472 F.2d 438 (5th Cir. 1973).

CHAPTER 14

Toward Legal Literacy for All

D uring their schooling, most parents learned little about the law, except, perhaps, a few historic cases. Today, many schools still teach little about our legal system that is relevant and useful, concentrating instead on presenting an idealized version of our system of government, or preaching the importance of respecting and obeying the law while sometimes violating the rights of parents and students. Instead of increasing respect for law, this approach often promotes legal cynicism.

In recent years, however, a new approach has been developed by lawyers and educators which gives students a more realistic understanding of the legal system and its relevance to their lives. By learning how the system works and how it can work for them, they gain a greater understanding and appreciation of our laws and develop a personal investment in supporting and improving our legal system.

This personal and dynamic approach to law-related education (or law studies) is becoming an increasingly important part of education throughout the country. Part of its success is due to the innovative methods and excellent materials that have been developed for teaching about law in the public schools. The American Bar Association Committee on Youth Education for Citizenship has published a series of useful booklets that can help parents become better informed about these programs, including an annotated bibliography of printed and audiovisual curriculum materials as well as a list of law-related education projects in each state.*

Most law materials are incorporated into social studies courses, and many are offered as high school electives. They include materials ranging from a theoretical and philosophical approach to law and courses on the Constitution to practical materials on criminal, contract, consumer, and environmental law. In addition, law studies include a variety of popular teaching techniques such as mock trials, role playing, and case analysis. Many courses bring lawyers or law enforcement personnel into the classroom or visit courts, prisons, and police stations.

Most schools that have introduced law into the curriculum have found that the experience is popular with teachers and parents as well as students—in elementary as well as secondary grades. Even so, less that 20% of our students have been exposed to law-related education. Parents can help expand these programs and promote universal legal literacy in several ways:

1. By encouraging schools to begin programs in law-related education. (Some parents learn as much from these programs as their children.)

2. By encouraging teachers and administrators to extend these programs to the "hidden curriculum" in schools. This hidden or informal curriculum is contained in the way schools teach through their policies and practices, rather than their texts and lessons. For example, schools teach as much (or more) about due process by the way they develop and implement their disciplinary codes as by what teachers say about this constitutional concept in class. Therefore, it is crucial to help schools realize the importance of having their hidden curriculum complement and reinforce their official curriculum.

3. By encouraging and assisting schools to begin (or extend) their efforts to keep all students, parents, and teachers informed about their rights and responsibilities under federal,

---

*To obtain these materials, write American Bar Association, Youth Education for Citizenship, 750 North Lake Shore Drive, Chicago, IL 60611.

state, and local laws and regulations. As education law changes and expands, this needs to be done on a continuing basis—with regular written communications and annual or semi-annual meetings or workshops.

Teachers, for example, can be taught about education law in courses or workshops sponsored by school districts, teacher organizations, or state colleges. And parents can be educated about their rights and responsibilities at PTA meetings, school-sponsored workshops, community college courses, or through parents' newsletters and magazines. In addition to discussing the kinds of information included in this book, such meetings or workshops could examine the ways in which federal laws and judicial decisions affecting parents' rights are carried out in your state and community. Local school administrators could be invited to discuss specific ways parents can participate in formulating policy and to suggest changes concerning school rules, texts, curriculum, or personnel matters. Representatives from the state department of education could be invited to explain new state policies or programs and how they affect schools and children—or an attorney who is familiar with education law might discuss recent judicial decisions of interest to parents.

If parents, teachers, and students are legally literate, each group's rights will be strengthened. In some legal areas, promoting the rights of one group may curtail the rights of another. But this is generally not the case with respect to parents' rights. For example, if schools do not respect the freedom of expression or due process rights of teachers, this will not expand the rights of parents. On the contrary, it will make it more likely that parental rights will also be ignored. Conversely, school districts that respect the free speech or due process rights of teachers and students are more likely to be aware and respectful of these parental rights as well.

Agenda for the Future. As we find ourselves in a judicial era dominated by a conservative Supreme Court, some people are concerned that the courts will not expand the rights of students and parents in the future as they have in the past. While this is probably true, we do not find the prospect threatening, because we do not believe that the judicial expansion of parent and student rights is the major issue today. It is far more important to help parents and educators become aware both of the legal rights that parents and students already have and of ways of protecting these rights in the public schools. In fact, courts may not be the best place for parents to turn to protect and expand their rights. There are parent councils, school administrators, and local school boards; state legislatures and state departments and boards of education; the federal Department of Education, Congress, and national citizen and parent organizations. Each of these groups can influence what happens in your school, and most provide ways for interested parents to learn more about their rights and to influence public education.

Helping all citizens of the school community learn about their rights and responsibilities will create a climate in which each individual will be more appreciative of the law and respectful of the rights of others. By teaching law through the formal and hidden curriculum to parents and teachers as well as students, our public schools can reaffirm their historic role of educating all Americans for more effective citizenship in a democratic society.

APPENDIX A

Constitutional Amendments

Most Relevant to the Rights of Parents and Students

Amendment I

Congress shall make no law respecting an establishment of religion, or prohibiting the free exercise thereof; or abridging the freedom of speech, or of the press; or the right of the people peaceably to assemble, and to petition the Government for a redress of grievances.

Amendment IV

The right of the people to be secure in their persons, houses, papers, and effects against unreasonable searches and seizures, shall not be violated, and no Warrants shall issue, but upon probable cause, supported by Oath or affirmation, and particularly describing the place to be searched, and the persons or things to be seized.

Amendment V

No person shall be held to answer for a capital, or otherwise infamous crime, unless on a presentment or indictment of a

Grand Jury, except in cases arising in the land or naval forces, or in the Militia, when in actual service in time of War or public danger; nor shall any person be subject for the same offense to be twice put in jeopardy of life or limb; nor shall be compelled in any criminal case to be a witness against himself, nor be deprived of life, liberty, or property, without due process of law; nor shall private property be taken for public use, without just compensation.

Amendment IX

The enumeration in the Constitution, of certain rights, shall not be construed to deny or disparage others retained by the people.

Amendment X

The powers not delegated to the United States by the Constitution, nor prohibited by it to the States, are reserved to the States respectively, or to the people.

Amendment XIV

Section 1: All persons born or naturalized in the United States, and subject to the jurisdiction thereof, are citizens of the United States and of the State wherein they reside. No State shall make or enforce any law which shall abridge the privileges or immunities of citizens of the United States; nor shall any State deprive any person of life, liberty, or property, without due process of law; nor deny to any person within its jurisdiction the equal protection of the laws.

APPENDIX B

How to Find Reports of Court Cases

It is not too difficult to find a law library. Every law school has one; many courthouses and universities have collections of law books, and lawyers, too, have libraries. In each of these places a librarian or friend can help you find cases of interest to you. The following is offered as a start into the mysteries of legal research, which is neither as mysterious nor as complicated as many laymen believe.

Appellate courts generally publish their decisions. The highest of these, the Supreme Court, publishes its most recent decisions in a weekly loose leaf volume called *United States Law Week*. A citation in this volume looks like the following:

Richard M. Nixon v. Administrator of General Services 45 U.S.L.W. 4917 (June 28, 1977).

This citation gives us the names of the parties to the suit, with the party appealing to the Supreme Court listed first. The entry further indicates that the case is reported in Volume 45 of *United States Law Week*, beginning at page 4917, and that the decision was rendered on June 28, 1977. Less recent Supreme Court cases can be found in the *United States Reports*. For example, the citation *Brown v. Board of Education of Topeka, Kansas*, 347 U.S. 483 (1954), refers to volume 347 of the *United States Reports* at page 483 and indicates that the decision was handed down in 1954.

Cases decided by the federal District Courts are reported in a publication entitled *Federal Supplement*, while those of the United States Courts of Appeals are reported in the *Federal Reporter, Second Series*. *Carmical v. Craven*, 547 F.2d 1380 (1977), would indicate that this case is reported in volume 547 of the *Federal Reporter, Second Series*, beginning at page 1380, decided 1977. Similarly, *Cook v. Brockway*, 424 F.Supp. 1046 (1977) would be found in volume 424 of the *Federal Supplement* at page 1046.

Decisions of state appeals courts are reported in regional reporters. These volumes group the decisions of neighboring states in the following regions: Pacific, North Western, South Western, North Eastern, Atlantic, South Eastern and Southern. For example, *Shrum v. Zeltwanger*, 559 P.2d 1384 (Wyo. 1977), indicates that this case reported in volume 559 of the *Pacific Reporter, Second Series*, at page 1384, is from Wyoming, and was decided in 1977. Similarly, *Wells v. Banks*, 266 S.E.2d 270 (Ga. 1980) is a case reported in volume 266 of the *South Eastern Reporter*, Second Series on page 270, is from Georgia, and was decided in 1980. The references to cases in this book from New York and California are to the *New York Supplement (N.Y.S.)* and the *California Reporter (Cal.Rptr.)*

The numbering system is consistent in official legal publications, while the titles of the reporters vary to reflect the courts, regions or states for which they report cases. The foregoing should enable the reader to find any case cited in this book. For other aids to legal research, including encyclopedias and digests, a friendly librarian is most helpful.

APPENDIX C

Two Supreme Court Decisions*

Tinker v. Des Moines
Feb. 24, 1969

Mr. Justice Fortas delivered the opinion of the Court.

Petitioner John F. Tinker, 15 years old, and petitioner Christopher Eckhardt, 16 years old, attended high schools in Des Moines, Iowa. Petitioner Mary Beth Tinker, John's sister, was a 13-year-old student in junior high school.

In December 1965, a group of adults and students in Des Moines held a meeting at the Eckhardt home. The group determined to publicize their objections to the hostilities in Vietnam and their support for a truce by wearing black armbands during the holiday season and by fasting on December 16 and New Year's Eve. Petitioners and their parents had previously engaged in similar activities, and they decided to participate in this program.

The principals of the Des Moines schools became aware of a plan to wear armbands. On December 14, 1965, they met and adopted a policy that any student wearing an armband to school would be asked to remove it, and if he refused he would be suspended until he returned without the armband. Petitioners

---

*These decisions have been substantially edited, and most case citations have been omitted.

were aware of the regulation that the school authorities adopted.

On December 16, Mary Beth and Christopher wore black armbands to their schools. John Tinker wore his armband the next day. They were all sent home and suspended from school until they would come back without their armbands. They did not return to school until after the planned period for wearing armbands had expired—that is, until after New Year's Day. . ..

I.

As we shall discuss, the wearing of armbands in the circumstances of this case was entirely divorced from actually or potentially disruptive conduct by those participating in it. It was closely akin to "pure speech" which, we have repeatedly held, is entitled to comprehensive protection under the First Amendment.

First Amendment rights, applied in light of the special characteristics of the school environment, are available to teachers and students. It can hardly be argued that either students or teachers shed their constitutional rights to freedom of speech or expression at the schoolhouse gate. This has been the unmistakable holding of this Court for almost 50 years.

In *West Virginia State Board of Education v. Barnette*, the Court said:

> The Fourteenth Amendment, as now applied to the States, protects the citizen against the State itself and all of its creatures—Boards of Education not excepted. These have, of course, important, delicate, and highly discretionary functions, but none that they may not perform within the limits of the Bill of Rights. That they are educating the young for citizenship is reason for scrupulous protection of Constitutional freedoms of the individual, if we are not to strangle the free mind at its source and teach youth to discount important principles of government as mere platitudes.

On the other hand, the Court has repeatedly emphasized the need for affirming the comprehensive authority of the

States and of school officials, consistent with fundamental constitutional safeguards, to prescribe and control conduct in the schools. Our problem lies in the area where students in the exercise of First Amendment rights collide with the rules of school authorities.

II.

. . .Only a few of the 18,000 students in the school system wore the black armbands. Only five students were suspended for wearing them. There is no indication that the work of the schools or any class was disrupted. Outside the classrooms, a few students made hostile remarks to the children wearing armbands, but there were no threats or acts of violence on school premises.

The District Court concluded that the action of the school authorities was reasonable because it was based upon their fear of a disturbance from the wearing of the armbands. But, in our system, undifferentiated fear or apprehension of disturbance is not enough to overcome the right to freedom of expression. Any departure from absolute regimentation may cause trouble. Any variation from the majority's opinion may inspire fear. Any word spoken, in class, in the lunchroom, or on the campus, that deviates from the views of another person may start an argument or cause a disturbance. But our constitution says we must take this risk, and our history says that it is this sort of hazardous freedom—this kind of openness—that is the basis of our national strength and of the independence and vigor of Americans who grow up and live in this relatively permissive, often disputatious, society.

In order for the State in the person of school officials to justify prohibition of a particular expression of opinion, it must be able to show that its action was caused by something more than a mere desire to avoid the discomfort and unpleasantness that always accompany an unpopular viewpoint. Certainly where there is no finding and no showing that engaging in the forbidden conduct would "materially and substantially interfere with the requirements of appropriate discipline in the operation of the school," the prohibition cannot be sustained.

In the present case. . .school authorities did not purport to prohibit the wearing of all symbols of political or controversial significance. The record shows that students in some of the schools wore buttons relating to national political campaigns, and some even wore the Iron Cross, traditionally a symbol of Nazism. The order prohibiting the wearing of armbands did not extend to these. Instead, a particular symbol—black armbands worn to exhibit opposition to this Nation's involvement in Vietnam—was singled out for prohibition. Clearly, the prohibition of expression of one particular opinion, at least without evidence that it is necessary to avoid material and substantial interference with schoolwork or discipline, is not constitutionally permissible.

In our system, state-operated schools may not be enclaves of totalitarianism. School officials do not possess absolute authority over their students. Students in school as well as out of school are "persons" under our Constitution. They are possessed of fundamental rights which the State must respect, just as they themselves must respect their obligations to the State. In our system, students may not be regarded as closed-circuit recipients of only that which the State chooses to communicate. They may not be confined to the expression of those sentiments that are officially approved. In the absence of a specific showing of constitutionally valid reasons to regulate their speech, students are entitled to freedom of expression of their views. As Judge Gewin, speaking for the Fifth Court, said, school officials cannot suppress "expressions of feelings with which they do not wish to contend."

In *Meyer v. Nebraska*, Mr. Justice McReynolds expressed this Nation's repudiation of the principle that a State might so conduct its schools as to "foster a homogeneous people." He said:

> In order to submerge the individual and develop ideal citizens, Sparta assembled the males at seven into barracks and entrusted their subsequent education and training to official guardians. Although such measures have been deliberately approved by men of great genius, their ideas touching the relation between individual and State were wholly different from those upon which our institutions rest; and it hardly will be affirmed that any Legislature could impose such restrictions upon the people of a

state without doing violence to both letter and spirit of the Constitution.

This principle has been repeated by this Court on numerous occasions during the intervening years. Mr. Justice Brennan, speaking for the Court, said:

> The vigilant protection of constitutional freedoms is nowhere more vital than in the community of American schools. The classroom is peculiarly the "marketplace of ideas." The Nation's future depends upon leaders trained through wide exposure to that robust exchange of ideas which discovers truth "out of the multitude of tongues," [rather] than through any kind of authoritative selection.

The principle of these cases is not confined to the supervised and ordained discussion which takes place in the classroom. The principal use to which the schools are dedicated is to accommodate students during prescribed hours for the purpose of certain types of activities. Among those activities is personal intercommunication among the students. This is not only an inevitable part of the process of attending school, it is also an important part of the educational process. A student's rights, therefore, do not embrace merely the classroom hours. When he is in the cafeteria, or on the playing field, or on the campus during the authorized hours, he may express his opinions, even on controversial subjects like the conflict in Vietnam, if he does so without "materially and substantially interfer[ing] with the requirements of appropriate discipline in the operation of the school" and without colliding with the rights of others. But conduct by the student, in class or out of it, which for any reason—whether it stems from time, place, or type of behavior—materially disrupts classwork or involves substantial disorder or invasion of the rights of others is, of course, not immunized by the constitutional guarantee of freedom of speech.

Under our Constitution, free speech is not a right that is given only to be so circumscribed that it exists in principle but not in fact. Freedom of expression would not truly exist if the right could be exercised only in an area that a benevolent government has provided as a safe haven for crackpots. The Constitution says that Congress (and the States) may not abridge the right to free speech. This provision means what it says. We properly read it to permit reasonable regulation of speech-connected activities in carefully restricted circumstances. But we do not confine the permissible exercise of First Amendment rights to a telephone booth or the four corners of a pamphlet, or to supervised and ordained discussion in a school classroom.

If a regulation were adopted by school officials forbidding discussion of the Vietnam conflict, or the expression by any student of opposition to it anywhere on school property except as part of a prescribed classroom exercise, it would be obvious that the regulation would violate the constitutional rights of students, at least if it could not be justified by a showing that the students' activities would materially and substantially disrupt the work and discipline of the school.

These petitioners merely went about their ordained rounds in school. Their deviation consisted only in wearing on their sleeves a band of black cloth, no more than two inches wide. They wore it to exhibit their disapproval of the Vietnam hostilities and their advocacy of a truce, to make their views known and, by their example, to influence others to adopt them. They neither interrupted school activities nor sought to intrude in the school or the lives of others. They caused discussion outside of the classroom, but no interference with work and no disorder. In the circumstances, our Constitution does not permit officials of the State to deny their form of expression. . ..*

Mr. Justice Black, dissenting:

The Court's holding in this case ushers in what I deem to be an entirely new era in which the power to control pupils by the elected "officials of state-supported public schools" in the United States is in ultimate effect transferred to the Supreme Court. . ..

Assuming that the Court is correct in holding that the conduct of wearing armbands for the purpose of conveying political ideas is protected by the First Amendment, the crucial remaining questions are whether students and teachers may use the

---

*The concurring opinions of Mr. Justice Stewart and Mr. Justice White have been omitted as well as the dissenting opinion of Mr. Justice Harlan.

schools at their whim as a platform for the exercise of free speech—"symbolic" or "pure"—and whether the courts will allocate to themselves the function of deciding how the pupils' school day will be spent.

While the absence of obscene remarks or boisterous and loud disorder perhaps justifies the Court's statement that the few armband students did not actually "disrupt" the classwork, I think the record overwhelmingly shows that the armbands did exactly what the elected school officials and principals foresaw they would, that is, took the students' minds off their classwork and diverted them to thoughts about the highly emotional subject of the Vietnam war. [And I repeat that] if the time has come when pupils of state supported schools, kindergartens, grammar schools, or high schools, can defy and flout orders of school officials to keep their minds on their own schoolwork, it is the beginning of a new revolutionary era of permissiveness in this country fostered by the judiciary. . . .

I deny [therefore] that it has been the "unmistakable holding of this Court for almost 50 years" that "students" and "teachers" take with them into the "schoolhouse gate" constitutional rights to "freedom of speech or expression." The truth is that a teacher of kindergarten, grammar school, or high school pupils no more carries into a school with him a complete right to freedom of speech and expression than an anti-Catholic or anti-Semite carries with him a complete freedom of speech and religion into a Catholic church or Jewish synagogue. It is a myth to say that any person has a constitutional right to say what he pleases, where he pleases, and when he pleases. Our Court has decided precisely the opposite.

In my view, teachers in state-controlled public schools are hired to teach there. . .certainly a teacher is not paid to go into school and teach subjects the State does not hire him to teach as a part of its selected curriculum. Nor are public school students sent to the schools at public expense to broadcast political or any other views to educate and inform the public. The original idea of schools, which I do not believe is yet abandoned as worthless or out of date, was that children had not yet reached the point of experience and wisdom which enabled them to teach all of their elders. It may be that the Nation has outworn the old-fashioned slogan that "children are to be seen not heard," but one may, I hope, be permitted to harbor the thought that taxpayers send

children to school on the premise that at their age they need to
learn, not teach. . ..

Change has been said to be truly the law of life but sometimes the old and the tried and true are worth holding. The
schools of this Nation have undoubtedly contributed to giving
us tranquility and to making us a more law-abiding people.
Uncontrolled and uncontrollable liberty is an enemy to domes-
tic peace. We cannot close our eyes to the fact that some of
the country's greatest problems are crimes committed by the
youth, too many of school age. School discipline, like parental discipline, is an integral and important part of training our
children to be good citizens—to be better citizens. Here a very
small number of students have crisply and summarily refused
to obey a school order designed to give pupils who want to
learn the opportunity to do so. One does not need to be a
prophet or the son of a prophet to know that after the Court's
holding today some students in Iowa schools and indeed in all
schools will be ready, able, and willing to defy their teachers
on practically all orders. This is the more unfortunate for the
schools since groups of students all over the land are already
running loose, conducting break-ins, sit-ins, lie-ins, and smash-
ins. Many of these student groups, as is all too familiar to
all who read the newspapers and watch the television news
programs, have already engaged in rioting, property seizures,
and destruction. They have picketed schools to force students
not to cross their picket lines and have too often violently attacked earnest but frightened students who wanted an education that the pickets did not want them to get. Students engaged
in such activities are apparently confident that they know far
more about how to operate public school systems than do their
parents, teachers, and elected school officials. It is no answer
to say that the particular students here have not yet reached
such high points in their demands to attend classes in order
to exercise their political pressures. Turned loose with lawsuits
for damages and injunctions against their teachers as they are
here, it is nothing but wishful thinking to imagine that young,
immature students will not soon believe it is their right to control the schools rather than the right of the States that collect
the taxes to hire the teachers for the benefit of the pupil. This
case, therefore, wholly without constitutional reasons in my
judgment, subjects all the public schools in the country to the

whims and caprices of their loudest-mouthed, but maybe not their brightest, students. I, for one, am not fully persuaded that school pupils are wise enough, even with this Court's expert help from Washington, to run the 23,390 public school systems in our 50 States. I wish, therefore, wholly to disclaim any purpose on my part to hold that the Federal Constitution compels the teachers, parents, and elected school officials to surrender control of the American public school system to public school students. I dissent.

Goss v. Lopez

Jan. 22, 1975

Mr. Justice White delivered the opinion of the Court.

This appeal by various administrators of the Columbus, Ohio Public School System ("CPSS") challenges the judgment of a three-judge federal court, declaring that appellees—various high school students in the CPSS—were denied due process of law contrary to the command of the Fourteenth Amendment in that they were temporarily suspended from their high schools without a hearing either prior to suspension or within a reasonable time thereafter, and enjoining the administrator to remove all references to such suspensions from the students' records.

Two named plaintiffs, Dwight Lopez and Betty Crome, were students at the Central High School and McGuffey Junior High School, respectively. The former was suspended in connection with a disturbance in the lunchroom which involved some physical damage to school property. Lopez testified that at least 75 other students were suspended from his school on the same day. He also testified below that he was not a party to the destructive conduct but was instead an innocent bystander. Because no one from the school testified with regard to this incident, there is no evidence in the record indicating the official basis for concluding otherwise. Lopez *Never Had A Hearing.*

Betty Crome was present at a demonstration at a high school different from the one she was attending. There she was arrested together with others, taken to the police station, and released without being formally charged. Before she went to school on the following day, she was notified that she had been suspended for a 10-day period. Because no one from the school testified with respect to this incident, the record does not disclose how the McGuffey Junior High School principal went about making the decision to suspend Betty Crome nor does it disclose on what information the decision was based. It is clear from the record that *No Hearing was ever held.* . . .

II.

At the outset, appellants contend that because there is no constitutional right to an education at public expense, the Due Process Clause does not protect against expulsions from the public school system. This position misconceives the nature of the issue and is refuted by prior decisions. The Fourteenth Amendment forbids the State to deprive any person of life, liberty or property without due process of law. Protected interests in property are normally "not created by the Constitution. Rather, they are created and their dimensions are defined" by an independent source such as state statutes or rules entitling the citizen to certain benefits. Having chosen to extend the right to an education to people of appellees' class generally, Ohio may not withdraw their right on grounds of misconduct absent fundamentally fair procedures to determine whether the misconduct has occurred. The authority possessed by the State to prescribe and enforce standards of conduct in these schools, although concededly very broad, must be exercised consistently with constitutional safeguards. Among other things, the State is constrained to recognize a student's legitimate entitlement to a public education as a property interest which is protected by the Due Process Clause and which may not be taken away for misconduct without adherence to the minimum procedures required by that clause.

The Due Process Clause also forbids arbitrary deprivations of liberty. "Where a person's good name, reputation, honor, or integrity is at stake because of what the government is doing to him," the minimal requirements of the clause must be satisfied. School authorities here suspended appellees from school for periods of up to 10 days based on charges of misconduct. If sustained and recorded, those charges could seriously damage the students' standing with their fellow pupils and their teachers as well as interfere with later opportunities for higher education and employment. It is apparent that the claimed right of the State to determine unilaterally and without process whether that misconduct has occurred immediately collides with the requirements of the Constitution.

Appellants proceed to argue that even if there is a right to a public education protected by the Due Process Clause generally, the clause comes into play only when the State subjects a student to a "severe detriment or grievous loss." The loss of 10 days, it is said, is neither severe nor grievous and the Due Process Clause is therefore of no relevance. Appellee's argument is again refuted by our prior decisions; for in determining "whether due process requirements apply in the first place, we must look not to the 'weight' but to the *Nature* of the interest at stake."

A short suspension is of course a far milder deprivation than expulsion. But, "education is perhaps the most important function of state and local governments". . .and the total exclusion from the educational process for more than a trivial period, and certainly if the suspension is for 10 days, is a serious event in the life of the suspended child. Neither the property interest in educational benefits temporarily denied nor the liberty interest in reputation, which is also implicated, is so insubstantial that suspensions may constitutionally be imposed by any procedure the school chooses, no matter how arbitrary.

III.

"Once it is determined that due process applies, the question remains what process is due." At the very minimum, therefore, students facing suspension and the consequent interference with a protected property interest must be given *some* kind of notice and afforded *some* kind of hearing. "Parties whose rights are to be affected are entitled to be heard; and in order that they may enjoy that right they must first be notified."

The student's interest is to avoid unfair or mistaken exclusion from the educational process, with all of its unfortunate consequences. The Due Process Clause will not shield him from suspensions properly imposed, but it disserves both his interest and the interest of the State if his suspension is in fact unwarranted. The concern would be mostly academic if the disciplinary process were a totally accurate, unerring process, never mistaken and never unfair. Unfortunately, that is not the case, and no one suggests that it is. Disciplinarians, although proceeding in utmost good faith, frequently act on the reports and advice of others; and the controlling facts and the nature of the conduct under challenge are often disputed. The risk of error is not at all trivial, and it should be guarded against if that may be done without prohibitive cost or interference with the educational process.

The difficulty is that our schools are vast and complex. Some modicum of discipline and order is essential if the educational function is to be performed. Events calling for discipline are frequent occurrences and sometimes require immediate, effective action. Suspension is considered not only to be a necessary tool to maintain order but a valuable educational device. The prospect of imposing elaborate hearing requirements in every suspension case is viewed with great concern, and many school authorities may well prefer the untrammeled power to act unilaterally, unhampered by rules about notice and hearing. But it would be a strange disciplinary system in an educational institution if no communication was sought by the disciplinarian with the student in an effort to inform him of his defalcation and to let him tell his side of the story in order to make sure that an injustice is not done. . ..

We do not believe that school authorities must be totally free from notice and hearing requirements if their schools are to operate with acceptable efficiency. Students facing temporary suspension have interests qualifying for protection of the Due Process Clause, and due process requires, in connection with a suspension of 10 days or less, that the student be given oral or written notice of the charges against him, and if he denies them, an explanation of the evidence the authorities have and an opportunity to present his side of the story. The clause requires at least these rudimentary precautions against unfair or mistaken findings of misconduct and arbitrary exclusion from school.

There need be no delay between the time "notice" is given

and the time of the hearing. In the great majority of cases the disciplinarian may informally discuss the alleged misconduct with the student minutes after it has occurred. We hold only that, in being given an opportunity to explain his version of the facts at this discussion, the student first be told what he is accused of doing and what the basis of the accusation is. . . .

Since the hearing may occur almost immediately following the misconduct, it follows that as a general rule notice and hearing should precede removal of the student from school. We agree with the District Court, however, that there are recurring situations in which prior notice and hearing cannot be insisted upon. Students whose presence poses a continuing danger to persons or property or an ongoing threat of disrupting the academic process may be immediately removed from school. In such cases, the necessary notice and rudimentary hearing should follow as soon as practicable, as the District Court indicated.

In holding as we do, we do not believe that we have imposed procedures on school disciplinarians which are inappropriate in a classroom setting. Instead we have imposed requirements which are, if anything, less than a fair-minded school principal would impose upon himself in order to avoid unfair suspensions.

We stop short of construing the Due Process Clause to require, countrywide, that hearings in connection with short suspensions must afford the student the opportunity to secure counsel, to confront and cross-examine witnesses to verify his version of the incident. Brief disciplinary suspensions are almost countless. To impose in each such case even truncated trial type procedures might well overwhelm administrative facilities in many places, and, by diverting resources, cost more than it would save in educational effectiveness. Moreover, further formalizing the suspension process and escalating its formality and adversary nature may not only make it too costly as a regular disciplinary tool but also destroy its effectiveness as part of the teaching process. . . .

On the other hand, requiring effective notice and informal hearing permitting the student to give his version of the events will provide a meaningful hedge against erroneous action. At least the disciplinarian will be alerted to the existence of disputes about facts and arguments about cause and effect. He may then determine himself to summon the accuser, permit cross-examination and allow the student to present his own witnesses. In more difficult cases, he may permit counsel. In any event, his discretion will be more informed and we think the risk of error substantially reduced.

Requiring that there be at least an informal give-and-take between student and disciplinarian, preferably prior to the suspension, will add little to the fact-finding function where the disciplinarian has himself witnessed the conduct forming the basis for the charge. But things are not always as they seem to be, and the student will at least have the opportunity to characterize his conduct and put it in what he deems the proper context.

We should also make it clear that we have addressed ourselves solely to the short suspension, not exceeding 10 days. Longer suspensions or expulsions for the remainder of the school term, or permanently, may require more formal procedures. Nor do we put aside the possibility that in unusual situations, although involving only a short suspension, something more than the rudimentary procedures will be required.

IV.

The District Court found each of the suspensions involved here to have occurred without a hearing, either before or after the suspension, and that each suspension was therefore invalid and the statute unconstitutional insofar as it permits such suspensions without notice or hearing. Accordingly, the judgment is *Affirmed*.

Mr. Justice Powell, with whom The Chief Justice, Mr. Justice Blackmun, and Mr. Justice Rehnquist join, dissenting.

The Court today invalidates an Ohio statute that permits student suspensions from school without a hearing "for not more than ten days." The decision unnecessarily opens avenues for judicial intervention in the operation of our public schools that may affect adversely the quality of education. The Court holds for the first time that the federal courts, rather than educational officials and state legislatures, have the authority to determine the rules applicable to routine classroom discipline of children and teenagers in the public schools. It justifies this unprece-dented intrusion into the process of elementary and secondary education by identifying a new constitutional right: the right of a student not to be suspended for as much as a single day without notice and a due process hearing either before or promptly following the suspension.

In an age when the home and church play a diminishing role in shaping the character and value judgments of the young, a heavier responsibility falls upon the schools. When an imma-ture student merits censure for his conduct, he is rendered a disservice if appropriate sanctions are not applied or if proce-dures for their application are so formalized as to invite a chal-lenge to the teacher's authority—an invitation which rebellious or even merely spirited teenagers are likely to accept.

The lesson of discipline is not merely a matter of the student's self-interest in the shaping of his own character and personality; it provides an early understanding of the relevance to the social compact of respect for the rights of others. The classroom is the laboratory in which this lesson of life is best learned.

In assessing in constitutional terms the need to protect pupils from unfair minor discipline by school authorities, the Court ignores the commonality of interest of the State and pupils in the public school system. Rather, it thinks in traditional judicial terms of an adversary situation. To be sure, there will be the occasional pupil innocent of any rule infringement who is mistakenly suspended or whose infraction is too minor to justify suspension. But, while there is no evidence indicating the frequency of unjust suspensions, common sense suggests that they will not be numerous in relation to the total number, and that mistakes or injustices will usually be righted by informal means.

One of the more disturbing aspects of today's decision is its indiscriminate reliance upon the judiciary, and the adversary process, as the means of resolving many of the most routine problems arising in the classroom. In mandating due process procedures the Court misapprehends the reality of the normal teacher-pupil relationship. There is an ongoing relationship, one in which the teacher must occupy many roles—educator, adviser, friend and, at times, parent-substitute. It is rarely adversary in nature except with respect to the chronically disruptive or insubordinate pupil whom the teacher must be free to discipline without frustrating formalities.

We have relied for generations upon the experience, good faith and dedication of those who staff our public schools, and the nonadversary means of airing grievances that always have been available to pupils and their parents. One would have thought before today's opinion that this informal method of resolving differences was more compatible with the interests of all concerned than resort to any constitutionalized procedure, however blandly it may be defined by the Court.

No one can foresee the ultimate frontiers of the new "thicket" the Court now enters. Today's ruling appears to sweep within the protected interest in education a multitude of discretionary decisions in the educational process. Teachers and other school authorities are required to make many decisions that may have serious consequences for the pupil. They must decide, for example, how to grade the student's work, whether a student passes or fails a course, whether he is to be promoted, whether he may be removed from one school and sent to another, whether he may be bused long distances when available schools are nearby, and whether he should be placed in a "general," "vocational," or "college-preparatory" track.

In these and many similar situations claims of impairment of one's educational entitlement identical in principle to those before the Court today can be asserted with equal or greater justification.

If, as seems apparent, the Court will not require due process procedures whenever such routine school decisions are challenged, the impact upon public education will be serious indeed. The discretion and judgment of federal courts across the land often will be substituted for that of the 50 state legislatures, the 14,000 school boards and the 2,000,000 teachers who heretofore have been responsible for the administration of the American public school system. If the Court perceives a rational and analytically sound distinction between the discretionary decision by school authorities to suspend a pupil for a brief period, and the types of discretionary school decisions described above, it would be prudent to articulate it in today's opinion. Otherwise, the federal courts should prepare themselves for a vast new role in society.

TABLE OF CASES

INDEX